Doing Politics
with Citizen Art

Frontiers of the Political: Doing International Politics

Series Editor: Engin Isin is Professor of International Politics, Queen Mary University of London (QMUL) and University of London Institute in Paris (ULIP). He is a leading scholar of citizenship studies and is a Chief Editor of the journal *Citizenship Studies*. He is author and editor of eleven books in the field, including *Being Political* and *Citizens Without Frontiers*.

This series aims to contribute to our understanding of transversal political struggles beyond and across the borders of the nation-state, and its institutions and mechanisms, which have become influential and effective means of both contentious politics and political subjectivity. The series features titles that eschew and even disavow interpreting these transversal political struggles with categories and concepts.

Doing Politics with Citizen Art

Fawn Daphne Plessner

ROWMAN & LITTLEFIELD
London • New York

Published by Rowman & Littlefield
An imprint of The Rowman & Littlefield Publishing Group, Inc.
4501 Forbes Boulevard, Suite 200, Lanham, Maryland 20706
www.rowman.com

86-90 Paul Street, London EC2A 4NE

British Library Cataloguing in Publication Information Available

Library of Congress Cataloging-in-Publication Data

Names: Plessner, Fawn Daphne, author.
Title: Doing politics with citizen art / Fawn Daphne Plessner.
Description: London : Rowman & Littlefield, [2022] | Series: Frontiers of
  the political | Outgrowth of the author's thesis (doctoral—Goldsmiths,
  University of London, 2019) under the title: 'Doing' politics within
  'citizen art'. | Includes bibliographical references and index.
Identifiers: LCCN 2021061735 (print) | LCCN 2021061736 (ebook) | ISBN
  9781538151471 (cloth) | ISBN 9781538151495 (paperback) | ISBN
  9781538151488 (epub)
Subjects: LCSH: Art—Political aspects. | Social practice (Art) |
  Citizenship—Philosophy.
Classification: LCC N72.P6 P59 2022 (print) | LCC N72.P6 (ebook) | DDC
  701/.03—dc23/eng/20211231
LC record available at https://lccn.loc.gov/2021061735
LC ebook record available at https://lccn.loc.gov/2021061736

In loving memory of Ern

Contents

Figures

Acknowledgments

I would like to thank Dr. Bernadette Buckley for her unwavering support, generosity, stimulating conversations, and friendship throughout the development of the doctoral research that forms the core of this book. This book would not have been possible without her insights and guidance. I thank also Dr. Nicholas De Genova, who hosted an invaluable series of interdisciplinary workshops at Goldsmiths and King's College, University of London, United Kingdom, on the important and pressing theme of "Borders, Citizenship & Mobility: On the Geopolitics of Encounter." I thank also members of the W̱SÁNEĆ First Nation in the province of British Columbia, Canada, and especially Kathy and Doug LaFortune, Mavis Underwood, Earl Claxton Jr., and Robert Clifford. I am indebted to them for sharing their insights and experiences of struggle under Canada's colonial regime. Their friendship has also given deeper meaning and purpose to my own citizen art interventions within their traditional territory. I also thank Emily Artinian, not only for her enduring friendship but also for her inspiring approach to our ongoing collaborative venture called *Clouded Title*, part of which is discussed in this book. I also thank all of my (now former) students who worked with me on the art interventions discussed in chapters 3, 4, and 6 and especially those who had a hand in the development of the *Citizen Artist News* interventions: Ilia Rogatchevski, Dovile Alseikaite, and Denise Holland. I am also indebted to the many conference respondents who shared their criticisms of papers (drafts of chapters) presented at the following: "Symposium Malerei," Technische Universitäte Dortmund, Germany, 2018; "Is There an Alternative? Management After Critique: Organising and Migration(s), Moving Borders, Enacting Spatialities, Enacting a Mobile Commons," University of Leicester, United Kingdom, 2015; "Political Action, Resilience and Solidarity," War Studies Department, Kings College, London, United Kingdom, 2014; "Resurrecting the Book," Birmingham Institute of Art & Design, Birmingham City University, United Kingdom, 2013; "Migrations and Militant Research: Borders, Migrants' Practices and the Critique of the Migratory Regime," Goldsmiths College, United Kingdom, 2013; "MELA [European Museums in an Age of Migrations] and MENS [Museums and New Societies]," University of Naples, Italy, 2013; "Art, Criticism and the Forces of Globalisation Conference," Winchester School of Art and Tate Liverpool, United Kingdom, 2012; "Art in Society Conference," John Moores University, Liverpool, United Kingdom, 2012: "Militant Research," workshop cohosted by the Paris Institute of Political Studies, Paris (Sciences Po), France, and Goldsmiths College, University of London, United Kingdom, 2012.

Aspects of chapters 4 and 5 have been published in:

- Forthcoming: "From Objects to 'Public Things': A Discussion of *Citizen Artist News* as an Artistic and Political Intervention." In *Presence, Process and the Pictorial Real: Perspectives on Painting*, edited by Tillmann Damrau. Bielefeld, Germany: Transcript Verlag.
- "What Is a University?" *Journal for Artistic Research* 6 (2014). https://doi .org/10.22501/jar.33909.

Introduction

In recent decades, an increasing number of artists have invoked the notion and name of citizenship within their (social and activist) artistic practices.[1] Following these developments, some art theorists have begun to assess the ways in which examples of "citizen art"[2] are expressive of citizenship within the existing lexicon of status, participatory, or cosmopolitan citizenship (Weibel 2015; Dzenko and Avilla 2018; Elliot, Silverman, and Bowman 2016a; Bishop 2012; Thompson 2012, 2015, 2017; Kwon 2002; Kester 2004, 2011; Papastergiadis 2012; Schmidt Campbell and Martin 2006; Polisi 2005; Frye Burnham and Durland 1998; Demos 2013; Meskimmon 2011; Love and Mattern 2013). However, within this emergent field of citizen art and its attendant body of literature, there is scant analysis of what constitutes citizenship itself; nor is there a fulsome discussion of how citizen art articulates and enacts alternative modes of political practices. This book sets out to reframe this discussion of citizenship by describing and examining how citizen art is a form of art practice that *does* politics and in turn enacts new modes of citizenship that do not reify or valorize the nation-state or cosmopolitan imaginaries. I will describe the manner in which citizenship is interrogated and performed within some examples of activist and social art practices that is only beginning to come into view in an emerging rubric of citizen art.

Assessing how citizenship is performed in citizen art is all the more pressing because the idea of citizenship is complex and contested and, indeed, under some considerable pressure in the shifting and increasingly fractious terrain of political membership within a number of state regimes (e.g., in the United Kingdom during and following Brexit;[3] in the United States in its populist discourses and immigration practices;[4] in the protracted (state) violence toward Indigenous peoples[5] in Canada that has become increasingly visible following the publication of a report by Canada's Truth and Reconciliation

1

Commission[6]). Understandings of citizenship that predominate range from a normative notion of membership as a legal status contingent on the state (Calhoun 2007) to a cosmopolitan conception of citizenship that advocates being a member of "the world" (Nussbaum 1996). Similarly, discussions within the literature on social practice and activist art focus on how art reifies or reinvigorates democratic values (Weibel 2015; Love and Mattern 2013; Elliot et al. 2016a) through "participation" (Bishop 2012; Kester 2004, 2011; Thompson 2012; Kwon 2002), describing how it fulfills the idea—or, indeed, the ideals—of a state's citizenship regime. Only a meager few have noticed or taken seriously the proposition that some art projects may be forging new political practices that reconfigure how politics is done and from where new political actors and new modes of citizenship emerge (Dietachmair and Gielen 2017; Hildebrandt et al. 2019). In essence, the literature within the field of art assesses citizen art practices as invoking and valorizing, in one way or another, citizenship as state bounded, participatory, or aspirational (i.e., cosmopolitan). However, this overlooks the emerging phenomenon of what I am foregrounding as citizen art. This book therefore examines whether or not new enactments of nonstatist and noncosmopolitan notions of citizenship are in play within citizen art. It distinguishes itself from other works by showing through certain examples how citizen art importantly and formatively (1) *troubles* normative notions of status, participatory, or cosmopolitan citizenship (i.e., citizenship formed through Enlightenment imaginaries) and (2) *enacts* new modes of citizenship that only come into view through its practice. This book asks two central questions: How does the practice of citizen art challenge normative (Western Enlightenment) notions of citizenship? And, how does citizen art reshape the manner in which politics is performed and through which new modes of citizenship come into being? As Nikos Papastergiadis says, "While [artists] do not have the answers to the issues that we face in the world, [they] have developed techniques for finding the questions with which they can cross-examine the perplexity of our common condition" (2012, 196). The purpose of this book as a whole is to demonstrate that citizen art has developed techniques for doing politics in significant and substantial ways and is instrumental in shaping new civic and civil spaces for the performance of (nonstatist) citizenship and to show why this is so.

To show that citizen art not only has developed techniques for "finding questions" but does politics in such a way as to create the material conditions for performing new and nascent modes of citizenship, I rely on the notion of "acts of citizenship" (Isin and Nielsen 2008). The notion of acts of citizenship is framed by Engin Isin (Ibid.) and will be discussed (in detail) throughout this book, specifically in chapters 2 and 3. It will also be discussed in relation to the theoretical work of Jacques Rancière (2010). Both authors argue for, but from different perspectives, the centrality of the political "act" in disrupting normative practices of citizenship and, in turn, fostering political conditions that resist the hegemony of state-bounded notions of membership. This is fundamental to supporting my observation that citizen art practices are instrumental in shaping the aesthetic conditions of new modes of citizenship. Citizen art (1) does politics in such a way as to make visible the problems produced through status citizenship regimes and cosmopolitan imaginaries and (2) generates strategies for enacting new modes of membership through its aesthetic practices. Citizen art projects bring to light the aesthetic and generative dimension of the perpetually "incipient" (Isin and Nielsen 2008) nature of citizenship. In making this point, this book distinguishes itself from other critical literature in the field that is subtended by notions of status citizenship or cosmopolitan imaginaries (Weibel 2015; Dzenko and Avilla 2018; Elliot et al. 2016a; Bishop 2012; Thompson 2012, 2015, 2017; Kwon 2002; Kester 2004, 2011; Papastergiadis 2012; Schmidt Campbell and Martin 2006; Polisi 2005; Frye Burnham and Durland 1998; Demos 2013; Meskimmon 2011; Love and Mattern, 2013). It will attempt what (most) others do not do, to challenge assumptions about citizen art as an expression of status or cosmopolitan citizenship.

To draw out my discussion of how the practice of citizen art produces new modes of citizenship, it is important to state upfront that I rely on examples of my own art interventions in addition to the work of contemporary artists. I do this to demonstrate how citizen art speaks to the complexities of citizenship through the lens of migration, solidarity, assemblies, and treatied and unceded lands, including engagement with an expanded conception of political membership that is extended to nonhuman beings as "kin" relations. Tania Bruguera's project *Immigrant Movement International*, Jonas Staal's *New World Summit: Rojava*, and two historical examples from the Guerrilla Art Action Group and the Artist Placement Group form my primary examples of citizen art and are discussed in relation to my own work. My own citizen art interventions discussed in this book are *The Mobile Armband Exhibition* (Plessner 2011), *National Student Surveys* (Plessner 2013b), *Citizen Artist News: The University as a Border Regime* (Plessner 2013a),[7] *Citizen Artist News: Clouded Title* (Plessner 2018), and *Citizen Artist News: Kinship* (Plessner 2019).

It is necessary to also point out that with regard to my own art projects, all my interventions were deliberately aimed at "doing politics" in response to the political conditions that I encountered in my employment as a senior lecturer in a university in the United Kingdom (1997–2013) and as a (returning) resident (2016–present day) of a small island on the southwest tip of Canada (Pender Island), which is the unceded territory of the W̱SÁNEĆ First Nation

People (pronounced wh sane, ech). My orientation as an artist therefore is one of deep entanglement in the aesthetic and material conditions of place. Equally, my artistic activities are centered on developing an art practice that is responsive to the (urgent) need for modeling new modes of citizenship within a locale. To clarify: two of my first interventions—*National Student Surveys* (Plessner 2013b) and *Citizen Artist News: The University as a Border Regime* (Plessner 2013a)—troubled the idea of a university's membership regime in the moment of governmental directives that required universities (administrators and teaching staff) to closely monitor and document the presence of their international students on behalf of the then UK Border Agency in 2012. As I was deeply implicated in these institutional mechanisms designed to expand the policing of international students, the need to address the implications of this racialized bordering regime was formative in the development of my art practice as a form of performative theorizing. That is, these early iterations were vital *practical* learning experiences and important tools for exploring how to effectively intervene in a civic space (a university); they also informed my subsequent activities in shaping a civil space that has interrupted how colonial-settler politics is enacted within the rural locale of Pender Island (i.e., the site of my subsequent interventions, *Citizen Artist News: Clouded Title* [Plessner 2018] and *Citizen Artist News: Kinship* [Plessner 2019]). Pender Island is a place that is dominated by British Canadian colonial imaginaries and ongoing dispossession of W̱SÁNEĆ lands and within which my family and I have been enmeshed for decades. Therefore, these latter interventions were implemented to forge a new political space on the island and to make way for the resurgence of W̱SÁNEĆ law and culture in situ. (I will discuss these points more fully and in chapters 5 and 6 and the conclusion.)

Therefore, civic and civil spaces, as distinguished from civic and civil publics, have become increasingly visible and relevant as landscapes in which citizen art projects operate as acts of citizenship. As preparation for describing how the design, techniques, and strategies of the art interventions of Bruguera, Staal, and others, as well as my own, construct a civil or civil-public space in the chapters that follow, the following will briefly turn to an excellent set of distinctions found in the work of Dietachmair and Gielen, who outline the difference between civic and civil space in the following way:

> "Civic" space describes a set of objectives that are defined by governments of states and carried out by their authorities and public institutions. These objectives cover a precisely pre-defined framework of "civic" tasks that the state provides for its citizens through particular services, initiatives and places it controls. . . . [T]hese "civic spaces" are already regulated, by law or otherwise. . . . By contrast, the civil space . . . is a space that remains fluid, a place where positions still have to be taken up or created. (2017, 15)

The authors also parse the notion of "civil and *public* space" (16). This too is important for understanding the scope and strategies of the citizen art interventions, as I will go on to show in the chapters that follow. Again, to quote them:

> The civil space requires collective actions, initiatives and organisations. People have to make an effort, organize something or simply "do" something in order to shape a civil space. By contrast, public space is the space we can enter into freely, that is or should be accessible to anyone. Or in following Jürgen Habermas, the space of public opinion where people can make their more or less idiosyncratic voice be heard, freely, and preferably with good arguments, like in the media, in public debate or in time-honoured salon conversations. . . . [W]hereas the public space is a space for the free exchange of thoughts, opinions ideas, and people, the civil domain provides the framework for organizing these thoughts, opinions, ideas, and people. Within the latter space, a thought or opinion or idea is expressed in a public action or in the form of an organization. (16)

The examples of citizen art that I discuss in the following chapters do not situate themselves as performing for a public; instead, as Dietachmair and Gielen (2017) point out, they "take up a position" within a "fluid" field of action and create the conditions in which their projects, organizations, and interventions forge new relationships, solidarities, assemblies, public disturbances, and troublings that alter the scene of politics and through which new and nascent modes of (nonstatist) citizenship begin to emerge. My own interventions *Citizen Artist News: Clouded Title* and *Citizen Artist News: Kinship* (as indicated previously and discussed in chapters 5 and 6) deliberately intervene in a small settler community to shape a new political space (via single-topic newspapers) and to focus residents' attention on the problematics of occupying and possessing appropriated W̱SÁNEĆ First Nation land. Put another way, the form of the newspaper is a widely recognized and respected mode of communication within the public sphere, but it was used as a tool for civil action. Indeed, both newspapers are not merely expressions of opinion or presentations of ideas or critiques; instead they staged public "thought experiments" that share the characteristics of "performative utterances" (Austin 1975). Their direct address to residents is akin to "the issuing of the utterance [as] the performing of an action—it is not . . . just saying something" (6). That is, newspaper interventions invited residents to fulfill a (tacit) "contractual" obligation (7) to actively examine their own situatedness within appropriated W̱SÁNEĆ territory. They also carved out a space for the contestation of the foundation of a status citizenship regime by pulling into the space of political practice W̱SÁNEĆ First Nation interlocutors to explore W̱SÁNEĆ law and governance that is centered on "reciprocal responsibilities" to human and nonhuman alike. The interventions thereby not only transformed the space of political action within the small rural settler community by altering what was seen as of political significance to the community but also shifted who had the prerogative to speak as the community. These citizen art interventions thereby interrupted the hegemony of settler-colonial logics of entitlement and local political practices that sustain settler privilege by situating W̱SÁNEĆ speakers at the seat of the local political community. I will discuss this point fully in chapters 5 and 6. For now, I simply want to flag up that by enclosing residents in a public dialogical act and calling into question residents' sentiments of belonging and membership while residing within appropriated lands, these interventions not only practice politics but are a new form of political practice that specifically constitute acts of citizenship. (This point too will be discussed in detail in the following chapters.) Both of these citizen art interventions—and, indeed, all of the citizen art interventions discussed in this book—were aimed at challenging the idea of who and what is seen as "belonging" (to the local community) and who is "visible" as a "member" and, most importantly, what it means to perform as a citizen. As Dietachmair and Gielen say, "Public space provides . . . both new ideas and new people (new citizens) but they can only claim and obtain their place in society through self-organisation in the civil domain" (2017, 17). Throughout this book I show how citizen art interventions are social, political, and aesthetic acts that not only disrupt a status quo but also in turn create subtle bonds between people, establishing new political relations and altering who is seen and heard as a political actor. Overall, I argue that citizen art interventions are self-organized strategies that not only carve out space to perform acts of citizenship but also enact new modes of nonstatist citizenship.

Before I turn to an overview of the contents of each chapter, the following will further elaborate on my choice of a printed newspaper as an artistic medium and a tool for doing politics and why it is significant to this discussion of citizen art as an act of citizenship (Isin and Nielsen 2008).[8] My use of the newspaper was influenced by the example of citizen journalists as they emerged in the mid-2000s and the nature of their unsolicited, unregulated, and random interruptions of mainstream news and media networks, systems, and structures. Their actions inadvertently exposed the mechanisms and gatekeeping that determine what is seen as a political topic and who is seen as a political subject. I realized that it was possible to model my own citizen art projects on the example of these maverick reporters who break (perceptual and conceptual) boundaries, trouble normative assumptions about who has a right to speak and be seen, and, importantly, dominate their own means of production. Citizen journalists also provided an important starting point for what has since become my primary interest in incorporating journalistic techniques into my artistic practices. Therefore, the newspapers, as an artifact produced by one artist rather than a media organization, bring to the fore perspectives that sit outside mainstream news media—mainstream media that of course also shape publics and establish normative assumptions of and for their readerships as a public. The interventions carve out different kinds of publics—publics within publics, so to speak. For example, as an artwork, the newspapers are legible as an artistic intervention to those who have the requisite knowledge (i.e., they've been informed that it is artwork; they are reasonably familiar with contemporary debates in art and aesthetics to anchor their reading of it as an art project, such as "dematerialization," "expanded practice," "social practice," "practice-based research," "interventionist art," "activist art" or "artivism," "aesthetic journalism" [Cramerotti 2009]; etc.). Otherwise, the newspaper as artwork is invisible to readers. This is important for escaping the designation of an artifact as an art object, which can enclose its interpretation and limit its reach. That is, "designations of certain practices as artworks, or restrictions of activities to the 'art field' can limit and even foreclose their potential" (Kelly 2005). This "inside" and "outside" of reading the newspaper as an art object or not is potent as it troubles the idea of a public readership; that is, new political spaces are shaped by art interventions of this kind in multiple and intersecting ways by readers who are situated either inside or outside the artwork and its aesthetics.

In recent decades, the printed newspaper has become somewhat antiquated, and because of this, it has certain liminal qualities that also make it an effective tool for my art interventions. As a printed artifact, against a backdrop of the ubiquity of the digital screen, the newspaper is strikingly odd and outdated; as a result, it has a particular aesthetic register that is enhanced in my view. Its aesthetic oddness is brought to the fore in comparison to the aesthetic qualities of the screen or "window frame" or the "interface" of our computers in acquiring "news." One might agree that the computer screen as a surface and as a window is experientially "ordinary" and routinized as a medium for the acquisition of information and news. The screen is in the background of our awareness. The printed newspaper, by comparison, is a communication medium in transition. On the one hand, it is an outmoded form of media, as I've suggested, but on the other hand, it retains authority as a medium of public knowledge. It is the slippage—the breakage in its technology—that makes it compelling and useful as an artistic medium and interventionist tool. The printed form of the newspaper oscillates between being ordinary (and therefore in the background) and extraordinary (i.e., visible as an aesthetic object in its own right). It comes into view through the oddness of its aesthetic register. These "affordances"[9] that present themselves in this technological shift make the newspaper a ripe artistic medium for my citizen art interventions because the aesthetic character of the newspaper is enhanced through the layering of familiarity and oddness.

The form of the newspaper, as a creative medium and interventionist tool, also allowed for the innovative assemblages of facts—that is, the editing and arrangement of images and text, the tenor and positioning of its various voices, the visual display of the newspaper's pages—to yield multivalent readings of a topic that in turn agitate in their suggestiveness, producing new imaginaries, new orientations, and new modes of becoming. In both interventions on Pender Island, this involved directly addressing residents and inviting them to engage in a public "thought experiment" that required them to navigate a set of local "problems"—that is, problems that are not in the purview of local or regional politics but that directly implicate the resident-reader, such as (1) the legacy of a (dubious) treaty that has produced the conditions of a silent apartheid, (2) the racialized and segregationist practices of the state's status citizenship regime that undergirds the disenfranchisement of First People's governance of their lands, and (3) a troubling of normative notions of political membership as applying to only human beings. In such a manner, the idiosyncrasies of the editorial role slip into the background and bring to the fore a provocation in speech and action not even conceivable, let alone achievable, within mainstream media. The interventions' direct address to residents, the arrangements of images and text, of quotations and transcribed conversations, the signification of printed media as archaic, and the novel method of dissemination charge the facts with new political meaning, carving out a new space for doing politics and enacting new modes of citizenship. This includes a belief that "representations of the real have *more* rather than *less* power to shape our world than heretofore [and further] that the production and control of the flow of historically based images [in my case, questioning historically based narratives of the legitimacy of the state] is increasingly the arena of social power that matters most" (Demos quoting Michael Renov, 2013, xvii). Hence, the aim of these newspaper interventions includes an intention to do politics in such a way as to address specifically "the kinds of knowledge that aesthetic experience is capable of producing" (Kester 2004, 9).[10] That is, the (formal) aesthetics of *Citizen Artist News* as an artistic object, on the one hand, and the aesthetic experience (affective, sensory, etc.) of the interventions as events, on the other, shape and advance political action in a civic and civil domain. Jacques Rancière's insights on the intersection of aesthetics and politics (which I will discuss further in chapter 2) are invaluable for articulating how all of the "citizen artist" newspapers, as artifacts *and* as art interventions, make visible the "partitioning" of beliefs and practices within specific communities and, by extension, who and what is seen as public and of importance. As Rancière says, art is a means for revealing "who ha[s] a part in the community of citizens" (2004, 12). In this way too, *Citizen Artist News* carries its information beyond its own limits.

Not only do the citizen art newspapers interrogate a single topic but the facts also are not presented in ways that meet the expectations of news as quick, digestible stories. Instead, they slow down the reader and prompt engagement with issues that not only implicate them in their problematics but also challenge normative assumptions. Citizen art newspapers prod at the affective, aesthetic, and subjective experiences of individuals to draw their attention to the facts that their own status as members (i.e., students, faculty, staff, etc., of a university or a community) and citizens (i.e., settlers on a small island in colonial Canada, etc.) are at the heart of the production of the problems of a (status) citizenship regime. In this way, too, the citizen art newspapers do politics through art. One might also say that the aesthetics of (mainstream) journalism are contested within the aesthetics of the citizen art newspapers. My editorial handling of facts disrupts notions of authority and the authoritative voice that is part of the posture of a newspaper's historical, social, cultural, and political legacy. There is an aesthetic dimension to the newspaper as originating from one (or a few) individuals and not an organization or agency. There is a bodily connection to the artifact as a form of media where, as Judith Butler would say, "the activation of the instrument is part of the bodily action itself" (2011, 9). "The use of the technology effectively implicates the body" (10), and in this sense, there is a bodily/aesthetic dimension to the newspaper that is framed through its authorship (by not just me but also those who are speaking through its pages), rather than legitimized through an organization or agency. However, the newspaper, as a highly coded artifact, also transcends the body. As Butler says, "The media is the scene or the space in its extended and replicable visual and audible dimensions. . . . [It] extends the scene in a time and place that includes and exceeds its local instantiation" (9). These citizen art interventions therefore are not an illustration of the theoretical positioning that is discussed in this book. and they do not aim to develop a theoretical position of their own. These citizen art interventions are not a mapping exercise or an exercise in hypothesizing or schematizing. They are an exercise in doing politics" and, in turn, performing new modes of citizenship. The citizen art newspapers are therefore not only an artistic medium but an aesthetic tool. They are also a political tool in which aesthetic and political characteristics intersect.

Chapter 1 lays out the problem of the lack of interrogation of the nature of citizenship by authors writing from within the nascent field of citizen art and more established literature on social and activist art practices. I not only distinguish what I am detailing as citizen art from other forms of social and activist art practice but also argue that the notion of citizenship as a status or as a cosmopolitan imaginary has been hollowed out. Therefore, it is significant to assess how new modes of citizenship manifest within citizen art. This chapter introduces how the term "citizen art" is signified in this book and in the context of the complex terrain of citizenship. I discuss how normative notions of citizenship as a status or cosmopolitan aspiration dominate the critical literature in this emergent field of citizen art and suggest that such perspectives miss important aspects of citizen art as enacting new nonstatist modes of citizenship. I also note that the term "citizen art" has widely differing uses—some skewed toward the marketplace or preoccupied with the ethics of artists' performing as "good" citizens—and that it is important to home in on and build on some of the literature on activist and social art practices to show that citizen art projects are not only distinctly self-organized performative practices (Hildebrandt et al. 2019) that alter politics "on the ground" but also creatively and practicably forge new political relationships within a locale. This chapter also specifies what this book does not do, such as characterize citizen art as a "participatory" form of political action in line with previous debates about social and activist art (Bishop 2012; Kester 1998, 2004, 2011; Thompson 2012, 2015, 2017; Kwon 2002). I argue instead that the form of citizenship that is enacted in citizen art is not reducible to a discussion about participation; nor is its performance necessarily a statist affair. This is done to set the stage for my wider argument in ensuing chapters where I show that citizen art does not emulate Western Enlightenment expressions of citizenship.

Chapter 2 focuses on contemporary theoretical debates within the fields of citizenship and migration studies, as well as that of aesthetics, to clarify how citizenship is to be understood within my own and other artists' projects. I argue that conventional notions of citizenship as participatory or as a status is replete with dilemmas (Heater 1999; Cole 2007, 2010; Bosniak 2006; Rygiel 2010; Delanty 2000; Isin 2002, 2012; Isin and Turner 2002) and impacts our understanding of the import of citizen art practices in shaping new modes of citizenship. This is especially important because art is not often seen as significant to a discussion about citizenship. Therefore, the first half of this chapter draws out the complexities and problems of citizenship as a legal status, framed and determined by a nation-state, and as a cosmopolitan aspiration. Neither of these understandings of citizenship illuminate the new and nascent forms of citizenship that manifest in citizen art. Therefore, it is necessary to discuss them in detail to show how citizen art differs from these normative imaginaries and practices. Troubling notions of status and cosmopolitan citizenship also distinguishes this research from that of other authors in the field of art who do not interrogate the problems of citizenship within their writings on citizen art. Such is the assumed normativity of status or cosmopolitan citizenship when discussing citizen art and other modes of social and activist art practices. The second half of this chapter outlines the importance of Engin Isin's notion of acts of citizenship and the work of Jacques Rancière for comprehending the aesthetic and nascent dimension of citizenship and its significance to citizen art as performative acts. Acts of citizenship are politically transformative acts that "break habitus creatively" (Isin and Nielsen 2008, 18) and in turn help to further distinguish citizen art as performing new and nascent modes of citizenship that unsettle conventional practices of politics within a locale. I argue that citizen art interventions not only disrupt a status quo but also in turn structure new (political) relations between people. Therefore, the entire chapter is dedicated to providing a foundation for the ensuing examination of citizenship within examples of citizen art.

Chapter 3 examines how citizen art interventions are tools for doing politics and enacting new modes of citizenship. A considerable part of this chapter describes what an art intervention is and outlines a range of its usages and meanings in the art world. I offer a rudimentary explanation of the nature of art interventions as either short and disruptive performative interruptions or as "projects" that are longer in duration and involve more comprehensive infrastructures for contesting normative practices of citizenship. Also, I distinguish between citizen art interventions and other interventionist strategies within the field of art to provide a map, so to speak, for understanding some core characteristics of citizen art projects discussed in subsequent chapters. I also draw a comparison between citizen art interventions and the concept of the "responsibility to protect" (RtoP) as a way of showing that citizen art interventions are determinable political acts and not only aesthetic gestures. To clarify how citizen art interventions do politics by structuring relations and embodying acts of citizenship, I discuss two historical examples of interventions by activist groups of the late 1960s and 1970s, namely, the Guerilla Art Action Group and Roger Coward of the Artist Placement Group, and one of my first interventions, *The Mobile Armband Exhibition* (Plessner 2011). These examples help to illustrate the characteristics of (and differences between) how citizen art interventions perform political acts as either short, sharp, public interventions or long-term projects that provide the architecture for shaping new political terrain and doing politics in a field of action.

Chapter 4 describes how four examples of citizen art interventions practice politics in such a way that exposes not only the pitfalls of a status citizenship regimes but also how they build infrastructures for new modes of political membership. I discuss Tania Bruguera's art project *Immigrant Movement International*, Jonas Staal's project *New World Summit: Rojava*, and two of my own citizen art interventions, *National Student Surveys* (Plessner 2013b) and *Citizen Artist News: The University as a Border Regime* (Plessner 2013a) to draw out (1) how acts of citizenship are realized through these projects and (2) how new modes of citizenship become visible through their aesthetic practices. I argue that these art interventions raise important insights about the perpetually nascent nature of citizenship by showing how they reconfigure political membership through their engagement with issues of migration, statelessness, and border regimes. These citizen art projects make real migrants' claims to rights *as migrants* (Bruguera); they make visible and challenge the practices of bordering regimes within universities (Plessner); and they enact assemblies within a nascent, democratic, stateless state (Staal).

Chapters 5 and 6 are dedicated to my most recent art interventions, *Citizen Artist News: Clouded Title* (Plessner 2018) and *Citizen Artist News: Kinship* (Plessner 2019), which are the most robust of my interventions to date. They were conceived as a pair and were launched successively on Pender Island and, therefore, should be read in relation to one another. Both chapters describe how these interventions shaped a new civil space for doing politics and performing acts of citizenship. I describe the strategies and techniques of the interventions as (1) pushing back at (local) colonial assumptions of entitlement and membership that are founded on the (dubious) scripting of a treaty as a "sale" of lands that is undergirded by Canada's status citizenship regime, (2) making visible how the state's citizenship regime disenfranchises Indigenous peoples' claims to land and governance, (3) interrupting Western Enlightenment assumptions that citizenship necessarily depends on the state or a world community or, indeed, on human actors, and (4) pointing out that aspects of the W̱SÁNEĆ worldview and forms of governance importantly pivot on aesthetic relations to land and, in turn, are demonstrative of new modes of nonstatist, noncosmopolitan citizenship. This is important for seeing how the contents of the interventions together not only challenge assumptions about the normativity of colonial practices of status citizenship but also call on residents to participate in a "thought experiment" that encloses them in a public act of "thinking through" the lens of local W̱SÁNEĆ descriptions of "being 'owned' by the land" (Tsawout First Nation 2015, 23). The interventions push residents to reorient themselves to the reality of W̱SÁNEĆ centrality in the political life of the island.

As indicated previously, chapter 5 describes how *Citizen Artist News: Clouded Title* raises the problem of how the Canadian state, through its imposition of the (dubious) Douglas Treaty on parts of W̱SÁNEĆ First Nation territory, instigated and sustains claims to the ownership of W̱SÁNEĆ territory. I describe how the state's insistence on its treaties as sales of land is the basis for the ongoing epistemic violence that is enacted daily by residents in the normalization of the appropriation of unceded and ceded W̱SÁNEĆ territory. Hence, I show how the intervention punctures widespread settler assumptions and practices of claiming to own lands that are, in fact, clouded in title. To further contextualize the scope and meaning of this intervention, I detail not only how local Indigenous peoples' identities and political status are managed and regulated by the Canadian state in ways that undermine W̱SÁNEĆ cultural and political agency and access to their wider territory but also how this sustains colonial fictions of settler entitlement that has produced a silent apartheid—a partitioning that has shaped the material reality of place. I discuss how the newspaper intervention prods island residents to reconsider their orientation to land, ownership, and assumptions about belonging by binding them together as (unwitting) subjects of the art project.

Chapter 6 documents how my second intervention, *Citizen Artist News: Kinship*, pushes residents to recognize the seriousness of W̱SÁNEĆ descriptions of reciprocal obligations and duties to nonhuman beings as foundational principles in W̱SÁNEĆ law and governance. This chapter also further troubles the notion of a status citizenship regime as normative. I draw out a discussion about the centrality of aesthetic relationships for navigating relationships with more-than-human beings and humans alike, showing how differing aesthetic experiences of (is)lands undergirds sentiments and enactments of belonging and membership. I also outline how this intervention does politics by circumventing local (political) gatekeeping in new and novel ways within the local settler community. I argue that the performative dimension of this intervention forges new modes of citizenship in their foregrounding of new political actors, establishing relations of trust among people who are psychosocially and politically segregated by British colonial histories and imaginaries of place but otherwise inhabit the land together.

These interventions together demonstrate that normative ideas of citizenship (as a status) or as a cosmopolitan imaginary cannot reconcile the complexity of relations between Indigenous people and settlers in virtue of the fact that, to date, island residents do not acknowledge the legacy of infrastructural privileges that have accrued to first British and then other settlers through the legacy of colonial state violence toward the W̱SÁNEĆ People (and, in fact, all First Nation Peoples). The legacy of the state's suppression of the W̱SÁNEĆ via the ongoing brokering of their appropriated lands, their economic, social, political, and cultural needs, and the management of their political status continues to disenfranchise the W̱SÁNEĆ (and other First Nations) in governing their traditional territory. The W̱SÁNEĆ People are further undermined by the obstinate rhetoric of (local) settler narratives of ownership of W̱SÁNEĆ lands to the present day. These interventions also expose how the state is dumb to the implications of indigenous knowledges, values, and relations to land in its practice of its status citizenship regime and control of lands. I will discuss and evidence these points extensively throughout chapters 5 and 6 because they are significant for seeing how these citizen art interventions open up new ways of cognizing and performing alternative modes of (nonstatist, noncosmopolitan) citizenship. The staging of these newspaper interventions, with their focus on W̱SÁNEĆ descriptions of being "owned by the land" (Tsawout First Nation 2015, 23), entangles residents in an act of thinking anew—an act not of their choosing. These interventions have thereby altered what is seen as the object of (local) politics, and they recenter who is seen as a political actor. They stage new interpersonal relations (especially among me, residents, and members of the W̱SÁNEĆ Nation) and scope out new potentialities for doing politics and performing new modes of membership at a critical moment when British Canadian colonial assumptions and practices continue to dominate in the local (provincial and national) settler community.

This book concludes with a discussion of the affects and effects of primarily these last two interventions so as to offer an overview of the consequences of these acts of citizenship. I present descriptions of what happened to me, including what was reported to me and my observations of how the interventions disrupted the smooth surface of colonial presence and entitlement by breaking the silence about the embodied apartheid that persists at a local level. I relate stories that tell of the inner workings of the interventions and their efficacy in interrupting the tenor of colonial politics within the locale and how they provide a material support for emergent relations and sensibilities that do not reify belonging and political membership as a regime of status and entitlement or as an abstract aspiration for a transcendent universal human community.

NOTES

1. The term "social art practice" is used synonymously with "activist art," "socially engaged art," "participatory art," "relational art," "community art," and "new genre public art." See Kester 2004, 2011; Kwon 2002: "social practice" is a field concerned with social and political issues and collaboration with people who are not necessarily artists, best understood as art in the public interest. See also Bishop 2012: the "surge of artistic interest in participation and collaboration . . . since the 1990s [has become known as] . . . social practice, . . . a genre in its own right" (1). I will refer to "social art practice" and "activist art" interchangeably.

2. When I commenced the research for this book in 2010, the term "citizen art" was not as much in use as it is today. For further discussion, see chapter 1.

3. Before and following the United Kingdom's departure from the European Union, the citizenship status of those of the "Windrush generation" was called into question. See Bulman 2018; Wikipedia, n.d.g. UK nationals resident in Europe no

longer enjoy the same rights as other European citizens, re: court cases emerging regarding legal principles such as "the idea that EU citizenship is a right that cannot be arbitrarily withdrawn" (Wesemann 2020).

4. The term "nationalism" has been used as a moniker by former president Donald Trump and far-right political groups to signify white supremacist ideology (Democracy Now 2018). Equally, debates on "Birtherism" (Zurcher 2016) and "nativism" speak to the xenophobic nationalism that percolates within right-leaning ideologies that define nationhood through ethnic, cultural, and religious terms rather than laws and values (Kleinfeld and Dickas 2020). Additionally, inhumane practices and fatalities in the handling of migrant children, who were forcibly separated from their parents and placed in detention centers, has been exposed (Rose 2018). The Deferred Action for Childhood Arrivals program, a path to citizenship for migrant children, is under threat of closure (Thanawala and Dalton 2018). See also travel bans barring Muslims from entering the United States (Zapatosky, Nakamura, and Hauslohner 2017) and Trump's (bizarre) proposal to erect of a wall along the US border (Timm 2017). Vice President Kamala Harris, when addressing the Guatemalan people, has said, "Do not come. Do not come. The United States will continue to enforce our laws and secure our borders" (*BBC News* 2021).

5. Terms such as "Indigenous" (Indigenous peoples), "Native," "Indian," "Aboriginal," and "First Nation" have complex histories and are somewhat contested within Canada; their use is also inconsistent. I rely on the term "Indigenous" to signify peoples and civilizations that preceded colonization of Canada. I draw on three sources—Joseph and Joseph 2002; First Nation Study Program 2009; and Underwood 2018—as well as my own personal informal discussions with individuals. "The term came into wide usage during the 1970s when Aboriginal groups organized transnationally and pushed for greater presence in the United Nations. In the UN, 'Indigenous' is used to refer broadly to peoples of long settlement and connection to specific lands who have been adversely affected by incursions by industrial economies, displacement, and settlement of their traditional territories by others" (First Nations Study Program 2009). The term "Indian" is a label that was affixed to the original inhabitants of North America by the early colonizers (Christopher Columbus) and was later used to denote their legal status under federal legislation and specifically under the Indian Act. It is a term that is seen as outdated and offensive because of the legacy of racism in Canada. However, some may self-describe as "Indian," indicating their legal status. The term "Native" has been used synonymously with "Indian" and is equally outdated in most respects (Joseph 2002; First Nations Study Program 2009). However, the terms "Indian" and "native" do not necessarily have negative overtones (Underwood 2018). The term "Aboriginal" emerged in 1982 under section 35 of the Canadian Constitution Act and continues primarily within government. It signifies all Indigenous populations (First Nations, Inuit, and Métis). "First Nation" came into use in the 1970s and 1980s and "was viewed as a liberating move away from the Indian Act identification of Indians living on numbered reserves" (Underwood 2018, 26). It does not apply to Inuit or Métis peoples. In many cases it has replaced the term "Indian band" or "tribe," although not entirely. In the case of the W̱SÁNEĆ First Nation, the term "First Nation" is used both collectively, to describe all of the nations (bands)

that constitute the wider group (e.g., W̱SÁNEĆ), and individually, as a descriptor of each "band."

6. See Truth and Reconciliation Commission of Canada 2015 re: acts of British Canadian colonial violence toward First Nations Peoples, such as residential schools, in which thousands of children were incarcerated and subjected to horrific abuse (i.e., sexual, psychological, and physical) and some were murdered. See also National Inquiry into Missing and Murdered Indigenous Women and Girls 2019: "The truth is that we live in a country whose laws and institutions perpetuate violations of basic human and indigenous rights. These violations amount to nothing less than the deliberate, often covert campaign of genocide against Indigenous women, girls, and 2SLGBTQQIA people" (5).

7. See also Plessner 2014.

8. From 1985 to 2008, my artistic activities centered on painting images, exhibiting artworks in galleries and museums, receiving commissions, grants, and awards, working with art dealers and collectors, and so forth, primarily in the United Kingdom and Europe. In 2009 I commenced my pursuit of interventions as an artistic practice (i.e., as an artistic medium and a tool for doing politics) that turned on my own disillusionment with painting as a means to mobilize dialogue about the issues and concerns that not only confronted me on a daily basis but that also informed the subject matter of my artwork. I started to think again seriously about what art can do politically and how it can be enacted in ways that do not depend on the apparatus of the "art world." More importantly, however, I was concerned with exploring what these interventions can do as practices of belonging and membership within a locale.

9. See Gibson 1986.

10. Compare the newspaper as an artistic medium with debates about "fake news," rooted in the nineteenth century, re: the yellow press and the production of sensationalist tabloid news (Public Domain Review, n.d.) or, currently, "post-truth politics" (Wikipedia, n.d.e), which appeal to people's emotions or are intentionally misleading. Fake news troubles the idea of the news media as presenting facts about the world. By comparison, the citizen artist newspaper interventions experiment with the aesthetic qualities of facts as presented and perceived and the evidence of matters of concern to reveal new meanings, but unlike fake news they do not misrepresent what is at issue. For further discussion, see chapters 4, 5, 6, and the conclusion.

Chapter One

What Is Citizen Art?

Its Meaning and Challenges

Within the field of contemporary art there has been a rapid expansion of artists doing politics as activists or through social art practice[1] rather than making or creating artifacts that represent or take inspiration from political themes and topics.[2] Emergent within activist and social art practice are numerous artists who either tacitly or overtly allude to the concept of citizenship, sometimes specifically using the terms "citizen," "citizen art," "citizen artist," or "artistic citizenship," to examine the idea of membership of a nation-state[3] or to engage with issues of migration,[4] inequality, social injustice,[5] and so forth. And yet, within the literature on social or activist art by its leading academic proponents[6]—barring some discussion of "artistic citizenship" in an edited selection of articles that focus on social responsibility and ethical praxis (El-liot et al. 2016a), within a recent edited volume by the authors Dzenko and Avilla (2018), or on the notion of performing citizenship (Hildebrandt et al. 2019), which I will discuss further—there is little substantial discussion of how the concept of citizenship is interrogated within such artists' projects. Indeed, there is no comprehensive study of citizen art in all its manifestations as it pertains to discourses within the study of citizenship. Equally, the complexities and tensions that surround citizenship's assumed boundedness to the state or the notion of fraternity as the glue of political belonging and so on have not been comprehensively factored into discussions, and yet untangling the problems and limitations of status or cosmopolitan citizenship is foundational to understanding the scope of the political within the emerging category of citizen art. More importantly, scoping out how artists critique the concept and practice of status citizenship is central to comprehending how citizen art produces new imaginaries and performances of citizenship that reframe or contest normative notions of citizenship. Therefore, examining how activist and social art practice is reflexive of citizenship in reconceptualizing the nature of the citizen and thus the scope and boundary of the state, shaping collectivities that speak to the bonds of fraternity and so forth, is germane to this analysis of citizen art.

I should add too that my own citizen art projects have emerged from re-flecting on my experiences of being a dual citizen (German and Canadian), in addition to being of mixed ethnicity (German-Jewish [Askenazi] and Ukrainian), neither of which are reflected in my citizenship statuses, and hav-ing lived in five different countries. Over the years, I have navigated various citizenship regimes (the United Kingdom, Ireland, Canada, the United States, and Germany), and this has prompted questions about the paucity of the state signifiers of membership and belonging. My own art interventions are deter-minably aimed at thinking through the limitations of Western Enlightenment framings of status and cosmopolitan notions of citizenship and productively doing politics in ways that explore alternative conceptions and enactments of membership and belonging. This has coincided with noticing that new and nascent forms of citizenship are emerging within citizen art more widely. Hence, examining how citizen art performs citizenship is germane to a dis-cussion of citizenship's changed conditions. I should add too that this discus-sion will begin by assuming that citizen art is not about democracy, per se. The central purpose of this book, as stated previously, is instead to assess the little understood roles and nature of (social and activist) art projects and artists who make claims to the status of and perform as citizens to determine not only how citizen art contests state-bounded notions of citizenship but also how it forges new approaches to doing politics.

This chapter will therefore outline how citizen art has been understood within the literature in art theory and to clarify what is (loosely) being delin-eated as citizen art within this book. I will also briefly outline the tensions that bear on citizenship as a status so as to provide a context for this emerging ter-minology. A preliminary outline of the problems and pitfalls of citizenship is necessary here to highlight the limitations of the literature produced so far on citizen art and, in turn, to foreground why an assessment of citizen art matters to a discussion about citizenship. My initial framing of the problems of citi-zenship will be developed in more detail in chapter 2, where I will trace a few arguments in the literature on citizenship to draw out some of its complexities at greater length. This is important for seeing how citizen art projects—and indeed my own citizen art interventions—are deeply engaged in the problems that are produced through a state's citizenship regime, especially as art is not normally seen as a central part of a discussion of citizenship.

As a proviso, the following will not define citizen art. This is not the pur-pose of this book. Instead, this inquiry proceeds on the understanding that such designations and categories as "citizen art," "political art," "social art practice," "activist art," and so forth, are slippery and at times opaque. However, there are some key characteristics of citizen art that stand out, such as (1) how it disrupts normative notions of citizenship by exposing the limitations of status citizenship regimes and cosmopolitan idealizations of universal membership, (2) how it performs new and nascent modes of citizenship that do not reify or valorize the nation-state or cosmopolitan imaginaries, and (3) how it performs new modes of citizenship that "are yet-to-come" (Isin 2019, 52), that is, modes of citizenship that unfold and become visible through the practice of citizen art that, in turn, structures new forms of political relations—new ways of doing politics between actors.

With this in mind, this chapter provides the necessary framing for my discussion in subsequent chapters where I show how the particular kind of political doing that manifests in citizen art, and indeed through my own citizen art projects, comes into view through the notion of acts of citizenship. Acts of citizenship enclose individuals in a (political) act that has "a necessary directedness towards some other person . . . [that] makes sense only where such directedness obtains" (Smith 1990, 3). In chapter 2, I will give a detailed review of the notion of acts of citizenship and its importance for understanding not only how new (nonstatist) modes of citizenship come into being but also how such acts reshape the performance of politics. I will now turn to a brief overview of the problems of (status and cosmopolitan) citizenship to contextualize my review (and critique) of current understandings of citizen art.

Citizenship is not just a heated issue in the rise of populist politics (e.g., before and after Brexit, in the "birtherism" or "nativist" debates in the United States, in the emergence of the Black Lives Matter and Proud Boys movements under former president Donald Trump) or brought into question in the interrogation of state-sanctioned (cultural) genocide and other crimes, such as in Canada (following the publications of *Honoring the Truth, Reconciling for the Future: Final Report of the Truth and Reconciliation Commission of Canada* [Truth and Reconciliation Commission of Canada 2015] and *Reclaiming Power and Place: The Final Report of the National Inquiry into Missing and Murdered Indigenous Women and Girls* [National Inquiry into Missing and Murdered Indigenous Women and Girls 2019]); there are other problematics. Currently, the COVID-19 pandemic, even though its effects and management play out differently in every locale and country (i.e., lockdowns, limitations on movement, etc.), has nevertheless sharpened awareness of our bodily interconnectedness and interdependencies across the world. Not only has the pandemic highlighted the precariousness of life and death for all, but it has made visible the deep undercurrents of migration, mobility, and "globalization" and, in turn, their influence on the sentiments of belonging, membership, collectivity, fraternity, social justice, and so on. "Globalization"[7] or "transnationalism,"[8] sometimes referred to as "denationalization"[9] (Bosniak 2000; Sassen 2000), has altered our experience as citizens of the nation-state.

These concepts—denationalization, globalization, and transnationalism—acknowledge the realities of social and political phenomena such as the flow and stoppages of peoples across borders, the economic interconnectedness of peoples and businesses over national boundaries, the impact of online digital technology (Jewkes and Yar 2009; Fenton 2010), and the adaptation of our imaginaries to a world beyond the limits of our own locales (i.e., "a new techno-social framework of contemporary subjectivation" [Berardi 2009, 1; 2010]). Transnationalism and denationalization critique the assumption of citizenship as membership of the geopolitical space of the state and also as a constituent element of a social contract[10] (between the individual and the state and in turn the justification for a democratic state), where citizenship is enjoyed as an entitlement to state protections and access to the benefits of civil and social goods under a government's management. The rights to cross borders and to the basic conditions needed to sustain human life, such as health care, food, and shelter, as well as legal representation, education, and so on, understood as "universal rights" (Kleingeld 2012),[11] reach beyond any one nation-state. So a paradox emerges: Membership is assumed to be implicitly tied to a nation-state, but our social imaginary, framed by the lived experiences of the pandemic, universal rights discourse, being mobile (or locked down), crossing borders, migration, and the changed habitude formed by online digital technology, alters our expectations and understanding of citizenship. Engin Isin and Greg N. Nielsen have discussed the impact of these conditions on citizenship in their book *Acts of Citizenship*:

> What has become apparent is that while citizens everywhere may be contained legally within state boundaries that enact rights and obligations, their own states are not subject to such containment. All states, through multilateral arrange-ments and international accords, implicate (or fail to implicate) their citizens involuntarily in a web of rights and responsibilities concerning the environment (wildlife, pollution) trade (copyright, protection), security, refugees, crime, minorities, war, children and many other issues. . . . What complicates the im-age further is that many citizens and non-citizens (illegal aliens, immigrants, migrants) of states have become increasingly mobile, carrying these webs of rights and obligations with them and further entangling them with other webs of rights and obligations. (Isin and Nielsen 2008, 15)

That we are "implicated" in a web of interconnected relations alters the material conditions for the production of art and especially art practices through which one seeks to *do politics as a citizen*.

Also, one's citizenship status, constituted of rights and obligations, is fur-ther challenged by the practices of nation-states. For example, in the United Kingdom, status citizenship has been debased through the diminishment of rights and protections under succeeding neoliberal governments' policies. Rights have been stripped away under antiterrorist legislation[12] (Agamben 2005; Carlile et al. 2012), and welfare as a mechanism for ensuring a level of equality among the populous has been diminished (the rolling back of welfare reforms that were introduced between 1906 and 1914). Equally pressing are the inequalities of citizenship status that come to the fore through the lens of migrants who are resident in the United Kingdom. The lack of formal, legal recognition (access to political and social rights) of immigrants of various statuses (noncitizens, dual citizens, the stateless, "illegal aliens," [i.e., a metic class, etc.]), who not only reside within the state but also contribute to the wealth and social fabric of a nation (Mezzadra and Nielson 2012; Cole 2010; Sassen 2007; De Genova 2009, 2010; Nyers 2008; Klicperova-Baker 2010), raises the specter of the marginalization or exploitation of people, who for all intents and purposes are one's equal and fellow inhabitants—indeed, one's neighbors—but who suffer (political) exclusion and (economic) disadvantage.

Additionally, there is an implicit structural problem in the governance of the state that skews the value of full membership and one's representation: The United Kingdom's monarchical parliamentary system, especially the existence and use of the royal prerogative (which was exploited under Tony Blair), set a precedent for narrowing and centralizing power in the hands of the executive (Marquand 2004), which in turn undermines the spirit and meaning of being enfranchised as a citizen within a democratic state. This, in addition to the rise in power of the party system in the latter half of the twentieth century has led to the entrenchment of a "selectorate," who are the gatekeepers of government (Marquand 2004; Graham 2002). These factors together have devalued the institution of citizenship, reduced the political rights of the citizen, expanded the powers of the executive, and limited democratic participation to voting for one or another political faction.

The conditions of citizenship then have multiple levels and layers of tension, and artists who invoke or challenge the normative idea of citizenship or display or critique its essential characteristics carry with them the baggage of these wider connotations. Indeed, given the rather divisive language and adverse practices of status citizenship regimes in the United Kingdom, in the United States, and in the ongoing colonial project in Canada (and elsewhere), there is a pressing need to scope out new formations of political membership by evaluating how citizenship is performed within citizen art.

With this in mind, the following will now clarify how the terms "citizen art," "citizen artist," "artistic citizenship," and so forth, herein referred to simply as citizen art, have been used within the field of art and outline how the term will be used throughout this book. This is necessary for the more comprehensive discussion of citizen art in the following chapters and to alert readers to the areas of discussion in the literature that this research will not cover. The central problem of understanding citizenship within an art world[13] context is that references to citizenship are not consistent, and the new modes of citizenship have not always been recognized within art practices that embody, in my assessment, acts of citizenship (discussed in detail in the following chapters). Again, the range of usages of the term "citizen art" do not denote a hard category; nor will I describe citizen art in this way. It is also important to appreciate that citizen art is invoked with varying degrees of sophistication. On one end of the scale, it is an unashamed sales tag for marketing artworks (prints, paintings, drawings, etc.) online (see www.citizen art.com, www.citizenatelier.com, www.citizen.net). The notion of citizen connotes a participant in an international (online) marketplace and, indeed, encompasses a neoliberal imaginary where citizen art is marketed as a (confusedly) egalitarian product within a world of consumers. On the other end of the scale, the terms "citizen art," "citizen artist," "artistic citizenship," and so on, emerge within activist and social art practice. I will focus on the latter.

These terms surface within a cluster of nebulous concepts such as community art, public art, activist art, and social practice. They are in many cases used synonymously and carry connotations of, on the one hand, the rejection of art production driven by the marketplace (usually steered by commercial galleries) and, on the other hand, the continuation of the tradition of modernist aesthetic ideals that challenged the material production of an "art object,"[14] which was considered to be implicitly capitalist, through the "dematerialization"[15] of the artwork. These new "expanded"[16] art practices (community art, socially engaged art, or activist art, etc.)—understood as expanded because they do not involve the creation of an art object or take place outside designated arts institutions (Sheikh 2009)—refer to artistic activity that engages directly with the public, involving the participation of community groups, schoolchildren, and so forth, and are committed to endorsing democratic values of equality. Some authors draw out a discussion of these art practices as the embodiment of democracy and, in turn, the artist-citizen as a fundamental actor (Weibel 2015; Love and Mattern 2013) or as expressive of trans- or postnational aspirations (Demos 2013) that are also captured in the values of cosmopolitan citizenship (Papastergiadis 2012; Meskimmon 2011). Additionally, other names have also been used synonymously with activist or social art practice, such as "experimental communities, dialogic art, littoral art, interventionist art, participatory art, collaborative art," (Bishop 2012, 1), where citizenship is either tacitly or overtly referenced (Thompson 2012, 2015, 2017; Kwon 2002; Kester 2004, 2011). This phenomenon has been described by one author as the "social turn" in art (Bishop 2006a). This social turn in art practice, with its emphasis on participation and community, pivots on a notion of citizenship derived from the civic republican tradition,[17] that is, a conception of membership as direct, active participation in the civic space.

However, the term "citizen art" has been used by only a small number of authors specifically to denote social or activist art (Weibel 2015; Dzenko and Avilla 2018; Schmidt Campbell and Martin 2006; Polisi 2005; Frye Burnham and Durland 1998). Or it has been used as a metaphor (Elliot et al. 2016a). As suggested previously, these authors fail to critique how citizen art embraces a set of characteristics that rely on and are complicated by the conditions of being a citizen. Instead, use of the term "citizenship" presupposes normative understandings of belonging to a state, in reaction to the state as a final arbiter (Dzenko and Avilla 2018; Azoulay 2008, 2011, 2012; Love and Mattern 2013; Elliott, Silverman, and Bowman 2016b), or as a universal aspiration (Meskimmon 2011; Papastergiadis 2012). Equally problematic is the claim by Elliot, Silverman, and Bowman in their edited volume *Artistic Citizenship* that "artistic citizenship is a concept with which we hope to encapsulate our belief that artistry involves civic-social-humanistic-emancipatory responsibilities, [and] obligations to engage in art making that advances social 'goods'" (2016a, 7). This requires further explanation because it not only yields interpretations of citizen art as expressive of statist or cosmopolitan imaginaries but also slants the meaning of citizen art toward a vision of the artist as a "good" citizen rather than as generating new concepts and modes of (nonstatist) citizenship. The ethical implications of citizen art are precisely the reading that my analysis does not encompass. Therefore, it is necessary to outline the discussion a bit more to set it aside in preparation for my own argument in following chapters.

The notion of the good citizen artist is captured in the work of Lynda Frye Burman and Stephen Durland (1998) and Joseph Polisi (2005) and in an edited volume by Mary Schmidt Campbell and Randy Martin (2006). These authors have specifically used the term "citizen artist" as a central concept in examining contemporary art practices from an ethical perspective, all with varying degrees of criticality of the concept of citizenship that they invoke. For example, Stephen Durland states, "Socially committed, community engaged artists add depth to our culture and re-enchant their chosen publics" (Frye Burnham and Durland 1998, 22). In the same publication, Lynda Frye Burnham states, "When art is allowed to flourish in society, it can help develop communities, address social ills, heal sickness, protect the environment and renew the urban landscape" (184). We see this overreaching ambition for citizen art paralleled in projects such as the Citizen Artist Incubator (funded by the EU-Eastern Partnership Culture and Creativity Programme) that instrumentalize and indeed *depoliticize* the idea of the citizen artist. For example, in its first iteration (2015–2017), selected artists were groomed to apply their artistic techniques to communicating what other "experts" ("leading academics, scientists, policy makers, and experts from the fields of change management, conflict resolution, systems analysis, fundraising and media" [Citizen Artist Incubator, www.citizenartist.eu, 2015–2017]) had formulated as solutions to Europe's social, environmental, and political problems but were not able to popularize. As stated on the website,

> The Citizen Artist Incubator aims to empower the next generation of artists with the skills necessary to actively implement change in our society and to explore unconventional partnerships and interdisciplinary exchange as part of an international network. . . . We aspire to deepen your artistic specialization through a constructive connection with other artists, scientists and experts. By sharing your experience, skills and knowledge, you can broaden your impact without blurring your focus. You'll find out how you can respond to current affairs, make sense of our changing world, convey key messages, leading by example etc. without compromising on your artistic vision. *A Citizen Artist can depoliticize the political, emotionalize the analytic, move people and help communities to look at issues from new perspectives.* There are endless ways to employ our craft and maximize impact. (Ibid., my italics)

These examples attribute to artists qualities and roles akin to those of idealized "communicators" and social workers.[18] Artists allegedly engage in "community building," where they "improve the quality of life" for the downtrodden, the dispossessed, or the resident alien and immigrant. Through collaborative community projects, artistic performances, or "public art" (i.e., the strategic placement of an artwork—a sculpture usually—in an area designated for "regeneration") (Wilson, n.d.), the artist is invested with the power to iron out the pain of inequality and marginalization or bring "culture" to the public space in preparation for redevelopment (i.e., the sanitizing aesthetic of big business). This vision of the artist as creating "an active impact on current issues and global challenges" (Citizen Artist Incubator [www.citizen artist.eu, 2015–2017]) or raising the dispossessed—those who do not yet feel the warmth of art's great goodness—to cultural and social understanding, synthesizing differences and discord, is aimed at attuning all concerned to a singular identity. And that identity is firmly located in the idea of the citizen as a member of a community bounded by the state. It is taken as a given that the artist behaves as a good member of the national community (or the European Union, in the case of the Citizen Artist Incubator). The notion of the good—indeed, super (ethical)—citizen artist who operates within a national framework is firmly in play, and yet it has yet to be fully critiqued within the literature.

Claire Bishop makes a similar observation regarding the claims to ethical values and actions within social and activist art, though without seeing the importance of an analysis of citizenship. Instead, she is primarily concerned with refuting the emphasis on the ethical versus the aesthetic as a criterion for judging social relations within a community of participants in social art practices. As Bishop says,

> We find a recurrent focus on concrete achievements and the fulfillment of social goals. In turn, these are elided into a hazy territory of assumptions not so much "practical and political" as entirely ethical. This is manifest in a heightened attentiveness to how a given collaboration is undertaken, rather than to the meaning of this collaboration and its production in toto. Artists are judged by their working process—the degree to which they supply good or bad models of collaboration—and criticized for any hint of potential exploitation that fails to "fully" represent their subjects, as if such a thing were possible. (2006a, 5)

Although I applaud Bishop's criticism of judging the processes of art production as ethical or not, she seems to miss the central problem: It isn't so significant that a discussion of the ethical dimension is left out in judging this or that work as good. After all, if the medium of the artworks is social relations ("Nicolas Bourriaud" 1998), then it is consistent to examine the ethical import of these relations and the power relationships between individuals, which are germane to understanding the social and cultural engineering taking place within the space of the artwork. What is missing in Bishop's analysis is how we are to understand the notions of community or membership, (political) subjectivity, or belonging that are in play here. What kind of politics is replicated within this form of art practice? The notion of the good citizen is (tacitly or overtly) in play, and yet the practice of citizenship, whether normative or radical, escapes observation and criticism. The problem is not how good the artwork is in ethical terms but what is meant by "good" within the politics referred to here. A critique of the politics of the artists—how their own (normative) assumptions about citizenship are reinforced or challenged—so far remains invisible or is elided by debates about citizen art that tend toward moralizing over an artist's behavior or praxis (i.e., how they conduct themselves or employ strategies to do good social work).

These oversights are paralleled by authors who have contributed to a book titled *Artistic Citizenship: Artistry, Responsibility and Ethical Praxis* (Elliott et al. 2016a). This publication is one of so few in the field that uses the term "citizen art" as a title (coined as "artistic citizenship" here) that I will refer to it in detail. In contrast to Bishop's work, this collection of articles presents a more pointed reflection on the intersection of art and citizenship; admittedly, the examination here is not restricted to statist imaginaries of citizenship alone but extends to a cosmopolitan vision of membership as a backdrop for various arguments.[19] I will discuss the problems of both status

and cosmopolitan models of citizenship for understanding citizen art throughout this book and in detail in chapter 2. For now, I want to draw attention to
the predominant view of citizen art as a discussion about ethics rather than
citizenship. These authors emphasize citizen art in relation to social injustice
(as seen in the articles by Diverlus 2016; Vujanović 2016; Wiles 2016) or as
a pedagogical tool for transforming individuals into good citizens (see Montgomery 2016; Elliott, Silverman, and Bowman 2016c; Peters 2016; Bowman
2016). As Wayne Bowman states, "Artistic citizenship necessarily entails a
relation of stewardship toward social values and practices that make artistry
possible," and "artistic citizenship suggests a necessary relationship between
artistry and civic responsibility" (Elliott et al. 2016a, 65). He goes on to say,

> Art is not . . . an autonomous domain whose values are intrinsic and whose
> practical concerns extend no further than its disciplinary boundaries. Artistic
> practices are not merely technical or aesthetic enterprises, but deeply ethical
> ones—vital ethical resources where we learn some of our most vivid and du-
> rable ethical lessons by exploring questions about what kind of person it is good
> to be, how we should live our lives, and to what values we should collectively
> aspire (Ibid., 66).

Although these observations are valuable, the point I wish to raise is that
examining the ethical dimension of citizen art presupposes a citizenship regime as either a statist or cosmopolitan project. Importantly, too, the authors
(either tacitly or overtly) assume that the idea of citizenship manifests only
within a civic republican or liberal-individualist[20] imaginary with a focus
on rights and responsibilities or the ethical complexities of "participatory"
agendas by artists. Literature within the field is limited to primarily envisaging citizenship through the lens of its Enlightenment framing. The question
remains, what kind of political regimes and social systems are played out
within an art practice that purports to "construct *new* subjectivities" and by
implication new societies ("Nicolas Bourriaud" 1998)—that is, new modes of
citizenship? What kind of sociopolitical being is imagined here? What kind
of new citizen? How does citizen art genuinely present alternatives to the
Western paradigm of citizenship as a republican or liberal, statist or cosmopolitan project? Art criticism that leaves out a discussion of the problems that
surround the core concept of citizenship is missing the point. What are the
actual potentialities of citizen art when governments perpetrate acts of violence against their own citizens or behave aggressively toward those residing
within or crossing through a terrain, when they have "hollowed out" (Marquand 2004) the social contract, when the world about us is either restrained
(under the pandemic) or on the move, when the condition of belonging is
precarious and borders and identities are blurred in the increasing globaliza-

tion and digitization of our social, political, and cultural experiences?[21] At stake here is the pressing need to reappraise how social and activist art practices redefine citizenship beyond the conventional view of art (either tacitly or overtly) seen as a product and expression of the state, or in resistance to the nation-state, or, indeed, in the service of humanity at large. Indeed, how does citizen art genuinely instigate new modes of citizenship that are not informed and, indeed, limited by a civic republican imaginary (with its emphasis on participation) or liberal-individualist imaginary (with its emphasis on rights) or an (empty) rhetoric of universal bondedness? How does citizen art shape new spaces for nonstatist modes of membership and belonging to be expressed and realized *in practice*?

This book therefore is not aimed at assessing the ethical significance of art in (re)shaping, repairing, or contesting a state's citizenship regime or resisting the consequences of the (neoliberal) policies of nation-states. Nor is it aimed at endorsing an idealist view of citizenship as universal. Instead, its purpose is to examine how citizen art frames genuinely alternative modes of citizenship that are separate from state practices and idealizations of a world community. It aims to shift the discussion to an examination of the initiatory nature of citizenship that is revealed through citizen art. This objective has, in part, been articulated, and only recently, in examples such as that of Philipp Dietachmair and Pascal Gielen, who, in assessing how activists carve out and define political issues within "civil spaces" (as opposed to "civic spaces" that are occupied and orchestrated through systems of state governance, as discussed in the introduction), notice that artists are undertaking "local, bottom-up initiatives of many varied forms of *self-governance*" (2017, 23, my italics). Equally, a research project conducted by a group of academics and artists in Hamburg, Germany, called *Performing Citizenship*[22] (2018), and their subsequent publication, *Performing Citizenship: Bodies, Agencies, Limitations* (Hildebrandt et al. 2019), have made similar observations to those of Dietachmair and Gielen. However, they focused their inquiry on the performance of citizenship through art. The objectives of their research project were announced as follows:

> New forms of citizenship are developing in the cities of the 21st century: self-organized and independent from the state and often creatively they do not only negotiate but also practically shape the way of how we live together. Performing Citizenship explores the articulations of this new urban citizenship, which puts into practice its desire and right for participation with performative means. Is it possible to think a "performative democracy" beyond our system of representative democracy? What comes into focus is a gap between traditional institutions such as political parties, public authorities or unions and a self-confident and

self-organized (nonviolent) new citizenry, which increasingly contributes to re-solving urban crisis situations with artistic means. (HafenCity Universität 2018)

The emphasis on performed citizenship is key to my discussion in subsequent chapters (and especially in relation to my own and other artists' projects in chapters 4 through 6). However, it is worth drawing attention again to the fact that a discussion of citizenship as participation, as intimated by these researchers (but subsequently critiqued in their book), can at face value suggest an inquiry into citizenship framed by notions derived from a civic republican tradition. That is, the fetishization of participation within the literature discussed previously (Bishop 2012; Kester 1998, 2004, 2011; Thompson 2012, 2015, 2017; Kwon 2002) produces the corollary problem that "participation can turn into a vector for dominant ideologies as easily as it can liberate" (see Kluitenberg in Elliot et al. 2016a, 265). As Paula Hildebrandt et al. subsequently noted in their book *Performing Citizenship: Bodies, Agencies, Limitations*, "Participatory [art] projects [although they] often seem to question given power relations . . . also produce and reproduce them" (2019, 8). Resisting this confusion is precisely why this book offers a fuller exposition of the problematics of status and cosmopolitan notions of citizenship and a more comprehensive discussion of art interventions that do politics and in turn perform new (nonstatist) modes of citizenship.

The performed aspects of citizenship that will be discussed in detail through the example of my own citizen art interventions (specifically in chapters 5 and 6) explore local indigenous understandings of political relationships extending to more-than-human beings. This reminds us that we need not stubbornly insist that citizenship is contingent on statist imaginaries. Nor is the concept and practice of citizenship original to the modern period or classical antiquity. David Wiles (2016), in "Art and Citizenship: The History of a Divorce," discusses the history of premodern notions of citizenship in Europe through an analysis of Japanese Noh theater in relation to Bertolt Brecht and draws attention to the existence of an "Eastern theory of citizenship . . . [with] a different ethical system that puts interpersonal relations before duties to an abstracted state, human responsiveness before moral responsibility, and consensus before choice" (Elliot et al. 2016a, 38). In chapters 5 and 6, I will extrapolate further on this shift in perspective when I discuss W̱SÁNEĆ First Nation approaches to membership, law, and governance founded on mutually reciprocal and interdependent human and more-than-human kinship relations, responsibilities, and duties (rather than individual "rights," etc.). Local indigenous concepts and practices of political membership show us that non-Western and sui generis formulations of citizenship are evident (but suppressed) within Canada. For now, I stress again here that the concept and practice of citizenship are not exclusive to its Western Enlightenment framings. This book therefore sets out to distinguish the idea of citizenship from the burden of its statist or cosmopolitan imaginaries as it manifests within what I am detailing as the practices of citizen art. Indeed, it examines the aesthetic foundation of new and nascent modes of citizenship as performed in citizen art. What kind of citizen is invoked and conceptualized within citizen art when, as Eric Kluitenberg says, it is not a "vector for dominant ideologies" (quoted in Elliot et al. 2016a, 265)?

NOTES

1. See introduction, note 1.

2. See Weibel 2015; Dietachmair and Gielen 2017; Elliott et al. 2016a; Artistic Citizenship (http://www.artistic-citizenship.com); Ramsden 2016; Thompson 2012; Thompson et al. 2004; Museum of Contemporary Art, Los Angeles 2012; Bishop 2006b, 2012; Kwon 2002; Kester 1998, 2004, 2011; Frieling 2008; Hewitt and Jordan 2004. Also see art exhibitions, conferences, and educational programs that explore the complexities and effects of globalization from the perspective of one's membership of and relation to a nation-state: *Artists as Citizens*, Reflective Conservatoire Conference, 2018, Guildhall (www.gsmd.ac.uk/about_the_school/research/events_researchworks /reflective_conservatoire_conference); *Looking Out, In, and Back: Artists on Citizenship*, 2018, Brooklyn Academy of Music (http://levyarchive.bam.org/Detail /occurrences/17222); *Am I Not a Citizen? Barbarism, Civic Awakening, and the City*, 2013 (https://giladreich.net/Am-I-Not-a-Citizen-Barbarism-Civic-Awakening -and-the-City); *It's the Political Economy, Stupid*, 2013 (www.e-flux.com/announce ments/33079/it-s-the-political-economy-stupid); *Histories of Now: Space for Dialogue, Art and Activism*, 2013 (www.artandeducation.net/announcements/108839/ histories-of-now-space-for-dialogue-art-and-activism); *Zizhiqu (Autonomous Regions)*, 2013 (https://timesmuseum.org/en/program/zizhiqu-autonomous-regions); *No Country: Regarding South and Southeast Asia*, 2013 (www.guggenheim.org /exhibition/no-country-contemporary-art-for-south-and-southeast-asia); *Revolution Happened Because Everybody Refused to Go Home*, 2012 (www.e-flux.com/announce ments/33607/revolution-happened-because-everybody-refused-to-go-home); *[Un] natural Limits*, 2013 (https://acfny.org/exhibition/unnatural-limits-january-23 -april-1-2013).

3. To name but a few, see US Department of Arts and Culture (http://usdac.us); Free Class FaM (http://freeclassfrankfurt.wordpress.com); Bambitchell (www.bam bitchell.com); Neue Slowenische Kunst 1984–1992; Hartley 2012; "Kaled Jarrar, State of Palestine (Interview)" 2014; Plessner 2010; Janez Janša (www.janezjansa.si); Freee Art Collective 2017; Centre for Political Beauty (www.politicalbeauty.com); Schlingensief 2000. Note: the US Department of Arts and Culture is not a government agency but an artists' collective.

4. To name but a few, see Bruguera 2010, 2011; Schneider 1997; Torolab Collective 2005; Plessner 2013a, 2013b; Werthein 2005.

5. To name but a few, see Plessner 2018; Critical Art Ensemble (www.critical-art .net); Democracia (www.democracia.com.es); Yes Men (http://theyesmen.org); Chto Delat? (http://chtodelat.org).

6. See Bishop 2012; Kester 1998, 2004, 2011; Weibel 2015; Thompson 2012, 2015, 2017; Thompson et al. 2004; Kwon 2002; Hewitt and Jordan 2004.

7. See David Held's definition of globalization: "Globalization has an undeniable material aspect . . . for instance, flows of trade, capital and people across the globe [and] refers to these entrenched and enduring patterns of world-wide interconnectedness. . . . [It] represents a significant shift in the spatial reach of social relations and organization towards the interregional and intercontinental scale. . . . It denotes the expanding scale, growing magnitude, speeding up and deepening impact of inter-regional flows and patterns of social interaction. It refers to a shift or transformation in the scale of human social organization that links distant communities and expands the reach of power relations across the world's major regions and continents" (Held and McGrew 2002, 3–4).

8. See Balibar 2002, 2004; Della Porta 2007; Della Porta and Tarrow 2005; Faulks 2000. The term "transnationalism" denotes social interconnectivity, networks, and affiliations of people across the boundaries of nation-states. It also refers to the social impact of mobile populations, globalization, the multinational practices of businesses (multinational corporations), and the economic interdependence of states.

9. See Bosniak 2000: denationalization is a "generic, shorthand term [for] globalization, transnationalization, and postnationalization of citizenship. . . . [The term is used to capture the sentiment (among scholars and activists) of a] growing inadequacy of exclusively nation-centered conceptions of citizenship" (449). See also Sassen 2000 re: a disambiguation of the terms "denationalized" and "post-national" (578). Denationalization concerns the transformation of the national and the relocation of sovereign authorities from the state to "other spheres [such as the] supranational, subnational, as well as private institutional domains" (578). The notion of the postnational by contrast, "has to do with new forms that we have not even considered and [that] might emerge out of the changed conditions in the world located outside the national rather than out of the institutional framework of the national. . . . [P]ostnational citizenship is an aspiration" and speaks to the sentiment of transcending the nation-state (578). See also Beck 2003.

10. Social contract theorists of the Enlightenment (notably Thomas Hobbes, John Locke, Immanuel Kant, and Jean-Jacques Rousseau) sought to examine the nature of political society via a heuristic method of positing man's transformation from a "state of nature" to political society and outlined a reciprocal and interdependent relationship between an individual and the political community via consent and thus a "contract" between the state and the citizen. See Locke 1690 re: consent entailing obligations to a government in virtue of the government being the sum total of the (majority) common will: "Every man, by consenting with others to make one body politic under one government, puts himself under an obligation, to every one of that society, to submit to the determination of the majority, and to be concluded by it; or else this original compact, whereby he with others incorporates into one society, would signify nothing, and be no compact, if he be left free, and under no other ties

than he was in before in the state of nature" (§ 97). See Kymlicka 1990 re: the contract is a moral obligation rather than a literal contract; "none of us is inherently subordinate to the will of others, none of us comes into the world as the property of another, or as their subject" (61). However, the notion of the contract is one that persists and conceptually frames a purported reciprocal relation between citizen and state, requiring the state to answer to the majority will.

11. See Kleingeld 2012 re: the notion of cosmopolitan right: "Earth citizens' [are] bearers of cosmopolitan rights," and this is understood as "an essential condition of a global rightful order" (73–75). Kleingeld draws on Kant, suggesting that "cosmopolitan right regulates the interaction between states and foreign individuals or groups, addressing them as world citizens rather than as citizens of a particular state. Independently of their affiliation with any particular state, and independently of any existing treaties between states, all humans have equal status under cosmopolitan rights, which lays down normative principles for their interaction with foreign states" (75).

12. See Agamben 2005 re: historically, the juridical use of the "state of emergency" is not only in Britain but in Italy, Germany, France, and the United States. Agamben outlines the subsumption and normalization of totalitarian practices within democracies in the twentieth century. For example, the juridical apparatus of emergency powers in France remained in place for two years following the Paris bombings of November 2015. President Immanuel Macron replaced state-of-emergency laws with a new counterterrorism law that critics say establishes a permanent state of emergency (Osborne 2017). Emergency laws continue to be exercised within the Egyptian state (Dewey 2013; *Independent* 2013; Webster 2011). Human Rights Watch (2013) has claimed that the current Egyptian government has ignored the right to trial: "The emergency powers give the police the authority to detain people in three cities for up to 30 days without any judicial review, and permit trials of those detained before emergency security courts. Judicial review of detention is a fundamental right that may not be removed, even during emergencies."

13. See Danto 1964 re: the term "art world" indicates the theoretical discourses that conceptually frame artistic activities and definitions of art; "without the theory, one is unlikely to see it [i.e., an artwork] as art, and in order to see it as part of the artworld, one must have mastered a good deal of artistic theory as well" (580). This conceptual shift distinguishes ordinary objects from artworks. See also Becker 1982 for the suggestion that the term "art worlds" better denotes the multiplicity of participants in the production of an artwork and acknowledges that there are various and differing discourses that surround the production of artworks.

14. The nature and status of the art object have been undergoing a critical re-examination (see Jackson 2011; Meier et al. 2014), which draws on the literature of object-oriented ontology (OOO), aka speculative realism. See also authors Jane Bennett, Graham Harman, Bruno Latour, et al., who have critiqued understandings of materialism that emerged in the Enlightenment when, to put it crudely, conceptions of the object as "other" are articulated as substance(s) or mental property. Instead, Bennett and Harman describe a conception of the object as a "thing in itself" (possessing "thing-hood," [i.e., autonomous]) and its ontological status as one that possesses agency (rather than being a representation) (Bennett 2010, 1–19; Harman

2007, 129–41). Agency is intrinsic to "things," and "things" have their own causal force and *act* in the world (Bennett 2010, 1–19; Harman 2007, 129–35, 161). OOO bears on how one might differently understand how we engage with (art) objects, not only as maps or markers of human (intellectual) understanding but also as possessing a capacity to "intra-act" (Dolphijn and van der Tuin 2012, 14) and frame the nature of aesthetic experience.

15. See Lippard 1973; Lippard and Chandler 1999. Lippard argues that (some) art was centered no longer on the process of making an object but rather on an (immaterial) "idea," hence, the "dematerialization" of the object. See also Sheikh 2009 re: the connection between dematerialization and the post-Fordist critique of capitalism, and Sholette 2011 re: artists who willingly refrain from partaking in the commercial production of artwork, museums, and not-for-profit spaces, preferring to remain invisible to the art world.

16. See Krauss 1979: "The expanded field which characterizes this domain of postmodernism possesses two features. . . . One of these concerns the practice of individual artists; the other has to do with the question of medium. . . . Thus the field provides both for an expanded but finite set of related positions for a given artist to occupy and explore, and for an organization of work that is not dictated by the conditions of a particular medium. . . . [I]t is obvious that the logic of the space of postmodernist practice is no longer organized around the definition of a given medium on the grounds of material, or, for that matter, the perception of material. It is organized instead through the universe of terms that are felt to be in opposition within a cultural situation" (41–43). Thus, expanded practice refers to theoretical and discursive "position takings" on the part of artists. See also Bishop 2006a re: the notion of an "expanded field" combined with social and activist art practice. See also Shannon Jackson, who states, "That made me interested in certain kinds of expanded art practices that not only celebrated freedom, but also explored interdependent relationships of obligation and care and sometimes even responsibility" (Linden 2011, 4).

17. I refer to civic republican notions of citizenship as an idealization of the role of the citizen as an active participant in the deliberations and constitution of the state, such as, "individuals best realise their essential social nature in a democratic society characterized by *active participation* . . . where individual freedom and civic participation [are interconnected] in the promotion of the common good" (Maynor 2018, my italics). See also Goodin and Pettit (1998) re: "'Republic' is the Anglicized form of the Latin *res publica*. . . . *Res publica* [is] the public realm of affairs that people had in common outside their familial life, and traditionally has been identified as the commonweal. *Res publica* also meant the institutional structures of public life and can often be translated as the 'commonwealth' or simply, . . . the state. . . . The crux of the ideal type of the Roman *res publica* was that the people (populous, giving the adjective *publicus*) had a decisive say in the organization of the public realm and this understanding linked the idea of an organized public realm in general to that of a specific form, or rather, source, of such organization—namely, 'the people'—thus creating the modern concepts of 'republic'" (569).

18. See also US Department of Arts and Culture, n.d.: "The work of artists is a powerful resource for community development, education, healthcare, protection of

our commonwealth, and other democratic public purposes. Indeed, artists' skills of observation, improvisation, innovation, resourcefulness, and creativity enhance all human activity. We advocate complete integration of arts-based learning in public and private education at all levels. We advocate public service employment for artists and other creative workers as a way to accomplish social good, address unemployment, and strengthen social fabric. We support artists who place their gifts at the service of community, equity, and social change." Public Art Online (2008) states, "Public Art . . . is a way of improving the changing environment through the arts." Mick Wilson 2010: "We in the creative arts make claims for ourselves as the privileged bearers of traditions, of creative practice, of creative learning and teaching, and of creative enquiry. . . . We cannot afford to protect our self-image . . . at the expense of our agency and responsibility as creative citizens. We might need to see . . . that the critical creative imagination is the very condition of possibility of our agency as citizens" (28).

19. See Elliot et al. 2016a, 2016c; Peters 2016.

20. Although liberalism is "more than one thing" (Stanford Encyclopedia of Philosophy, n.d.), I use the term to indicate its classical formulation as emphasizing the freedom of the individual citizen as "primarily concerned with rational autonomy, realizing one's true nature, or becoming one's higher self" (Ibid.). See also John Locke (1823) re: the individual (citizen) and protections for freedom are anchored in the possession of attributes, such as rights. Rights are a form of "property," undergirded, in Locke's argument, by possession ("ownership") of one's body. Rights are dependent on a social and political organizational imaginary that posits the notion of "property" and its protections as foundational to the role and rationale of the nation-state (see discussion in chapters 2 and 6). Also, rights are conceptualized as universal and underpin arguments for cosmopolitan notions of citizenship (see chapter 2). Freedom then, within this liberal individualist paradigm (including neoliberal framings), is conflated with individual "ownership" of "property" (in all its forms). Liberal theory, from the Enlightenment to today, not only posits the individual citizen as a possessor of rights but also rights and "property" are constitutive of the liberal democratic state. The idea of citizenship is understood as contingent on the state as the ultimate arbiter (through legislation, policing, etc.) for protection of the individual citizen's rights and "property."

21. To name a few, for example: #metoo and #blacklivesmatter attest to the social, cultural, and political shifts that have formed around online digital technology.

22. See HafenCity Universität 2018.

Chapter Two

The Problem of Status and Cosmopolitan Citizenship and the Value of "Acts of Citizenship" for Understanding Citizen Art

In previous chapters, I indicated that an examination of citizenship is germane to understanding the manner in which citizen art does politics and enacts new modes of citizenship. I also pointed out that, barring some recent developments in the study of artists performing citizenship (Hildebrandt et al. 2019), to date no robust analysis of this fact has been achieved within the literature on social and activist art. The central question of this chapter, therefore, is how are we to understand citizenship within this form of art practice—where artists do politics and claim, either tacitly or overtly, to be citizens, especially as the institution of (status) citizenship carries with it implicit problems and is under some considerable strain, as indicated in chapter 1? The following discussion therefore maps some key debates within the citizenship and migration studies literature so as to further illuminate the problems of normative notions of citizenship and to ground my observations about how citizen art performs new modes of citizenship in the ensuing chapters. This literature also helped to inform the development of my own citizen art interventions discussed in this book. That is, it not only provided an important support for articulating my art interventions as determinably acts of citizenship, discussed here and in chapters 4 through 6, but also facilitated my understanding of what I have observed as acts of citizenship in the work of some other artists (discussed further in chapters 3 and 4).

The following will therefore address the fundamental problem of how citizenship is to be understood within citizen art and this book. I will look at some key arguments that critique the idea of citizenship conceived of as a (legal) status and a cosmopolitan ideal. This will be done for three reasons: (1) to draw attention to the prevalence of the notion of status citizenship as normative and to guard against confusing state-bounded notions of citizenship with practices in citizen art, (2) to demonstrate how the changed conditions

35

of contemporary membership and belonging inform the nature of citizenship within citizen art, and (3) to clarify how we might understand citizenship as separate from the state and, in turn, how citizen art enacts nascent forms of membership that are not expressive of cosmopolitan or state-centered notions of citizenship. My wider claim is that citizen art interventions not only trouble normative understandings of status and cosmopolitan citizenship in important and generative ways but also shape new civil spaces (Dietachmair and Gielen 2017) for doing politics in the performance of new modes of citizenship.

In addition to outlining some of the problems and pitfalls of status and cosmopolitan citizenship, this chapter, most importantly, will examine the work of Engin Isin and Jacques Rancière (and others) to establish that new modes of citizenship as enacted within citizen art come into view through the notion of acts of citizenship. I will discuss Isin's analysis of acts of citizenship to ground my discussion in subsequent chapters of how citizen art interventions disrupt normative notions of citizenship and scope out new approaches for doing politics. This includes discussing Isin's work in relation to Rancière's (2010) concept of "dissensus." I aim to show that Isin's and Rancière's insights support my argument that citizen art *performs new modes of (nonstatist)* citizenship and *does* politics in ways that have yet to be properly recognized or analyzed. This latter point is foundational to my (further) discussion (chapters 5 and 6) of how citizen art forges new practices of citizenship that do not pivot on Western Enlightenment framings of status or cosmopolitan citizenship. Two questions need clarification here: (1) How is citizenship to be understood if one strips away its boundedness to the state? (2) How are we to recognize enactments of nonstatist citizenship? This matters for evaluating how citizen art functions and to guard against conflating (even tacitly) its qualities and characteristics with normative conceptions of status citizenship or cosmopolitan ideals. My claim is that citizen art activities, which at face value may not appear to embrace citizenship practices, exemplify a form of political engagement that falls outside the normative vision of political participation (i.e., as seen in voting, protesting, etc.), on the one hand, and the instantiation of the legal status (rights and obligations) of citizenship, on the other. In subsequent chapters, I will show that citizen art is not reactionary (i.e., it does not reify the concept, values, or sentiments of a nation-state) and it is not an expression of cosmopolitan aspirations. Instead it is a nascent form of membership that may not yet be fully acknowledged or, indeed, easily recognizable as citizenship per se. The ultimate aim of this chapter is therefore to provide a foundation for examining the uniqueness of citizen art in how it does politics by first reviewing some contemporary discourses within the academic literature that assesses the role of the individual in enacting and performing, indeed, generating and instantiating new conceptions and practices of membership.

The intellectual architecture that informs citizenship obviously has a formidable history, and it is something of a truism to say that the concept of citizenship is contested. Even in antiquity, Aristotle noted that definitions vary and are contingent on the constitution under which one lives (Aristotle 1992) and that it has multiple uses and understandings and is not definable per se (Heater 1999). But this requires qualification: Although Aristotle does claim that the "state" (the city state) and the citizen conceptually exist on the same continuum, he also assigns an active role to the citizen within his definition and claims, "A citizen is one who participates in giving judgment and holding office" (Aristotle 1992, 167). Putting aside the narrow social and class restrictions in ancient Greece that prevented anyone other than property owning men from participating in political life, Aristotle's words illustrate belief in the presence and participation of the citizen as a key component of a sovereign political order.

This aspect of citizenship, as active participation in civic duties, continues to inform a civic republican view that emerged in the Enlightenment in the context of new conceptions of the individual as an autonomous moral and rational agent (exemplified in Immanuel Kant's "Copernican turn"[1]) and the concomitant development of the nation-state. Here citizens actively constitute the "body politic" in virtue of a contractual[2] obligation with the sovereign (advocated by, for example, Thomas Hobbes, Jean-Jacques Rousseau, John Locke). The notion of participation flows from a description of freedom, equality, individual deliberation (free will), and responsibility (duty) to the greater "self," thereby constituting the political reality of the state.

This narrative of a (social) contract—the boundedness of citizens to a sovereign state and in turn the justification of the existence of the state in virtue of its participant members—in addition to the advent of discourses on "rights" (e.g., Locke, Kant), gave impetus to the primacy of the nation-state as the entity to which citizens owe their title as citizens. The status of the citizen as a bearer of rights is legitimated by the nation-state, and this determines the what and the whom of entitlements and protections. Liberal democratic states in the modern period emphasize the rights of an individual in terms of the protections and benefits one accrues under the state's jurisdiction (e.g., human, civil, and social rights, freedom from harm, the right to vote), which are instantiated as either negative or positive rights that are enforceable by law. Rights, then, are conceived of as predicates and are conditional upon the status of the subject as citizen (Rawls 1971; Nozick 1974; Arendt 1976; Cole 2007). This also entails that individuals, via their participation (voting, protesting, assembling), inform the ways that political rights are conceived and implemented.

The assumption of the nation-state as "*the* characteristic form of political community of the modern age" (Fine 2007, 10) on which normative conceptions of citizenship depend is pervasive if now also widely critiqued. It has been characterized within the social sciences as "methodological nationalism" (Fine 2007; Beck 2003, 2008, 24–32; Chernilo 2006). Methodological nationalism has been criticized as a tacit (and analytic) presupposition that

> naturalises or rationalises the existence of the nation-state. It locates the development of the nation state in a teleological framework as the apex of a modern political community. It imposes the concept of the nation upon all political formulations which have emerged or survived in the modern period, including multi-national empires, totalitarian regimes, east and west power blocs, city states, and transnational bodies such as the European Union . . . [and] it presumes its solidity, centrality and increasing pervasiveness. (Fine 2007, 10)

It is imperative for my analysis of citizen art that one resist thinking of citizenship as constitutive of the nation-state for these reasons: The normative notion of citizenship does not capture the realities of cross-border affiliations, population flows, or the affective experience of pandemics (and death), the sentiments of belonging, or, indeed, "reconciliation" of the social, political, and cultural effects and *affects* of state-sanctioned genocides and so forth, that characterize contemporary life and in turn the context in which citizen art performs acts of citizenship. There are substantial qualitative differences between normative notions of citizenship and the changed conditions in which we find ourselves today. By contrast, citizen art initiates new forms of political practices that sidestep the nation-state. It is at the forefront of enacting new modes of citizenship that is responsive to local and global political entanglements.

However, one must also guard against assuming that citizen art is an expression of cosmopolitan citizenship. This point requires more explanation, beginning with a critique by authors who write from a cosmopolitan perspective (Sassen 1999, 2002a, 2002b; Beck 2003, 2008, 2012; Held and Mc-Grew 2002; Nussbaum 1996; Braidotti, Hanafin, and Blaagaard 2013). For example, in his characterization of methodological nationalism, Ulrich Beck draws our attention to how analyses of "global data, which presuppose nation state statistics . . . exclude transnational 'networks,' 'flows,' and 'scapes.' In membership and statistical representation, methodological nationalism operates on the either-or principle, excluding the possibility of both-and. But these oppositions—either 'us' or 'them,' either 'in' or 'out'—do not capture the reality of blurring boundaries between political, moral, and social communities" (2003, 455).[3] Beck illustrates how status citizenship is deeply tied to the creation of categorical binaries that are inadequate for understanding how membership is actually enacted in the context of shifting populations and, I would add, in the context of the pandemic, the intensification of techno-psycho-social relations, social justice movements (e.g., Black Lives Matter), the heightened awareness of state-sanctioned violence against citizens in some liberal democratic regimes (police violence, the use of "goon squads" in the United States), and so forth. This is also why citizen art is valuable to a discussion of citizenship: It provides models for how new (nonstatist) modes of citizenship are enacted in these new and changed conditions of shifting populations, global interdependencies, the entrenchment of techno-social relations, and so on, that produce an affective and relational experience of borderless affiliations. It is helpful then to take Beck's observation seriously and to beware of conceiving of citizenship as a set of qualities reducible to the state and its gift or relying on theoretical positions that enclose citizenship within the nation-state. Instead networks, flows, and scapes—that is, the crisscrossing and conceptually borderless domains in which human beings live and move (and die) in a globalized space—are the appropriate backdrop for discussing citizenship practices within citizen art. This helps us to understand the conditions in which citizen art performs and shapes emergent forms of belonging and membership. It is important too to recognize that memberships within the networks, flows, and scapes have been transfigured as multiple (i.e., the rise in dual nationalities and multiple identities and affiliations) and mobile, in parallel with nation-states that are seemingly transforming into transnational entities (Beck 2003; Sassen 1999, 2000, 2002a, 2002b; Klicperova-Baker 2010).

Cosmopolitanism then (in its contemporary form[4] within the humanities) pivots on a critique of the assumption of the primacy of the nation-state as the locus within which politics is exercised and citizenship is realized. The following will outline one central thesis from a cosmopolitan perspective that does not factor in the nation-state. This is significant for mapping the tensions between differing understandings of citizenship in some of the academic literature and also for contextualizing citizen art practices, given that the ultimate goal of this book is not only to discuss how nonstatist practices of membership and belonging are generated through art but also to warn against assuming that citizen art reifies cosmopolitan ideals of citizenship. Therefore it is important first to examine the debates in the literature on the relation of the individual to other citizens, which in turn allegedly constitute a cosmopolitan political domain.

At its foundation, cosmopolitanism follows the moral universalism of Kant and, in so doing, sees the human being as the primary unit of social and political life. Utterances such as having "a right to have rights" (Arendt 1976)[5] and "I am a citizen of the world" or "a citizen of a world of human beings" (Nussbaum 1996, 6) posit the primacy of the individual as the holder of rights ("Human Rights") and as having ethical responsibilities that transcend the boundaries of the state. Rights are not a gift of the state. Instead, they are intrinsic to human beings,[6] and one's responsibility to others in the world is contingent on this.[7]

In her article "Patriotism and Cosmopolitanism," Martha Nussbaum goes even further and argues that it is imperative that one's emotional connection and identity with the nation-state (which she argues is morally arbitrary) be overcome and replaced by a commitment to basic human rights that "join [a state] to the rest of the world" (1994, 5)—that is, that one join with others via an ethical commitment that surpasses the boundaries of the state. She is not claiming that this includes a formal legal status in a world polity (Bosniak 2000). Instead, it is through a sense of citizenship to the world first and foremost that self-knowledge is discovered through contact with difference,[8] the ability to solve problems that require international cooperation is achieved, and the ability to recognize moral obligations to others in the world is accomplished (Nussbaum 1996). Identity with the state or even one's ethnicity should be understood as having a second-order value. Nussbaum's citizen is set apart from the state. Moral commitment to others is a first-order aspiration for membership, and it speaks to the lived experience of mobility and cross-border affiliations.[9]

Authors such as Kwame Anthony Appiah, also speaking from within the literature on cosmopolitan citizenship, criticize Nussbaum for suggesting that one's affective experience of and identification with the state is (or should be) morally arbitrary. Instead, Appiah argues,

> States[10] matter morally, intrinsically. They matter not because people care about them but because they regulate our lives through forms of coercion that will always require moral justification. State institutions matter because they are both necessary to so many modern human purposes and because they have so great a potential for abuse. . . . [T]he state, to do its job, has to have a monopoly of certain forms of authorized coercion, and the exercise of that authority cries out for (but often does not deserve) justification. (1997, 623)

Appiah clearly recognizes the apparatus of the state as a key component of its own justification, and he also points to how political deliberation is an embodied discipline of the citizen. However, for now, the problem of his argument is that it misses the implications of Nussbaum's insight that the "transnational" affective and ethical affiliations and obligations of people inform the material reality and the lived imaginary of a "postnational" membership.

This matters when framing the context within which to understand citizen art because the affective and aesthetic experience of membership can easily be overlooked, especially within citizen art practices (a point that will be fully illustrated in following chapters). For example, Appiah supports a belief in the process of political deliberation as determining the moral legitimacy of the state. But this confuses the form and apparatus of governance with the reality of the psychosocial shifts that are present under the conditions of globalization: the "transterritorial quality of political and social life . . . [that require] a commitment to a vision of citizenship that is multiple and over-lapping" (Bosniak 2000, 450). However, the transterritorial reality does not necessarily entail the same universalist ideals expressed in Nussbaum's appeal to "world citizenship" (Bosniak 2000). For the purposes of the argument here, we need only hold on to the fact that affiliations (affective ties) between people situate new modes of cross-border membership that displaces the state and skews status citizenship.

To briefly recap, the arguments in the literature have so far caught us in a curious paradigm. On the one hand, an imaginary of the nation-state is in play as determining one's identity, status, and entitlements as a citizen, not only as a normative claim but also tacitly presupposed in theoretical discussions (hence, "methodological nationalism") within the literature. On the other hand, we are presented with a somewhat idealized but otherwise aspirational conception of global belonging, as captured in Nussbaum's comments. It is not particularly convincing that one's sense of belonging or the manner in which one practices political membership is explicable through generalized and abstract universal ideals of world citizenship. Equally, neither perspective sheds any light on the (nascent) forms of membership that are practiced within citizen art. This is significant if we are to recognize that citizen art and its enactments do not necessarily reiterate state-bounded conceptions of citizenship; nor does citizen art necessarily articulate the utopic vision of global citizenship. Instead, it is best understood in the *context* of the transformation of the nation-state (Sassen 2000, 2002a, 2002b) and the flows, networks, and scapes (Beck 2003)[11] that have framed and instigated our affective and aesthetic embodiment of multiple and overlapping memberships (Bosniak 2000, 2006). However, forms of citizenship practices are more readily visible in citizen art against a version of cosmopolitanism that recognizes and takes seriously the "immanence [of the] *material conditions* of global interdependence" (Braidotti et al. 2013, 4, my italics). It is the affective embodiment of the changed material conditions of membership—including affiliations that are not contingent on the nation-state—and the implications of this for political agency, rather than an articulation of an ideal or a reiteration of normative politics, that constitute the terrain of citizen art.

To further support my observation that the nature of citizenship within citizen art is not expressive of status citizenship, I will briefly list some additional key arguments in the literature that home in on the specific material conditions that manifest within a status citizenship regime. This is necessary for (1) seeing the full import of how citizen art performs new modes of belonging and membership in the examples of art projects that I discuss in subsequent chapters and (2) introducing and detailing the value of Isin's and Rancière's insights to an analysis of citizen art. The intention is to distinguish between citizenship as the embodiment of a legal status as opposed to an affective (and aesthetic [i.e., sensed]) and enacted experience that has real purchase on the formation of the material conditions of membership and belonging as seen in citizen art. This is key to discussing how citizen art contributes to newly developing practices of nonstatist and noncosmopolitan modes of membership and belonging.

First, it is not obvious that one's legal status is a necessary or sufficient condition for entitlements as a citizen.[12] Much work has been done to map how "undocumented" and "stateless" people embrace civic behaviors, such as being an active member of a local community, or make claims to rights and entitlements within a region, regardless of their formal status (Oliveri 2012; Nair 2012; Glick Schiller 2009; Nyers 2008). These behaviors, of course, do not make them citizens qua (legal) citizens; nor am I (or the authors) suggesting that stateless and undocumented people do not have to endure tremendous hardships in securing rights and recognition. But these claims and behaviors do begin to capture the ambiguity of citizenship understood solely as a legal status. This point is best drawn out through the example of the mass mobilizations of undocumented migrant workers (primarily Latin Americans) in 2006 in the United States, protesting against the introduction of the Border Protection, Antiterrorism and Illegal Immigration Control Act (passed on December 16, 2005), which further affixed and aggregated the criminalization of "illegal migration" with antiterrorism. The protests are testimony to the "incorrigibility" (De Genova 2010, 101, 103) of undocumented workers and their claim to be "present"—present in the sense of a de facto entitlement to protest against the oppressive legislation of the state and present as a claim to be seen and understood as members of the society and bearers of rights (De Genova 2010).[13] It seems, then, citizenship conceived of only as a legal status is too thin a criterion especially in the context of examples where the state's scope for the legitimation of membership (even if expressed negatively as curtailing nonmembers' identity and presence) is contestable in practice. It is worth briefly noting that these observations of the "incorrigibility" of migrants (De Genova 2010) give deeper significance to Tania Bruguera's project (*Immigrant Movement International*) in how it functions as an act of citizenship (to be discussed further in chapter 4).

Second, rights alone cannot define citizenship. Rights require that individual nation-states uphold and enforce them. International accords that set out to establish standards for civil, social, and cultural rights are primarily symbolic (Bosniak 2000; Geuss 2008). As yet, there is no "transnational body that can ensure states' compliance with major human rights norms" (Bosniak 2000, 468). Some authors argue, "Since the notion of natural right is from the start no more than a moralizing conception about what would be desirable without any concrete specification of an enforcing agency, there seems no particular reason to exclude woods, mountains, or other inanimate objects from the realm of purported rights" (Geuss 2001, 142).[14] The point here is that there is nothing binding in an a priori claim to rights in virtue of being human. Being human in itself is not a necessary or sufficient condition for the enforcement of rights. Equally, the development of a vocabulary of "universalist sentiment," where protagonists "reach beyond state law to press claims of right against the state itself," signals a loosening of the national grip on citizenship (Bosniak 2000, 470).[15] This indicates a profound conceptual shift: The state is seen on an equal basis to the citizen. Citizens (regardless of the state in which they reside), in principle at least, can call any state apparatus to account when contravening the moral import of (universal) human rights. Citizen art also "reaches beyond state law" by setting itself apart and "presses at the state itself" in its articulation and manifestation. I have in mind here art interventions that take command of citizenship issues such as Khaled Jarrar's *State of Palestine* (where people entering the West Bank were offered a passport stamp that Jarrar designed as a claim to a "State of Palestine"), Tania Bruguera's *Immigrant Movement International* and *Migrant People Party*, Jonas Staal's engagement in Rojava and the staging of "stateless" parliamentary democracy. (Bruguera's and Staal's projects will be discussed in detail in subsequent chapters.)

My third critique of status citizenship picks up on the theme of participation introduced at the beginning of this chapter. The practices of direct action[16] within activist circles (and by extension, citizen artists) and the notion of "commoning"[17] outstrip the idea of participation as expressed through voting and protesting. Two points follow: (1) Activism at the local level is grounded in the direct involvement of individuals in shaping local institutions and organizations—an aspiration that is evidenced in some examples of social art practices as discussed by Claire Bishop (2012) in her book *Artificial Hells: Participatory Art and the Politics of Spectatorship*, where she writes, "The recurrent characteristics [of community art, aka social art practice] can be summarized as follows: . . . [I]t aimed to give shape to the creativity of all sectors of society, but especially to people living in areas of social, cultural and financial deprivation. For some, it was also a powerful medium for social and political change, providing the blueprint for a participatory democracy" (177). (In chapters 3 through 6 I will take up this point again in relation to citizen art interventions). (2) Activism at the transnational level can be seen in the growth of nongovernmental organizations and other "grassroots social movements" and organizations that organize around an issue or common cause (e.g., environmentalism, racial justice, women's rights, labor rights). Unlike the republican and liberal democratic traditions that see participation (e.g., voting, protesting) in relation to a polity, what is conceived of as the "common good" or the "public domain" by activists is "drawn [out] more expansively than they usually are within the tradition" (Bosniak 2000, 479). Equally, it is important to recognize that citizen art too embodies activist strategies of direct participation that expands our understanding of citizenship. Indeed, many authors (Kwon 2002; Bishop 2006a, 2006b, 2012; Kester 2004, 2011) have discussed activist art as a "participatory" practice,[18] but none have homed in on what this actually entails in terms of understanding citizenship and they have not examined what citizenship might look like if they were to put aside their preoccupation with activist art as art. I am concerned here with identifying how citizen art functions as a mode through which citizenship is framed and performed, and not with questions concerning how this kind of political behavior can be judged as art. Hence, the purpose of my argument here is to situate my claim that citizen art is transformative; it does politics in the same manner in which political activism performs more generally. This latter point needs a bit more elaboration.

The notion of a public domain is expanded through the practices of activists. This is where differing attitudes to governance find real purchase and push at the normative conception of the bounded character of citizenship. Activists compete with state authorities over claims to the governance of natural resources, cultural products, and public spaces via differing attitudes to stewardship (Della Porta 2006).[19] The notion of the commons is invoked by activists not only as a challenge to conceptions of (and claims to) property and ownership within state(s) but also as an alternative form of governance involving commoning[20] within a locale, in a symbiotic relation to an expanded conception of the global, understood as "planet Earth" (Helfrich 2014; www.bollier.org). The local is the site of politics proper, and governance stands in relation to other locales on Earth, rather than to the state per se. Citizenship in this scenario is constituted of individuals who conceive of themselves as directly governing at a local level and managing the resources on which they depend, thereby requiring active negotiation between members of the community, contra the passive or reactive conception of participation within the civic republican tradition (e.g., voting and protesting) (Bosniak 2006).[21] Commoning and, by extension, stewardship therefore conceptually equalizes the state and the citizen. Indeed, it exceeds the state. Political membership as evidenced here is legitimated not by the state but by the participants in action and the duties and obligations that they take on themselves as stewards. Similarly, citizen art claims and, indeed, shapes political space in the field of action, and this is significant for seeing citizen art as an emergent and enacted form of citizenship that does not reference the state and sidesteps the apparatus of government and its articulation of membership.

Fourth, the condition of citizenship as a legal status is further undercut by changes to bordering practices and the regulation of individual bodies. There is an extensive body of literature on the topic of the border, and it is far beyond the scope of this chapter to discuss this material in detail. However, some contemporary literature (Nyers 2008; Rygiel 2010; Mezzadra and Neilson 2008, 2012) homes in on the "shift from territorial borders to borders based on governing populations" (Rygiel 2010, 142). What is at issue here is an analysis of border regimes (e.g., the use of transit spaces and internment camps, procedures for regulating access to a region, biometric data systems) as a "method" of population control (Mezzadra and Neilson 2008, 2012) rather than a simple matter of permitting (or disallowing) border crossings.

Kim Rygiel argues that following 9/11 in 2001 and the increased securitization of nation-states such as the United Kingdom, the United States, Canada, and the European Union, the adoption of technological systems of biometric data collection (in addition to internet data collection) individuates and traces the behavior of both citizen and noncitizen alike (and more specifically citizens who are already visible to the state because they are already embedded in its apparatus). As she says, "Practices and technologies of citizenship are increasingly used to govern 1) by displacing power from state authorities on to international organizations and private [e.g., security] companies and 2) by disciplining individual bodies"[22] (Rygiel 2010, 51–52). Management regimes are dispersed within a state territory (such as that of a university, to be discussed in chapter 4 in reference to *Citizen Artist News: The University as a Border Regime*) and are globalized under international organizations (such as the International Civil Aviation Authority) (Salter 2008). The data that attaches to one's "body" is traced and stored, and this frames the conditions on which one not only moves across borders but also within the space of the state itself. The border no longer is at the geographical perimeter of a state but is fluid and "performed" and contingent on the individual body, on the individual citizen and their behavior.

This shift in managing populations on the basis of individual data is concerning, and Rygiel draws our attention to the implications of "reading" the body as "information" and what this does to undermine the former conception of the citizen as a political agent. Indeed, it explodes the presupposition of a citizen as a political subject. As she says, "Mobile citizens are increasingly conceptualized less as political subjects with rights and more as authorized (depending on risk and desirability) mobile bodies. This shift not only blurs the distinction between citizen and non-citizen but also undermines (and potentially renders meaningless) the notion of citizens as political beings with rights to [in this case] mobility" (Rygiel 2010, 144). The geographical boundary of the state is superseded by the management of individual citizens. Understanding how citizen art is responsive to the realities of individual bodies being classified and "bordered" leaves open a discussion about the subversive potential of citizen artists when staking claims to being citizens. This point will be taken up in chapter 3 in the context of a discussion of how interventionist strategies within citizen art impact claims of citizenship.

In sum, "we can either presume that citizenship is necessarily a national affair, so that these developments cannot be captured in the language of citizenship by definition, or we can approach the question of where citizenship is enacted as one to be determined in light of developing social practices" (Bosniak 2000, 489). Analyzing the nature of political enactment, then, is germane to this discussion and will help to establish a foundation for understanding how citizen art practices carve out new civil spaces for doing politics and performing (nonstatist) modes of membership. The following will outline what is involved in the doing of politics as a citizen and by extension a citizen artist (versus weighing up what one possesses in terms of status and properties or data). What exactly are we to understand of how citizenship is enacted? Guidance can be found in the work of Engin Isin, who focuses on the nature of the act and sees in it a foundation for citizenship proper. I will discuss Isin's work to demonstrate how acts of citizenship (re)frame (transnational and/or local) sociopolitical bonds. I will argue that acts of citizenship and in turn citizen art are not only *based on* affective ties between peoples but the *basis for* binding social commitments, obligations, and duties that stages a "miniature civil society" (Smith 1990, 30). This is how new, emergent, and binding forms of citizenship are coming to fruition and not necessarily through our (legal) status as members of a nation-state or, as Nussbaum suggests, our care and concern for others in (relation to an abstract concept of) a "world" polity. In chapter 5 through the conclusion, I will further develop this observation by arguing that the aesthetic (affective and sensory) dimension of relations (including relations to "land" as nonhuman actors within W̱SÁNEĆ First Nation law and culture) illustrates that citizenship is conceptually expanded in practice and challenges normative assumptions (and practices) of the citizen as possessing legal status contingent on the state. Isin's work is an important start to this discussion.

In *Acts of Citizenship* (Isin and Nielsen 2008), Isin sets out to investigate how acts are a mode through which individuals transform themselves into citizens. He discusses how those who are deemed to be stateless or without political representation make claims to rights and entitlements that are regarded as exclusive to status citizens. The backdrop to this within the field, he argues, is "that most critical studies on citizenship focus on how [the legal] status [of citizenship] becomes contested by investigating practices through which claims are articulated and subjectivities are formed" (17). Political subjectivity is understood as "habitus," "(internalised or embodied ways of thought and conduct) . . . [evident in] routines, rituals, norms and habits of the everyday through which subjects become citizens" (17). Furthermore, these routines, rituals, norms, and so forth, are typically analyzed in virtue of their duration in time. By contrast, the problem that Isin is concerned to draw our attention to is one where "internalised or embodied ways of thought and conduct" are formed "within relatively short periods of time," such as in momentary acts (17). He sees acts of citizenship (citing examples such as the Montgomery Bus Boycott in 1955 or Marion Wallace Dunlop's hunger strike in Holloway prison in 1909) as creative breaks or "ruptures" from social habits and behaviors that do the job of "transform[ing] subjects into citizens as claimants of justice, rights and responsibilities" (18). It is the capacity of the act to "break habitus creatively . . . transforming oneself from a subject into a claimant" (18). This is precisely how citizen art should be regarded as well: as transformative acts that reframe how politics is done and how citizenship is performed and from where new political actors emerge.

Isin continues to detail how the act of making claims (to equality or justice, etc.) cannot be explained as issuing from the (legal) status of citizenship because claims to rights (i.e., the embodied sense of having "rights to rights"[23]) can be made and are made by people who are stateless or "illegal," as mentioned previously. Equally, acts cannot be understood as actions either—or rather, they are not reducible to actions. And to this he offers a more detailed discussion about the characteristics of acts versus actions. Isin draws on the work of Robert Ware to compile a working list of the characteristics of both acts and actions. Briefly, they are as follows:

> First, . . . an act is to indicate a doing. . . . Actions . . . also involve a doing . . . [but] they involve movement, change, and motion of objects and bodies. . . . Second, acts are doings of actors. Actions can happen without actors. . . . Third, acts happen because of a decision to perform an act . . . [and] will always involve a decision. Fourth, . . . acts take time and space for doing . . . [but] they do not have spatio-temporal coordinates. . . . Fifth, acts must have completion.

> . . . [Isin quoting Ware:] "The accomplishment of something is not an action although it may take action to accomplish something, and doing something will usually involve action" (p. 407). . . . Sixth, acts build upon acts. . . . They accrete over time. (Isin and Nielsen 2008, 23)

From this list we begin to see that there is a qualitative difference between these two forms of behavior. To guard against possible category mistakes, Isin notes that acts are necessarily deliberate, they require actors and "completion," and they aggregate (in meaning and significance). However, it is in discussing the work of Adolf Reinach that Isin fleshes out the full import of why acts are useful analytical markers of political subjectivity and generative of new forms of citizenship and, therefore, are worthy objects of investigation. At the core of the argument is the observation that the nature of an act requires an interlocutor. Acts, such as "willing, promising, commanding, requesting and contemplating . . . [are expressions of] a need by one party to be heard by another" (Isin and Nielsen 2008, 24). Someone has to hear (i.e., comprehend) what is being said and done for the act to be a social act and for it to have any reality. The point can be illuminated best in Barry Smith's discussion of Reinach's work:

> A command is not "a desire expressed by language" (Reinach 1969a, 61). A promise is not "some kind of will, consent, or intention, which may be expressed, or may not be expressed" (op. cit., 453). Social acts are such as to have a necessary directedness towards some other person, and the relevant linguistic expression makes sense only where such a directedness obtains. In a promise, for example, "the prestation promised must be understood by both parties" (op. cit., 446). Social acts thereby constitute a miniature "civil society," a special kind of structured whole, embracing both the one who initiates them and the one to whom they are directed. (1990, 30)

Acts, then, in virtue of being dialogical, are intrinsically social and binding and distinct from actions that are not necessarily so. Importantly, too, acts are qualitatively different from any other form of performed behavior in constituting, as Smith says, a "miniature "civil society" (1990, 30) in virtue of the dialogical contract between interlocutors. This is important for understanding the nature of the political relationships that are enfolded within citizen art interventions (discussed in following chapters). Isin's description of the nature of acts (as opposed to actions) and Smith's clarification about social acts as constituting a miniature civil society illuminate how citizen art interventions also enclose individuals in new relationships with social and political bonds. This can be further clarified through John Austin's insights about performative statements. Statements, such as "I do" at a wedding ceremony, do not describe (i.e., represent) a state of affairs but are the action itself. To say "I do" at a wedding ceremony is not to report on the ceremony but to perform an act: "it is to do it" (Austin 1975, 6). By comparison, citizen art and especially the *Citizen Artist News* interventions do not describe (or critique) a political theme or topic but instead perform an act and specifically an act of citizenship. Citizen art "has a necessary directedness to some other person" (Smith 1990, 30). It too encloses both "the one who initiates" the intervention and "the one to whom [it is] directed" (30). It too establishes a boundedness between interlocutors—a miniature civil society. Hereafter, I will reference Smith's phrase "miniature civil society" (30) or my own phrase "mini social contracts" to emphasize the subtle nature of the social and political obligations that transpire within citizen art in the performance of acts of citizenship, which in turn constitute a boundedness of relations within new and emergent modes of citizenship.

Isin goes on to make a further clarification: "acts are a class of phenomenon that indicate transcendent qualities . . . of an action, whereas an action indicates a deed, a performance, something that is done" (Isin and Nielsen 2008, 25). Acts, then, "have a virtual existence that can be actualized under certain conditions" (25). As a class of acts they constitute a conceptual and contractual hub, so to speak, of the ethical and political dimensions of social life and when instantiated by actions are given (spatiotemporal) reality. As he says, acts and actions are to be analytically distinguished (so as not to confuse what is at the foundation of political deliberation) but considered together (as and when occurring).

But one may wonder why this is important to citizenship. Isin is keen to draw our attention to not only how acts of citizenship generate and actualize political agency but how they in turn "rupture the given" (i.e., habitus) and thereby transform subjects into claimants of rights, justice, and so forth (Isin and Nielsen 2008, 27). As he says, "the essence of an act, as distinct from conduct, practice, behavior and habit, is that an act is a rupture in the given" (25). Apart from his adoption of Rancière's notion of dissensus (Nyers 2008; Rygiel 2010), which will be discussed, Isin continues with a fuller definition of an act: "To act means to set something in motion, to begin not just something new but oneself as the being that acts to begin itself. . . . To act, then, is neither arriving at a scene nor fleeing from it, but actually *engaging in its creation*. With that creative act *the actor also creates herself/himself as the agent responsible for the scene created*" (Isin and Nielsen 2008, 27, my italics).

Isin pinpoints the nature of acts as cognizant and cognizable moments that not only set the stage for the enactment of ethical relations (i.e., we make claims and "take responsibility") but also, importantly, function as mini social contracts that are perpetually negotiated and renegotiated, newly formed or broken, binding one person to another through their daily social relations.

These acts happen independently of the state and, indeed, are distinct from statist notions of political action. These small moments, these acts, determine obligations, affinities, and solidarities. Acts inform and shape our imaginary of the larger sociopolitical body and are at the center of how the scope of political life is determined. This helps us to better understand the nature of the citizen proper, not in the formal sense of being a holder of rights or as a willing (or unwilling) participant but through acts as fertile and generative behavioral moments that emerge and transform the body politic anew, displacing or disturbing normative conceptions of membership in the formation of a miniature civil society (Smith 1990).

Acts of citizenship, then, are core to my analysis of how citizen art practices are properly political and, in turn, how this kind of transformative art practice demonstrates a reframing of membership and belonging that does not align itself with status or, indeed, cosmopolitan citizenship. This point needs further explanation and will be at the center of a discussion in subsequent chapters. For now, though, the purpose of my argument here is to draw attention to how acts of citizenship break with normative conceptions of status citizenship and to establish that this is necessary for seeing how citizen art is instrumental in framing new notions of citizenship. This is important because, as discussed in chapter 1, the debates within the literature on social and activist art have missed this point. What has been missed is seeing how the political and aesthetic (affective and sensory) dimension of some social and activist art is deliberate in its modeling of new citizens. The point is that citizen art is alive to the real pressures and complexities of (statist) membership and cosmopolitan imaginaries and that its emergence is the practice of political acts that stake claims through doing politics and enacting new modes of citizenship. As Peter Nyers notes, "What is at stake is the model by which the political community constitutes its subjects, audiences and spaces [in the understanding that] the political community is also an aesthetic community" (Isin and Nielsen 2008, 164). Citizen art is at the locus of these two trajectories; it enacts the political and the aesthetic.

But this raises a question: How exactly are we to understand the role of the aesthetic in politics and, in turn, citizen art? This needs clarification, and the connection between the two is to be found in the work of Jacques Rancière. I rely on his insights about the role of the aesthetic in politics and especially his notion of the "distribution of the sensible" (2011b, 7) because this too is central to the positioning of my wider argument about the significance and capacity of citizen art to do politics and, in turn, reframe notions of citizenship. His insights are also important for articulating how my own citizen art interventions, which were modeled on the random interruptions of citizen journalists (as discussed in the introduction), expose "the configuration" of a specific community, its habits, and its practices. His discussion also, importantly, helped me to think through the point and purpose of the *Citizen Artist News* interventions. That is, Rancière's insights about aesthetics (sensory experience) as an a priori condition of politics align with how my own interventions (see especially chapters 5 and 6) alter *what* is *seen* as a political object and *who* is perceived as a political subject. The following will therefore review what Rancière says so as to establish how his work informs my discussion of the citizen art projects discussed in this book.

Rancière offers us a two-pronged analysis of the relationship between aesthetics (i.e., sense perception) and politics. One is his conception of how "the distribution of the sensible" is an a priori condition of political visibility (presence, voice, etc.), and the second is the role of some acts (as discussed previously) in constituting politics proper—that is, as points of disruption that expose inequalities and determine genuine democratic practices. Rancière calls such acts a "dissensus." I will discuss each of these claims in turn and then close with a summary of the implications for citizen art. First, Rancière's use of the term "aesthetics" is nuanced and deeply interwoven with his notion of the political and pivots on his discussion of the "partitioning of the sensible," discussed in terms of "the perceptible" (2011b, 7). As Rancière says,

> My work on politics was an attempt to show politics as an "aesthetic affair." . . . This term has nothing to do with the "aestheticization of politics" that Benjamin opposed to the "politicization of art." What I mean is that politics, rather than the exercise of power or the struggle for power, is the configuration of a specific world, *a specific form of experience* in which some things appear to be political objects, some questions political issues or argumentations and some agents political subjects. I attempted to redefine this "aesthetic" nature of politics by setting politics not as a specific single world but as a conflictive world: not a world of competing interests or values but a world of competing worlds. (7, my italics)

Hence, the partitioning of the sensible is a distinction between what is sensed and perceived rather than a judgment of taste—that is, an aesthetic (or indeed, a rational) judgment. As Davide Panagia says in his discussion of Rancière,

> Aesthetics names the affective pragmatic for the realignment of the dynamics of sensibility that render anything whatsoever or anyone whosoever sensible and thus perceptible. . . . Aesthetics is always political and politics is always aesthetic: because any system of representation is a carrier of a normative set of assumptions about political inclusivity and exclusivity expressed in terms of who or what counts as worthy of perceptibility or sensibility (2018, 10).

Rancière's conception of the aesthetic, then, entails not judgment—who and what is to be worthy of intelligibility—but "a pre-subjective, but also a pre-objective, moment when distensions of sensation have yet to assign value to specific persons, things and events. This is the aesthetic moment of indistinction, which is also the political moment of equality, when anything whatsoever or whosoever can count" (10). This matters to understanding the nature of citizen art as not only challenging the normative ordering of the sensible but also enacting new modes of citizenship (as I will discuss further in subsequent chapters).

Rancière's notion of the distribution of the sensible necessitates more detailed discussion because it provides the appropriate context for understanding how doing politics underpins citizen art as an act of citizenship. In his text *The Politics of Aesthetics*, Rancière defines the distribution of the sensible in the following way: It is "the system of self-evident facts of sense perception that simultaneously discloses the existence of something in common and the delimitations that define the respective parts and positions within it. A distribution of the sensible therefore establishes at one and the same time something common that is shared and exclusive parts" (2004, 12). What he means by this is that by virtue of one's privilege, status, and labor within a community, there are not only different and unequal (of course) shares in what is "common to the community" (12) but varying degrees of what is and can be performed, determined, and described as common to the community, and these are predetermined by the differential between members' "visibility" (or invisibility, as the case may be). As he says, "Having a particular 'occupation' thereby determines the ability or inability to take charge of what is common to the community; it defines what is visible or not in a common space, endowed with a common language, etc. There is thus an 'aesthetics' at the core of politics" (12–13). Our sensed experience and, therefore, our sociopolitical experience, is partitioned. Aesthetics (in terms of sense perception), then, predetermines one's understanding of and access to what is common to the community. It determines how visibility in the common space is divided and who has access to what is given. Drawing on Kant, he suggests that aesthetics "can be understood as the system of *a priori* forms determining what presents itself to sense experience. It is a delimitation of spaces and times, of the visible and the invisible, of speech and noise, that simultaneously determines the place and the stakes of politics as a form of *experience*" (13, my italics). This is where the acts of citizenship performed in citizen art projects have real purchase. They alter what is perceived as politically significant and reconstitute what is experienced as new modes of citizenship. Politics, then, is not solely contained within activities such as voting, protesting, or exercising one's status as a holder of (legal) rights but, instead, is intrinsically shaped and determined by the sensed (and affective) experience of our daily lives. This point is central to Rancière's second line of argument: his discussion of politics as a particular form of action.

At the start of his book *Dissensus*, Rancière states, "Thesis 1: Politics is not the exercise of power. Politics ought to be defined in its own terms as a specific mode of action that is enacted by a specific subject and that has its own proper rationality. It is the political relationship that makes it possible to conceive of the subject of politics, not the other way round" (2010, 27). Citing Aristotle, he has in mind here the conception of the political subject (i.e., the citizen) as embodying a contradiction: the activity of "partaking" "in the fact of ruling" and a sensitivity to or awareness of the "fact of being ruled" (27). Considered in this way, Aristotle's definition of citizenship as "participation in giving judgement and in holding office" is the corollary of being subject to a ruler's judgments. Rancière draws out the internal contradiction in Aristotle's logic of ruling and being ruled, noting that this is conceptualized within political philosophy as a normative and necessary condition for democratic politics itself (27–29). This is important to my argument here because he makes a distinction between political theories that frame an understanding of power as formalized rather than contingent on individual actions (i.e., "acts"[24]). He continues, "Thesis 2: What is specific to politics is the existence of a subject defined by its participation in contraries. Politics is a paradoxical form of action" (29). In drawing out how a subject is both an agent who can initiate action (can create and begin a thing) and a subject on which an action is performed, Rancière goes on to argue that it is necessary to break with the logic of the presupposition that "a determinate superiority is exercised over a determinate inferiority" (30). Instead, Rancière subverts the normative view of the political as actors acting on each other from determined social positions of power. As he says, "Thesis 3: Politics is a specific break with the logic of arkhe [i.e., the logic of ruling]. It does not simply presuppose a break with the 'normal' distribution of positions that defines who exercises power and who is subject to it. It also requires a break with the idea that there exist dispositions 'specific' to these positions" (30).

Politics, then (and by implication the mode in which politics is performed in citizen art), is not evident in the normal distribution of positions (i.e., actions such as voting or demonstrating, commanding or ruling). Politics proper (i.e., forms of action that do not simply passively reiterate the habits and practices of a status quo) requires breaking with the conception of the interplay of ruled and ruler and the endorsement of a governing order within which citizens do not (indeed, cannot) play a part in determining what constitutes the political. Citizen art does just this too: It interrupts the manner in which normative politics is determined and the mode through which it is constituted.

This is important to my discussion of the art intervention as a tool for doing politics (chapters 3 through 6) in that citizen art interventions restructure what is seen as the subject of politics and who is seen as a political actor.

As Todd May says in his discussion of Rancière's work, for Rancière, "politics . . . concerns equality" (2008, 40), by which he means that it is a foundational belief. Rancière argues that in the context of the status quo, which he calls a "police order" (Rancière 2010, 36),[25] this presupposition results in a tension (a dissensus) that emerges from the agent acting on the premise of their equality and coming into conflict with a governing order that denies or delimits that fact. "A dissensus is not a conflict of interests, opinions or values; it is a division inserted into 'common sense': a dispute over what is given and about the frame within which we see something as given" (Rancière 2010, 69). Disputes expose the structures and practices that delimit equality, and this is the point at which we are enabled as political subjects. Dissensus, then, is a cognitive shift that reveals "the political," founded on the presupposition of equality, and this is the basis upon which one acts (May 2008).

Rancière's observations were immensely useful to the creative development of my own art interventions. His theory was especially important in how he positions the actions of artists and their creative methods of hybridizing and appropriating ideas and mediums in generating new conceptions and modes of political experience. In particular, he outlines how aesthetic practices determine what is visible and, by implication, how they can make apparent or disturb the partitioning of the sensible (i.e., who and what is seen as the subject and object of politics). But also, his discussion articulates how new subjects and objects of politics are revealed *in practice*. As Rancière says, "Artistic practices are ways of 'doing and making' that intervene in the general distribution of ways of doing and making as well as in the relationships they maintain to modes of being and forms of visibility" (2004, 13). These insights about how creative practice is in itself a tool for redistributing what is seen illuminate how the manner of doing politics is differently arranged in citizen art through its aesthetics. As Panagia says, "What carries weight in these instances of aesthetic and political simultaneity is the capacity to arrange relations, and therefore worlds, anew regardless of one's assigned ways of being and doing" (2018, 3). This is precisely what citizen art does too. Although Rancière relies on a conventional notion of art practice as solely located within an "interface created between differing 'mediums'" (2009, 16), which he bolsters by a discussion of how art is delimited by a discourse surrounding representation (the mimetic in Plato and Aristotle, etc.), his appreciation of how art can interrupt normative conceptions of the politic and, indeed, intervene in the practice of politics is key to understanding how citizen art has the potential to reframe practices of citizenship. As Rancière says, "Aesthetics has a politics—which . . . is a metapolitics, a manner of 'doing politics' otherwise than politics does" (2011b, 8). By comparison, the specific doing and making that is at the center of citizen art is an act of intervening—an *act* of citizenship (Isin and Nielsen 2008, my italics). Citizen art practices employ tactics of intervention to interrupt the daily doing and making and partitioning of the sensible.[26] Put another way, new and nascent modes of citizenship become apparent in the practice of doing politics within citizen art interventions. Hence, citizen art *performs* new modes of citizenship through its interventions. I will elaborate on this point in chapter 3 to draw out how citizen art interventions structure relations that afford a redistribution of the sensible.

Isin's and Rancière's observations open up possibilities, first, for rethinking what it is to be a political subject and, second, for seeing in this how certain forms of behavior (acts) shape a political domain that creates and constitutes a citizen. And this has a bearing on how we recognize the political in citizen art practices that at face value we do not associate with doing politics and enacting new modes of citizenship. Citizen art actively forms and generates new political subjectivities, behaviors, and relations that alter the scene of politics, which in turn reframes the practice of citizenship. Again, I will develop this line of argument further in the following chapters to demonstrate the significance of the material reality of citizen art as performed through acts of citizenship.

I have argued that citizen art is best understood as forging new and nascent forms of membership and belonging in line with contemporary literature that criticizes normative notions of citizenship in favor of a conception of citizenship as active and emergent and able to intervene in and change the scene of politics. I have demonstrated that conceiving of citizenship as contingent on or determined by the state is increasingly incoherent in virtue of the affective ties of cross-border affiliations, moments of claim making enacted by people who have no legal status, and activists competing with states over governance (of resources), and so forth. I have shown that arguments in favor of cosmopolitan citizenship, by contrast, recognize the immanence of cross-border affiliations and the affective bonds between peoples as having altered the scene of membership however limited by its adherence to abstract notions of "world" membership. I have drawn attention to the fact that citizen art is not an expression of abstract cosmopolitan aspirations but is instead inherently engaged in doing politics. That is, it is a practice and not an idealization of membership. I have demonstrated that Engin Isin's analysis of acts helps us to better understand the immanent character of political agency and that the formation of miniature civil societies (Smith 1990) stands as a foundation for the bonds of membership and citizenship proper within citizen art. I have also outlined how acts provide some leverage in shaping and altering the scene of politics through momentary events that disrupt what is taken as normative and shown that, through the lens of Rancière, we begin to see how art practices can be instrumental in reframing notions of membership. What has not been discussed are examples of acts of citizenship as art interventions performed within citizen art and, in turn, a fuller consideration, on the one hand, of how citizen art thereby exposes the problems produced by status citizenship and, on the other, how it forges new modes of membership. How exactly are we to understand citizen art interventions as tools for doing politics and forming new modes of membership? This is the subject of chapter 3.

NOTES

1. See Kant 1987 (110, Bxvi) re: the revolution of the planets as a metaphor for shifting the foundation of propositional knowledge from the divine (truths, etc., founded in the word of God) to man and man's innate ability to reason.

2. See Hobbes 1999 re: "contractual" understood as the rational choice to surrender ones autonomy (i.e., "right of governing my selfe") in exchange for the greater protection of the "Common-Wealth . . . which [to define it] is One Person, of whose Acts as a great Multitude, by mutual Covenants one with another, have made themselves every one the Author, to the end he may use the strength and means of them all, as he shall think expedient, for their Peace and Common Defence" (120).

3. See also Appadurai 1990 re: the impact of the "global" on the nation-state by the increase of mobile bodies (shifting "ethnoscapes"), the speed with which technology is reproduced across national boundaries ("technoscapes"), the movement of financial capital ("financescapes"), the reproduction and dissemination of information ("mediascapes"), and the spread of Enlightenment "ideoscapes," exacerbating the nation-state's struggle to sustain itself as a homogenous cultural and economic sphere. Scapes "are not objectively given relations that look the same from every angle, but rather, . . . they are deeply perspectival constructs, inflected . . . by the historical, linguistic and political situatedness of different sorts of actors: nation-states, multinationals, diasporic communities, as well as sub-national groupings and movements (whether religious, political or economic), and even intimate face-to-face groups, such as villages, neighbourhoods and families. . . . [T]hese landscapes are the building blocks of . . . 'imagined worlds' . . . which are constituted by the historically situated imaginations of persons and groups spread around the globe. An important fact today is that many people live in such imagined 'worlds' and not just in imagined communities, and thus are able to contest and sometimes even subvert the 'imagined worlds' of the official mind and of the entrepreneurial mentality that surround them" (Appadurai 1990, 296).

4. See Fine 2007 re: cosmopolitanism as a critical space within a range of fields (international law, public relations, sociology, politics, cultural studies) that have

emerged since the 1980s and that (1) contest the assumption of the centrality of the nation-state, (2) recognize the interdependency of peoples and (transnational) organizations (such as the United Nations, nongovernmental organizations, the European Union), and (3) frame the development of new imaginaries and appeals to values such a "world citizenship," "global justice" and "cosmopolitan democracy."

5. See Arendt 1976 re: the "right to have rights" is an appeal to sustain rights for all within the jurisdiction of the state (invoking Kant's notion of the intrinsic nature of right) in her analysis of stripping legal status from the individual to "kill the juridical person" that thereby positioned categories of people (e.g., Jews) outside the visibility and responsibility of the state and humanity (145).

6. See Teitel 1997 re: the history of the human rights movement as emerging out of the values of social contract theory and, hence, the assumption of human rights as intrinsic qualities. Postwar politics of human rights "gave rise to a new paradigmatic view of rights as extraordinary and discontinuous from prior expectations . . . [an] utterly transformed model regarding individual/state responsibility and relations . . . [The human rights movement] drew their normative force . . . not necessarily from social consensus, but from the exercise of judicial power." For instance, the Nuremburg Trials used a normative vision, where norms were later ratified. In play was a new paradigm, a shift from human rights within a "social contract" (i.e., where individuals are entitled to rights/protections under a state) to individual rights bearing no particular relation to the state's assumption of duties (indeed, the state, as Teitel argues, is instead perceived of as a potential source of evil). Accordingly, rights protection moved to alternative sites and systems, to international human rights conventions, mechanics, and processes (Teitel 1997).

7. See Pollis and Schwab 1980 re: charters such as the Universal Declaration of Human Rights being particular to the cultural values and political ideology of the West, where "economic rights are given priority over individual civil and political rights" and the "philosophical underpinnings defining human nature and the relationship of individuals to others and to society" are exclusive to Western individualism (1).

8. See also Papastergiadis 2012 re: the epistemological value of "contact with difference." Artists are instrumental in problematizing and shaping a social imaginary that speaks to the conditions of difference as experienced in population flows and globalization: "Art is now a mode through which cosmopolitan ideals have materialized both in visual forms and through collective social actions. . . . [Cosmopolitanism] requires a greater commitment towards openness and an appreciation that differences really matter . . . [and] is often explored with vibrant effect in artistic practices" (14).

9. See Della Porta and Tarrow 2005 re: the politics of activists who form solidarities and networks that reach far beyond their own locales.

10. Appiah 1997 sees nations, not states, as arbitrary; referencing Benedict Anderson he argues that they are "imagined communities" of culture, whereas states are spaces in which political and ethical values are contested and determined (63n10).

11. See also Hardt and Negri 2000 re: "deterritorialised multitude" similarly denoting the phenomenon of "flows" and "scapes."

12. See Bosniak 2000 re: Yasmin Soysal's coinage of "reconfigured citizenship" (452).

13. See also Nair 2012.

14. This observation that rights in principle can apply to "woods, mountains, or other inanimate objects" (Geuss 2001, 142) is developed more fully in chapter 6.

15. One example is Indigenous peoples presenting claims for political recognition (including property rights and protections) to the United Nations (United Nations 2007).

16. See Graeber 2009: "Direct action implies one's acting for one's self, in a fashion in which one may weigh directly the problem with which you are confronted, and without needing the mediation of politicians or bureaucrats" (201, quoting Sans Titre Bulletin).

17. See Helfrich et al. 2009 re: definitions of "the commons" (res commune) as communal ownership of material (and immaterial) property such as natural resources (water, air, minerals, DNA, photosynthesis, wind, solar energy, seeds, etc.), sometimes conceived of as "gifts"; cultural products (language, medicine, internet, open source software, music instruments, frequency ranges, etc.) "produced by persons or groups not always clearly identifiable" and handed down through the ages; and public spaces and goods (res publica), primarily produced through state institutions (roads, playgrounds, social security, capital markets, political institutions, universities, libraries, laws, etc.). However, a distinction is made between "the commons" and "public goods/spaces": "Public goods require that the state plays a dominant role. The commons require, above all mature, engaged citizens. Living in a commons based culture requires one *taking* one's life into one's *own* hands" (9).

18. See also Meskimmon 2011: "While participation is a term frequently invoked by political theorists and art critics alike it is not an easy term to use well. For participation to have any meaning in either the political or the aesthetic sense, it must move beyond passivity, merely 'going through the motions'; participation must be engaged and active" (71). This supports my point that 'the subject must become part of the process, must actualize the event or, . . . be itself transformed'" (71).

19. Della Porta 2006 re: "Social movements criticize the 'organized' democratic model, based on the mediation by mass political parties and the structuring of 'strong' interests, and seek to switch decision-making to more transparent and controllable sites. . . . [T]he people themselves must assume direct responsibility for intervening in the political decision-making process" (239–40).

20. "Commoning" is "a social process where rules and norms are to be negotiated in processes that are often conflict ridden" (Helfrich et al. 2009, 11). See also Ostrom 1990, contra Hardin 1968.

21. Examples include Ecuador: "The Inter-American Court of Human Rights (IACHR) ruled in favor of a Sarayaku community that claimed the Ecuadorian government violated their rights by allowing a foreign oil company to operate on their lands without acquiring FPIC [Free Prior and Informed Consent]" (Pelosi 2012). See also the "Report on the Workshop and Panel on Indigenous Knowledge (IK) and Natural Commons in Myanmar," which summarizes issues and problems facing indigenous people's management of "1) Forests and shifting cultivation, 2) Resistance to land grabbing and legal means and political action to support the right of the Commons on their land, 3) Defense of local seeds and promotion of ecological agriculture

(based on indigenous heritage), 4) Indigenous knowledge on water, irrigation and soil management" (Bühnemann, Tillmann, and Ganjanapan 2013).

22. Rygiel 2010 further states, "Through the institution of citizenship, and the discourses, practices, and technologies of governing that it entails, individuals (and individual bodies) are disciplined and calibrated to the needs of the broader population and species-body" (101). See also Foucault 2013 re: the shift in political power as the dominion over the life and death of a juridical subject to that of the management of "living beings": "Life as a political object was in a sense taken at face value and turned back against the system that was bent on controlling it. It was life more than the law that became the issue of political struggles, even if the latter were formulated through affirmations concerning rights. The 'right' to life, to one's body, to health, to happiness, to the satisfaction of needs, and beyond all the oppressions or 'alienations,' the 'right' to rediscover what one is and all that one can be, this 'right'—which the classical juridical system was utterly incapable of comprehending—was the political response to all these new procedures of power which did not derive, either, from the traditional right of sovereignty" (48–49).

23. See Arendt 2009.

24. Rancière does not distinguish between acts and actions. However, Rancière's use of the word "action" is not undermined if it is understood as "act(s)" for the very reason that both Isin and Rancière conceive of acts/actions as doing the same thing—as disrupting normative notions and practices of politics. I will use the terms interchangeably from here on.

25. Rancière 2010 states, "The essence of the police lies in a partition of the sensible that is characterized by the absence of void and supplement: society here is made up of groups tied to specific modes of doing, to places in which these occupations are exercised, and to modes of being corresponding to these occupations and these places. In this matching of functions, places and ways of being, there is no place for any void. It is this exclusion of what 'is not' that constitutes the police-principle at the core of statist practices" (36). Rancière (2011b) also says, "Politics does not stem from a place outside the police. . . . But there are conflicting ways of doing things with the 'places' that [the police order] allocates: of relocating, reshaping or redoubling them" (6).

26. See also De Certeau 1984 re: the practice of walking as a potential form of resistance within a city. Its subversive potential resides in circumventing, through the act of walking, a city's organization (i.e., the power structures evident in its social architecture expressed through its buildings and roadways and main flows of the populous, etc.). De Certeau argues that via detours, reversals, shortcuts, the forging of new pathways, and so forth, the practice of walking, as an act of appropriation (i.e., being bodily engaged in disruption), is a form of resistance.

Chapter Three

Art Interventions as Tools for Doing Politics and Shaping New Terrain

In previous chapters, I have spoken at length about why it is valuable to assess the manner in which politics is performed within citizen art, indicating that citizenship itself is reconfigured through its practices. However, the term "intervention," as used within this book, is in need of clarification. The aim of this chapter is therefore to first outline some of the various understandings of an art intervention within some of the literature in contemporary art criticism to show how it is understood in terms of actions, projects, and tools.[1] I will then draw out a comparison with the responsibility to protect (RtoP) (an obvious example of a political intervention) and argue that citizen art and RtoP share some key characteristics in their active restructuring of (status) citizenship. This is important for recognizing the uniqueness of citizen art projects in how they do politics and practice new modes of citizenship through interventionist strategies. Equally, it is important to distinguish between different forms of art intervention because the term has wide use and varied meanings and is not a coherent or cohesive category. It is noticeable too that a comprehensive study of art interventions is lacking in the literature even though the term is frequently used by artists and academics from a variety of fields (e.g., in the art world, management studies, the literature on RtoP). This chapter in no way can fully capture the complexities of the subject. However, for now it is necessary to delineate some of the core distinguishing features of citizen art interventions in preparation for my discussion in following chapters. The purpose is to distinguish citizen art interventions from other forms of art intervention and also to demonstrate that they produce genuine political acts that have real purchase in the doing of politics.

I will detail how citizen art projects structure social and political relations, in and through their practice, in such a way as to create new subjectivities, new "forms of life" (Martin 2013, 200), that do not reify normative imaginaries of citizenship. As Chantal Mouffe says, "Critical art practices can play an important role in the creation of a multiplicity of sites where the dominant hegemony would be questioned. They [art interventions] should be seen as counter-hegemonic interventions, which, by contributing to the construction of new practices and new subjectivities, aim at subverting the dominant hegemony" (Martin 2013, 213). I argue that citizen art projects do this and more. They also create new pathways and models for performing nonstatist citizenship. This includes recognizing the perpetually nascent and emergent nature of citizenship rather than seeing membership and belonging as flowing from a set of (theoretical) rules and principles. Citizen art projects do not rearticulate the nation-state as the entity to which one owes one's title as citizen (as discussed in chapter 2), and they are not a mechanism for generating a kind of agonism on which democratic practices are realized and performed (as might be assumed if one were to read through the work of Mouffe). Therefore, it is essential to map the basic characteristics of citizen art interventions so as to recognize their value to the production of nascent and nonstatist modes of citizenship.

This chapter will discuss some of the key characteristics of art interventions through two historical examples (two artists' collectives of the 1960s and 1970s) and my first intervention, *The Mobile Armband Exhibition* (Plessner 2011), for two reasons. First, I will demonstrate that these early iterations draw on a rejection of "studio art" that, importantly, frames the critical purchase of citizen art interventions in the present day. This is also to acknowledge the deep legacy of artists interrogating the practice of citizenship within citizen art, even though so little research has been done to identify and analyze this phenomenon within art criticism. Second, I will more carefully describe not only how citizen art troubles norms and conventions of status and cosmopolitan citizenship but also how it carves out new spaces of criticality and, indeed, devises inventive political strategies that counter normative practices of membership. New political strategies include experimenting with forms of sociality, (re)framing our experience of each other, and altering our relation to the normative conception and regime of citizenship. I will show how sociopolitical relations are structured within citizen art (and its "acts of citizenship") to illustrate the manner in which some interventions are effective tools for doing politics.

This chapter is divided into two sections: short disruptive interventions and the interventionist project. This distinguishes between primarily two forms of art intervention: Some are public, "stunt-like" criticisms that are short in duration, and others involve more comprehensive and long-term "project-based" approaches that often include working with other (nonartistic) people. However, these categories are not mutually exclusive. I merely aim to loosely map their form so as to provide a foundation for my discussion of contemporary examples of citizen art interventions in subsequent chapters. I should say here too that *The Mobile Armband Exhibition* was my first step in experimenting with art interventions. I will therefore discuss how the kind of "making and doing" (Rancière 2004) that manifested in its creation and execution not only involved me in enacting a critique of the workings of a state's citizenship regime (in this case, a protest march) but also, as a rudimentary step, helped me to think through in *practice* the potential for an art intervention to prod, interrupt, and, indeed, purposefully alter the aesthetic conditions of a political event. It also helped me to grasp how art interventions can collapse into acts of citizenship.

As indicated previously, I sum up this chapter with a brief comparison of citizen art interventions and the notion of humanitarian intervention such as the RtoP (Evans 2006; Verellen 2012; Cannizzaro 2015; Bajoria and McMahon 2013; Kardas 2001; Ryniker 2001; UN General Assembly 2005). The purpose of this comparison is to further demonstrate that citizen art interventions are comprehensive and deliberate political acts and not artistic gimmicks staged for private (aesthetic) experience. The comparison is valuable for illustrating how RtoP and citizen art delink the idea of a citizen and state, without either invoking or advancing cosmopolitan notions of citizenship (contra Papastergiadis 2012; Meskimmon 2013; Byrne and Schoene 2013).[2] Equally, the comparison is helpful for showing how citizen art expands understandings of citizenship beyond its normative imaginaries, extending the insights of Engin Isin, Jacques Rancière, and others.

The leading question then is how interventions are understood within the art world. Numerous contemporary authors in art theory and criticism have turned away from theorizing artworks as aesthetic "objects" toward the notion of "projects"[3] (Staal 2015b; Kester 2011; Miessen 2011; Thompson 2012; Wochenklauser 2009; Carroll La 2016), "actions" (Gray 1993; Hendricks and Toche 1978; Scholl 2010), or "relations" (Bourriaud 2002). In line with these distinctions the use of the term "intervention" has emerged to denote "art designed specifically to interact with an existing structure or situation, be it another artwork, the audience, an institution or in the public domain" (Tate, n.d.). Although the definition offered here by the Tate Gallery may be vague and sweeping, the use of the term is an indication of its common parlance in contemporary art.[4] The term "artistic intervention" has also been used synonymously with the term "artists' residencies"[5] in business contexts and health sectors (primarily in Sweden, Denmark, France, Austria), which are the subject of analysis in business schools and management studies programs[6] (Styhre and Fröberg 2016; Berthoin Antal 2014; Soila-Wadman and Haselwanter 2014). However, it is important to stress that not all art interventions share the same characteristics; nor do they all do politics in the manner that is significant to citizen art. The following will offer a brief examination of the constitutive elements of art interventions to prepare for the more complex examples of citizen art projects in the following chapters.

SHORT DISRUPTIVE INTERVENTIONS

The idea of art interventions became more fully articulated in the 1960s and 1970s with the intersection of conceptual art, the proliferation of performance art, and, more widely, the desire of artists to engage more directly in the political and social issues of their times. Artists' collectives such as the Guerilla Art Action Group (GAAG; 1969–1976), the Artist Placement Group (APG; 1966–1980s), Experiments in Art and Technology (1966–2001), the Event-structure Research Group (1969–1979), the Zoo Group (1968–1970, under the leadership of Michelangelo Pistoletto), Fluxus, Viennese Actionism, the Situationists, and numerous other groups of artists and individuals[7] employed what today would be labeled as interventions. In these early iterations, the term "action art" (Gray 1993) was often invoked to distinguish performative event-based practices from formal studio art (understood primarily as painting and sculpture) and also to signal artists' direct engagement with political issues. In the case of the GAAG, their interventions were short in duration, decisive, and politically pointed, and the form these interventions took intersected with the activities of other artists of the time who interrogated the basis of art production, its meaning, and its role, especially in relation to the state. GAAG's interventions took the form of public protests and helped to lay the foundation for the use of stunt-based "guerilla"[8] tactics by numerous contemporary artists, such as the Yes Men (http://theyesmen.org), the Art Not Oil Coalition (www.artnotoil.org.uk), the Laboratory of Insurrectional Imagination (https://labofii.wordpress.com), and Liberate Tate (www.liberatetate .org.uk/liberating-tate), to name but a few.[9] The following will briefly outline one example of GAAG's interventions to open my discussion of how citizen art interventions disrupt hegemonic political narratives—what Chantal Mouffe (2007) sees as the central value of art interventions and what Rancière describes as "rupturing the given" (2010, 36) or creating "a fissure in the sensible order by confronting the established framework of perception, thought, and action" (2004, 85).

On January 3, 1970, at the Museum of Modern Art (New York), members of GAAG and other artists assembled in front of Pablo Picasso's *Guernica*, a painting commemorating the bombing of the Basque town of Guernica, Spain, in 1937 during the Spanish Civil War and the massacre of its women and children. The purpose of GAAG's intervention was to hold a memorial service for "dead babies murdered in Songmy" (Hendricks and Toche 1978), also known as the My Lai massacre, by US soldiers during the Vietnam War. Members of GAAG and other participants assembled in front of the painting, placing wreaths and flowers beneath it. A woman affiliated with GAAG sat on the floor in front of the wreaths holding a baby, while a priest conducted a memorial service (Hendricks and Toche 1978). The implementation of this (unauthorized) event within a national museum, positioned in front of an iconic and evocative painting that is symbolic of state violence, illustrates the potency of interventions of this kind for doing politics. GAAG's intervention agitated in a number of ways. First, by conflating references to the bombing of Guernica with My Lai and in turn linking German and Italian fascism and the Spanish state with US state violence, the intervention drew attention to the US government's actions in Vietnam as akin to the horrors perpetrated by state actors during World War II. Second, the intervention troubled the role of (studio) art (in the example of Picasso's painting) in the context of a national museum that is, in practice, a valorization of the nation-state and the political establishment. It thereby disrupted the lazy assumption that art is distinct from politics and, indeed, revealed how the role of art within state institutions (e.g., museums) can perpetuate the normalization of state violence. Third, the intervention, as an unauthorized performative spectacle, created space for their actions to be seen to do the work of exposing the social and political structures in which they found themselves.[10] That is, the intervention had an expressive character in virtue of staging a public refutation to mainstream political narratives and, as a tactical strategy, disrupted everyday life.

Artistic disruptions such as this can confound and confuse in their disturbance of hegemonic norms, especially when the intervention is a means to another end. That is, art interventions of this kind "are not an external practice to comment on the struggle or influence its representation in the Media" (Scholl 2010, 69). Instead, an art intervention such as this "contribute[s] to the *clarification* of social struggles by *immersing* itself [i.e., the art intervention] into them [i.e., the struggle]" (69, my italics). I would hold that this immersive quality of an intervention and its performative capacity to reveal new dimensions of the political conditions of an event, as well as one's physical encounter with a regime (i.e., a bodily encounter with the status quo), permit individuals to see, grasp, think through, and develop new understandings of the political complexities they confront. This is one of the key characteristics of the interventions that are created and effected as citizen art practices. To explain this point more carefully, I will turn to the example of the first of my art interventions: *The Mobile Armband Exhibition* (MAE; Plessner 2011) (see figures 3.1, 3.2, and 3.3). *MAE* further illustrates the nature of these temporal stuntlike interventionist tactics for troubling normative assumptions about a state's (status) citizenship regime.

Figure 3.1. The *Mobile Armband Exhibition*, Trade Union Conference Rally, March 26, 2011, London, United Kingdom. Top: one of the armband slogans; bottom left: a costumed protestor wearing one of the armbands; bottom right: the citizen artist team joining the rally carrying a supply of armbands. *Photo courtesy of F. D. Plessner and Sophia Selby*

Figure 3.2. Left: members of the Anonymous Hacktivist group wearing the armbands; right: a member of the citizen artist team soliciting a protestor to participate in the *Mobile Armband Exhibition. Photo courtesy of F. D. Plessner and Sophia Selby*

PROTEST– ONCE YOU HAVE IT, YOU LOVE IT	**PROTEST LIFESTYLE**	PROTEST: MAKING PEOPLE SUCCESSFUL IN A CHANGING WORLD
THE ART OF PROTEST	BE YOUNG, HAVE FUN, TASTE PROTEST	**ENJOY PROTEST**

Figure 3.3. Examples of the armband slogans worn by protestors during the *Mobile Armband Exhibition*, Trade Union Conference Rally, March 26, 2011, London, United Kingdom. *Photo courtesy of F. D. Plessner*

MAE (Plessner 2011) set out to interrogate the aesthetics of political resistance that manifest within the space of a protest rally (in this instance, the Trades Union Congress Rally, aka March for the Alternative or the Anticuts Protest, March 26, 2011). *MAE* intentionally drew on the short, stuntlike interventionist form, parsing studio art and performative acts by using the rally as an exhibition space. My aim was to experiment with "hijacking"[11] the aesthetic (visual and performative) display of a protest rally, turning the rally into an object in itself and, specifically, an arena for the display of objects. By asking the citizenry to wear armbands that parodied the protest, the intervention embodied a newly declared public exhibition space. It was also an important stepping-stone in the development of my art interventions in that the moment of the rally provided an opportunity to act and to theorize through practice. On the one hand, the purpose was to draw attention to the space of the rally as an aesthetic and affective performance of (status) citizenship[12] (i.e., the public refutation of a state's policies). On the other hand, the aim was to critique how protests can operate as a normative expression of status citizenship that itself produces elisions in who and what is seen.

Protests admittedly can be immensely valuable and operative expressions of resistance to a state, but they also embody a "partitioning of the sensible" (Rancière 2004) in that they too produce elisions in what is seen as politically significant and also who is seen as a political actor. How actors are visible (or not) within the doing of politics had quickly unfolded as a key concern of mine (I will return to this point in chapter 5 through the conclusion). I therefore set out to first explore how the aesthetics and performative displays within a rally influence the field of action. How can one subvert the aesthetics in play so as to open up a new space of critique? How can one make visible some of the problems and pitfalls of exclusions within a rally, subtended by a state citizenship regime?

We are all familiar with the rhetoric that is used when reporting the tensions between citizens and state during a march: Protesters are often caricatured as a violent "mob" (Addley 2010; Harrison 2010; Coughlan 2010), and this in turn serves as justification for provocative and aggressive actions of the state in its policing of such events. When and if protesters display force, the state is seen as a just arbiter instead of accountable for the political issues. And yet, despite these portrayals conveyed in mainstream or broadcast media, one peculiarity of many rallies is the atmosphere of a carnival (e.g., Wikipedia, n.d.a; Occupy Wall Street 2011; Hartman 2010).[13] The performance of satire infuses the spirit of a march, and that was a source of inspiration for *MAE*.

Six people collaborated on designing and fabricating 120 original cloth armbands printed with satirical protest slogans.[14] These slogans were generated online by the Sloganizer, which combined movie tag lines and commercial promotional phrases with the key word "protest," resulting in a vast array of hideous but amusing new slogans, such as "I lost weight with Protest," "Be young, have fun, taste protest," "Protest, the real thing," and "Protest: One Name. One Legend," among others. The armbands were distributed to individual protestors at the rally, and in handing them out, we were in essence playing a double game. On the one hand, we were participating in the march and the fact of our presence contributed to the practicalities of the event (i.e., as visible markers of the citizenry's rejection of government economic policy). On the other hand, we were offering up a subtle criticism, through parody, that questioned the *sentiment* of the march as a space of entertainment. The aesthetic of carnival has come to characterize political events such as these, turning marches into festivals (or entertainment) rather than protests per se.

There are two perspectives on the efficacy of the protest as carnival, and both had influenced the reasoning behind *MAE* and its attempt to trouble the sentiment of playful resistance and question what is enclosed in public gestures of this kind. For example, some authors interpret this carnivalesque turn as an integral part an antiauthoritarian stance (Tancons 2011, 2012) or, as Simon Critchley has said, as a "rendering visible of an opposition, an alliance, in the most colourful way" (Gullestad 2010). Equally, authors such as David Graeber (2007) see carnivalesque (and circus) metaphors that inform the design of props within rallies, such as large, often misshapen puppets, costumes, banners, clowns, and the like, as not only tools for diffusing tensions between police and protesters but as a provocation of the idea that one is making "constituent power" within the act of the performance itself.[15] Puppets and other such props embody alternative frames of reference that are seemingly politically wayward but also, importantly, generative. As Graeber says,

What this means on the streets is that activists are trying to effectively collapse the political, negotiating process into the structure of the action itself. To win the contest, as it were, by continually changing the definition of what is the field, what are the rules, and what are the stakes—and to do so on the field itself. A situation that is sort of like nonviolent warfare becomes a situation that is sort of like a circus, or a theatrical performance, or a religious ritual, and might equally well slip back at any time. (2007, 407)

This is exactly what *MAE* set out to explore as well: how an art intervention can change, as Graeber says, what is delineated within the field, its rules, and what is at stake. The "installation" of the exhibition within the space of the rally (soliciting people to wear the armbands and then photographing them) was to perform a double game of satirizing the carnival atmosphere as a kind of consumer activity (in the messages of the slogans) but also actually participating in the rally (we were among the many thousands of bodies moving through the streets also creating fun). As an intervention, *MAE* temporarily corralled a portion of the crowd at a rally into the performance of an art exhibition. It was an opportunity to experiment with probing, interrupting, and reconfiguring the performance of the event itself. It was a rudimentary attempt to explore the performance of an act of citizenship within a politically codified civic space and to see what this would look like in action.

The idea then of distributing the armbands, with their crude, self-critical, parodic slogans, was, as I described previously, to reframe the notion of the protest itself and to play on the idea that the carnival can, in part, contribute to the reproduction of familiar political gestures and normative beliefs that are representative of a political status quo. As Judith Butler suggests in her discussion of protest rallies, the public space is created through the assembly of bodies, and "collective action collects the space itself" (2011, 2). She continues, "As much as we must insist on there being material conditions for public assembly and public speech, we have also to ask how it is that assembly and speech reconfigure the materiality of public space, and produce, *or reproduce*, the public character of that material environment" (1, my italics).

Protests critique the status quo, but they are not immune to a partitioning of the sensible (Rancière 2004). I will draw on one notable example to illustrate this point more carefully. Eve Tuck and Wayne K. Yang (2012) report on the experiences of Joanne Barker, an American Indian scholar of Lenape origin. During the Occupy Movement protests in 2011, a number of groups from

Boston, Denver, Austin and Albuquerque had . . . tried to engage in discussions about the problematic and colonial overtones of occupation. . . . [Barker and others had] called for the acknowledgement of Oakland as already occupied and on stolen land; of the ongoing defiance by Indigenous peoples in the U.S. and around the globe against imperialism, colonialism and oppression; the need

for genuine involvement of Indigenous people in the Occupy Oakland movement; and the aspiration to "Decolonize Oakland," rather than re-occupy it.
(Tuck and Yang 2012, 25)

The response from Occupy Oakland was ironic. Activists were themselves
reluctant to relinquish their own privilege, even theoretically, when it came
to discussions about their own material advantage and possession of assets
such as appropriated land. (See also my discussion in chapter 5 through the
conclusion). Even within the space of street protests and in their display of
resistance, public rallies can enclose and endorse hegemonic beliefs and practices about what is to be seen and heard within the doing of politics. The point
and purpose of *MAE*, then, was to problematize the tension between differing
perspectives (the sentiments of antiauthoritarianism versus a reiteration of the
status quo) in the action and moment of the rally.

These short and disruptive interventions expose important aspects of a political issue that are otherwise elided within conventional practices of political
action. They publicly trouble normative assumptions and employ aesthetic
gestures to expose what is otherwise hidden, suppressed, or deflected within
mainstream politics. By disrupting what is seen and heard, they undoubtably
perform acts of citizenship. However, the temporal nature of these short and
disruptive interventions is clearly limited with regard to establishing long-term
relations between actors (i.e., social relations that translate into new forms of
citizenry).[16] Understanding how citizen art structures relations is important for
understanding how citizen art interventions are determinable acts of citizenship. The following will turn to a more fulsome analysis of how citizen art interventions that do more critical work in effecting new modes of membership
primarily follow a project-based model. This form of project-based intervention will be explained and discussed in detail. These interventions also have
their roots in the 1960s and 1970s, and key concepts such as structuring social
relations help to clarify how citizen art is a tool for doing politics.

THE INTERVENTIONIST "PROJECT"

Interventions that are longer in duration and that rely on a project-based format differ in character from the form of intervention already discussed in that
they effect critical realignments in the aesthetic and political conditions of a
locale. The examples of citizen art discussed in chapters 4 through 6 emulate
this project-based form; therefore, it is important to clarify what its terminology entails. These art projects not only evidence the productive dimension of
citizen art as a "dissensual" prop or tool exposing the systems and structures
of a status quo (the manner in which the "sensible" is "distributed") but also

(re)structure relations between (political) actors. My wider argument is that they do this in such a way as to effect new modes of "incipient" citizenship (see chapter 4 through the conclusion).

The following discussion will begin with a brief outline of a historical example—the work of Roger Coward from the APG—to illustrate how this early intervention deliberately facilitated new political relations that upended the protocols and practices of a government office (the Department of the Environment) at a local level. The discussion of Coward's intervention also provides an important anchor for my criticism that follows of the work of theorists such as Nicolas Bourriaud and others, writing decades after Coward, who make a distinction between studio art and activist and social art practice to foreground social relations as an artistic medium in their own right. Unlike Bourriaud, I distinguish between the way in which relations that are structured through citizen art interventions significantly differ from how Bourriaud describes those within social practice art. I argue instead that citizen art projects are distinct and deliberate political acts and not convivial social moments celebrated as art. This matters to my discussion of the work of Tania Bruguera and Jonas Staal and my own citizen art projects in subsequent chapters and to an appreciation of the full import and complexity of the political acts performed within citizen art. Coward's project, as I will show, is an early iteration of citizen art as structuring relations, altering (political) sensibilities, and purposefully reframing, in his case, the material conditions of a civic space.

Under the leadership of artist and APG founder Barbara Stevini,[17] artists, such as Coward, were embedded, or "placed" (hence, APG's moniker), in host organizations (e.g., Department of the Environment, Scottish Office, London Zoo, Department of Health and Social Security, Esso Petroleum Corporation, Ocean Fleets Ltd., and British European Airways, among others), sometimes for several years at a time. APG "aimed to find ways to relocate their [artistic] practices from the studio to the industrial or governmental workplace, and in the process alter the perception of the artist as marginal to the key social issues of the day . . . pioneering the shift in art practice from studio and gallery to process-based forms of social engagement" (Hudek and Sainsbury 2012, 3). Hence, APG sought more radical and calculated organizational change, and in turn "societal change," through direct involvement of the artists in day-to-day politics and decision-making practices within their host organizations. Their interventions were therefore intended to effect a more totalizing and reformist worldview than momentary interventionist stunts. The following will outline how Coward's placement inside the Department of the Environment (1975–1977) not only structured social relations to form new "mini social contracts" and political memberships but also exposed the limitations of status citizenship in the doing and making of his interventions.

There were two phases to Coward's project: (1) the preparation of a feasibility study and (2) a proposal outlining the art project's main objectives that was used to negotiate his placement within the Department of Environment (Coward 1976). Once the terms of the placement were agreed, this was followed by the execution of individual art projects that included creating audiovisual material for the department's "Inner Area Study" (Coward 1975). This study comprised a government report on inner-city deprivation in Birmingham. As Coward states, the placement was "to investigate through sociological research[18] and *action projects* the problems of the deprived and blighted inner city area of Small Heath" (1976, 9, my italics). It is important to note that although this intervention was framed around servicing local government research, Coward's approach was to effect change through investigating and structuring new relationships between actors. As he says, "Effective change cannot take place unless there is an accurate understanding of the internal relationships between the different levels of human experiencing: physical, emotional, mental and intuitional in each individual, as well as of the process of change from past to future, in time. . . . Every relationship is a social responsibility. . . . As soon as we are concerned with relationships we are concerned with society" (Coward 1976, 3).

The aim of Coward's intervention was to investigate and make visible the aesthetic and ethicopolitical dimension of relations between members of the community and local government. To do this, he assembled a team of artists (Gavin Brown, Roland Lewis, Evande Stevens, and Frances Viner) to collaborate with the community of Small Heath in gathering and collating the perspectives of community members.[19] Coward describes two stages of the intervention and his approach to structuring social relations. It involved a "period of research," including photographing the locale, meeting members of the community and connecting people, meeting with city councilors, and sourcing potential support agencies (such as a television unit and community drama groups), and the creation of a "participatory video project" where he assembled a working group with individuals who represented different streets in the area. The goal was to produce a video of residents meeting with city councilors but quickly manifested as "an appeal to form a Residents Association which actually occurred shortly afterwards. The video group formed the core of the committee . . . and brought people together for . . . viewing, tea and a chat" (Coward 1976, 9). The video and, importantly, the method of its making had the effect of creating "an *image* of the community [which helped] to *make* the community" (9, my italics).

Coward understood very well not only the value of both the process and the act of making an intervention for forming bonds between individual residents and communicating with their audience—the policy makers—but also the importance of cocreating and making filmic imagery for *seeing oneself as a group of political agents*. That is, doing politics in this example was not about announcing oneself as a resident in the community and thereby deserving of representation by virtue of one's status as a citizen; instead it involved residents in negotiating and enacting obligations, creating mini social contracts, consulting on the terms of their association and, importantly, shaping the mode of their representation. The process also required that residents "a) [clarify] what they meant by 'community'; b) decide what they wanted and what others wanted for their area; c) the video equipment was an excuse to go into each other's houses. Somebody noted that neighbors had started to call on each other once again after the video visit" (Coward 1976, 11). To see oneself as affiliated with others—especially in this instance, where the point and purpose of their association was to visually represent themselves to policy makers and communicate their personal experiences of the inner city and its deprivation—is to also perform oneself as a member of a political group and shows how interventions of this kind create new political alliances and membership regimes.

Coward's entire project was concerned to create new social and political relations and make visible the tensions between various actors that were manifesting through the intervention. For example, the placement included projects under the following titles: *Participatory Video Projects, City Council Video Project—Participation in Decision Making*, and *Drama Project* (Coward 1976). The development and execution of all these projects depended on the involvement and, indeed, leadership of residents. How this was achieved had much to do with Coward's own role. As he says, "My role was to initiate activity, organize equipment . . . and suggest a working structure to make sure that what [the residents] wanted to do actually happened viz. got them to appoint a chairman and a coordinator and helped the chairman to prepare an agenda to guide the meetings" (Coward 1975). In short, Coward had facilitated the residents in such a way as to help them formalize their community as a political organization—a residents' association—that was recognizable to and indeed mirrored local government. Coward's interventions continued in this vein throughout his placement, during which he produced "participatory video projects" that documented the chain of decision-making within government administration. One of the video projects, titled *City Council Video Project—Participation in Decision Making*, traced the trajectory of a problem "as it progresse[d] vertically from street to council Chamber and horizontally from department to department" (Coward 1976, 12). Coward and his team of residents recorded meetings of the residents' association and of the residents and local councilors, as well as communications between local councilors and senior Whitehall staff. At one point his team met with resistance from the leader of the local council who stopped the artists' work, which was later overruled through ministerial pressure. Coward also made a "feedback film" titled *The Most Smallest Place in the Spaghetti Junction* to expose the communication problems between the residents and government officials (Hudek and Sainsbury 2012).

Coward's interventionist projects unmasked the asymmetrical power structures within local and national government and how government offices in fact produce representations of the citizens. The ability to expose how political norms and power relations are constructed is a key characteristic of citizen art interventions generally and will be discussed further in chapter 4 through the conclusion. However, in this example, not only had Coward's intervention facilitated the residents in being visible to local and national bureaucrats and assisting them in learning about how government functions, but the project also revealed the system and its strategies through which individual relationships, statuses, and social hierarchies are structured and sustained. The intervention enabled those who were "outside" the system to witness how their own problems and issues were being interpreted and discussed and, indeed, how they were represented within government agencies. Coward's intervention was radical rather than ameliorative in the sense that it provided the residents with a tool with which to investigate the imbalance of power between councilors and residents. The intervention also produced visual material with which to evidence a new image of the citizenry not as a collection of poor, blighted inner-city subjects but as engaged, skilled, and knowledgeable individuals capable of determining their own forms of political organization and representation. This example also shows how citizen art projects that do the work of making visible the apparatus of a government regime and its problematic management of citizens can subvert normative politics in new and unexpected ways. Hence, my suggestion (inspired by Isin) that citizenship is, in practice, fluid and nebulous and perpetually open to new formulations.

Coward explains the importance of providing a framework for "social-relational matters." As he says, "A group is in some way a microcosm of society and so its dynamics give the artists direct experiences which are significant for the subject they are dealing with and *the structure becomes part of what the work is about*—as is usual in an art-work" (Coward 1975, my italics).

That is, the structure of Coward's process-based art projects depended on the *relations* that he instigated among the artists, residents, and government officials, and the work of the intervention therefore was not focused on the artifacts that were produced or what might have been contrived as studio art. Instead, the relations between the interlocutors *is* the content and form of the art work.[20] I will discuss this point in the context of the work of Nicolas

Bourriaud to differentiate between how sociopolitical relations are structured within citizen art and Bourriaud's own assessment of participation within social practice art because he and a number of authors who have written about social and activist art practices (sometimes called "participatory art") miss seeing the significance of a discussion about relations to the practice of especially new modes of nonstatist citizenship. However, the important point to note here is that artists' groups of the 1960s and 1970s, such as APG and GAAG, had expanded this constructed dichotomy between studio art (and its association with a social and political status quo) and action, process, and project-based interventions that were entrenched in specific social and political problems of their time. The products of their art interventions were not objects, per se, but engineered social and political relationships and a reworking of the visual signifiers of political representation, or deliberate disruptions in public places (museums, etc.) that interrupted the smooth flow of daily habits and practices. That is, these early iterations of citizen art interventions disrupted sedimented behaviors and uncritical assumptions that tacitly endorsed the political realities of, say, the Vietnam War, as expressed in GAAG, or the problems of the state's representation of the inner-city poverty of a local community in Coward's project.

The traces of this split between studio art and interventions matter to understanding how citizen art does politics today. Contemporary art critics reiterate this dichotomy, using it as a crutch, so to speak, to delineate their own theoretical logics and hypotheses. For example, Bourriaud analyzes the phenomenon of the increased attention to social relations within contemporary art practice in his book *Relational Aesthetics* (2002)—a text that is often cited as a key theoretical source for social art practice (Jackson 2011; Kester 2004, 2022; Bishop 2006a, 2012; Thompson 2015, 2017). Bourriaud echoes the previous declarations of APG and GAAG and suggests that "the role of artworks is no longer to form imaginary and utopian realities, but to actually be ways of living and models of action within the existing real" (2002, 13). He draws on the impulse of (some) artists to merge art and life[21] and the desire to reject the value, status, and relevance of ("studio") art that is symbolically representative of social, political, or cultural experience.[22] He suggests that artists are interested in directly exploring the nature of social relations through participation with nonartists. At face value, this is prefigured in the action interventions of Coward (and other artists of his kind), but there are significant differences, as I will show. As Bourriaud says,

> The artist embarks upon a dialogue. The artistic practice thus resides in the invention of relations between consciousness. Each particular artwork is a proposal to live in a shared world, and the work of every artist is a bundle of relations with the world, giving rise to other relations, and so on and so forth,

ad infinitum. . . . As part of a "relationist" theory of art, inter-subjectivity does not only represent the social setting for the reception of art, which is its "environment," its "field" (Bourdieu), but also becomes the quintessence of artistic practice. (22)

For Bourriaud, it is relations rather than objects that are the locus of social and activist art practices, and he makes a case for how "the possibility of *relational* art (an art taking as its theoretical horizon the realm of human interaction and its social context, rather than the assertion of an independent and *private* symbolic space), points to a radical upheaval of the aesthetic, cultural and political goals of modern art" (2002, 14). The assertion that structuring relations *is* the subject matter and medium of relational art has attracted sharp criticism, primarily from Claire Bishop. She demonstrates that to evaluate artworks based on the extent to which they generate dialogue does not entail critical insights about the kinds of relationships generated within relational art. As she says, "The *quality* of the relationships in 'relational aesthetics' are never examined or called into question" (Bishop 2004, 65).[23] For these reasons, Bourriaud's analysis is also not particularly useful for understanding the nature of interventions that are constitutive of citizen art. To ward off any confusion and to further distinguish citizen art from other manifestations of social art practices that have been modeled on Bourriaud's theory, it is important to remember that citizen art makes visible the tensions in relations between actors that in turn productively forge new modes of membership (e.g., as seen in the example of Coward). By contrast, Bourriaud's thesis celebrates the artistic staging of *conviviality* ("Nicolas Bourriaud" 1998; Bourriaud 2002) within art institutions—an approach that is strikingly reactionary and at odds with the form of citizen art practices that this book is attempting to explain. For Bourriaud, not only is the museum (or gallery) framed as a smooth, uninterrupted space within which to perform genial acts—say, artists offering food to museum visitors (Rirkrit Tiravanija) or seeking out companionship in an effort to talk about loneliness (Georgina Starr)[24]—but also more problematically, the staging of such daily habits and practices within the museum environment undergirds a sentiment of complacency that in turn reifies a status quo. There is serious slippage in the cogency of Bourriaud's argument when he suggests, even rhetorically, that the performance of such convivial social encounters within art institutional spaces can "define new . . . political goals" ("Nicolas Bourriaud" 1998). He claims, "Art is a site that produces a specific sociability; what status this space has within the range of 'states of encounter' proposed by the Polis remains to be seen. How can an art that is centered on the production of such modes of conviviality succeed in relaunching the modern project of emancipation as we contemplate it? How does it allow us to define new cultural and political goals?" (Ibid.).

Bourriaud does not see that enacting conviviality as a focus of artists' interventions *fails* as a mode through which to discern or "define new cultural and political goals" and, by implication, new modes of citizenship. The kinds of relations Bourriaud celebrates are feel-good moments that venerate unproblematic social conventions rather than (re)structure social relations between participants in ways that instigate new political subjectivities or organizations. His assessment of how artistic interventions can generate new modes of sociality that are productive of political emancipation is lacking. By contrast, citizen art is firmly embedded within a mode of social practices that involves "open[ing] up a *new* regime of the symbolic" (Kershaw 2015, 26). A "*new*" regime of the symbolic," effected through interventions, is a declaration of the potential for art to trouble and alter what is to be seen and acted on in the public space—not, as Bourriaud would have us believe, regarded as a performance of social consensus. Citizen art exposes the problems produced by a (statist) membership regime (e.g., inequality, exclusions, racism), and it structures, in practice, new modes of (nonstatist) citizenship that manifest as solidarity or assembly or mini social contracts, and the like. As Shannon Jackson says, "Some socially engaged art can be distinguished from others by the degree to which they provoke reflection on the contingent systems that support the management of life" (2011, 29). That is, socially engaged art practices "make art from, not despite, contingency" (28). To intervene in society is to do politics, that is, to determine what is to be seen and acted on. Therefore, citizen art should be understood as distinct from the kinds of socially convivial art interventions that authors such as Bourriaud celebrate, but it is otherwise at the intersection of political acts and aesthetics. It emerges from within this milieu of social and activist art practice; however, it is not defined by it. Citizen art embodies citizenship as perpetually nascent and emergent—indeed, contingent—and hence, it not only troubles the notion of a status citizenship regime but also is genuinely productive of new and nascent modes of membership made visible through the doing of its politics. This point will be made even clearer in subsequent chapters.

CITIZEN ART INTERVENTIONS AND THE RtoP

To demonstrate that citizen art interventions are genuine political acts and not discrete artistic performances staged for (private) aesthetic reflection, the following will first briefly outline a description of social and activist art as a tool for doing politics and then turn to a comparison between citizen art interventions and the logics of the responsibility to protect (RtoP). This is germane to understanding that citizen art interventions carry real weight in their political intentionality and capacity to contest the effects of a status citizenship regime in their enactment of new forms of (nonstatist) citizenship. Comparing citizen art with RtoP is also important for appreciating the uniqueness of the performance of citizen art interventions for doing politics in their synthesis of aesthetic and political practices rather than, say, flattening citizen art into a debate about art as participation within a continuum of the avant-garde (as indicated previously and in chapter 1). I argue that it is in the nature of these (project-based) citizen art interventions (discussed in more detail in subsequent chapters) that politics is enacted in new and novel ways so as to produce nascent modes of citizenship, as it manifests through acts of citizenship—that is, acts that do not reify statist notions of citizenship centered on the state's gift of legal rights or on cosmopolitan aspirations.

To say that art is a tool is to suggest that it is "useful"[25]—it has "utility"— and as Tania Bruguera says, "Artists have become interested in providing concrete social solutions by using art as a problem solver, a direct social tool" (Internationale Sommerakademie für Bildende Kunst 2013, 233). Indeed, she goes even further by stating, "We need to move from 'saying something' about [i.e., representing] our society to 'doing something' about it" (Ibid., 234). Hence, doing politics is expressed here as the intention to alter a field of action and echoes Rancière's insights about the capacity for art to interrupt what is aesthetically partitioned. In reading through the lens of Rancière and by conceiving of citizen art as an interventionist tool, citizen art can be understood to create the terms in which social and political concerns that are otherwise suppressed, elided, or simply lacking in formulation are made visible. Citizen art not only interrupts normative social and political practices and habits but also generates new possibilities for political action, but it also shapes new conceptions of what it is to be a self-deliberating citizen. As Bruguera says, "useful art" (which she has coined as "Arte Útil") is aimed at "an activation of yourself as a citizen" (2013, 239). It is also a tool for transforming an audience (spectators) into performing as agents of change.

Importantly, citizenship as articulated here is not a reiteration of the roles assigned to one as a status citizen, where one meets the challenges of political life through, say, voting or protesting, or as a discriminating spectator (Green 2010); nor is it an articulation of a utopian cosmopolitan ideal that, say, fetishizes the abstract idea of equality as a universal good. Instead, to be a citizen in this iteration is to *determine* what is to be spoken of and what is to be acted on, and this includes exposing, at one and the same time, the limitations of status and cosmopolitan, civic republican and liberal individualist citizenship regimes. Citizen art interventions are therefore tools for excavating and problematizing discourses and carving out, shaping, and mobilizing a field of action and, in turn, individuals in their daily lives. As Markus Miessen says,

"The moment of the political is when agency is assumed, when one becomes visible" (2011, 103). What Miessen points to (but does not discuss) is the role that creative practice plays in shaping our understanding of what it means to be a political subject as constitutive of the generative nature of belonging and membership. My claim is that citizen art interventions are practical tools that stage a "generative friction" (101) between the undisclosed and the apparent and thereby bring to the fore (i.e., make visible) the perpetually emergent and creative nature of a citizen qua citizen.[26]

To further demonstrate the political leverage and potency of citizen art interventions as tools for shaping a field of action and forging new modes of (nonstatist) membership, it is constructive to briefly outline how humanitarian and military interventions, and specifically the RtoP, compare with citizen art practices. The aim of the comparison is to briefly draw out parallels between citizen art interventions and the more obvious form of political intervention of RtoP to further illustrate that citizen art alters the concept and scene of citizenship (albeit in different ways in practice). Relevant questions then include the following: How does RtoP alter the notion of citizenship? How, in principle, does the RtoP function as a tool?[27] And importantly, how does RtoP compare with citizen art interventions? I will limit my discussion to a simple summary of the rationale that underpins the responsibility to protect within the literature in international relations because the intention is to briefly illustrate how citizen art practices and RtoP are alike in altering the scene of politics and, more widely, to challenge normative conceptions of (status) citizenship and the presumption of state sovereignty as absolute. In no way am I suggesting that the two are alike in practice, especially because RtoP involves military violence. The aim is simply to draw attention to how RtoP and citizen art reflect the changing meaning of citizenship and, further, to indicate that the idea of RtoP interventions manifestly disrupts statist and cosmopolitan imaginaries (for good or ill). My discussion of RtoP will not involve a deeper analysis of the politics and problematics (and failings in practice) of RtoP or its ethical controversies because this is beyond the scope of this book.[28] Instead I will show that this form of intervention, articulated within some literature on RtoP, shares characteristics with the interventionist acts seen in citizen art. The purpose is to demonstrate, via the comparison, that, like RtoP, citizen art interventions are determined and persistent practices that do politics in a manner that parallels politics proper. This will become even more evident in my discussion of Jonas Staal's, Bruguera's and my own citizen art interventions in subsequent chapters.

The military interventions envisaged under the banner of RtoP alter the imaginary of (status) citizenship akin to that seen in citizen art. It arose out of a growing concern by the United Nations (UN) to develop protocols and to establish a norm for military intervention against states that perpetrate violence against their own citizens on a massive scale following the failure of the international community to respond to Rwanda (1994), Somalia (1993), Srebrenica (1995), Kosovo (1999), and so forth. In the wake of the NATO bombing campaign of Kosovo, this (illegal[29]) action set a new precedent and instigated a redefinition of humanitarian intervention in terms of a state's responsibility to protect citizens. It also supplanted the normative notion of state sovereignty as absolute with a conception of the citizen as sovereign. In a preliminary version of his speech to the UN General Assembly[30] Kofi Annan states:

> State sovereignty, in its most basic sense, is being redefined—not least by the forces of globalisation and international co-operation. States are now widely understood to be instruments at the service of their peoples, and not vice versa. At the same time individual sovereignty—by which I mean the fundamental freedom of each individual, enshrined in the charter of the UN and subsequent international treaties—has been enhanced by a renewed and spreading consciousness of individual rights. When we read the charter today, we are more than ever conscious that its aim is to protect individual human beings, not to protect those who abuse them. (Annan 1999)

Since its adoption in 2005,[31] RtoP posits a conception of sovereignty that radically shifts the relation of citizen to state. It "invented a new way of talking about humanitarian intervention" and state sovereignty (Chandler and Neumark 2006, 708). Instead of talking about rights per se, RtoP insists that the essence of sovereignty "should now be seen not as *control* but as *responsibility*" (708)—that is, state sovereignty should be conceived of as limited to and contingent on the rights and protection of citizens.[32] Under RtoP's directives, the citizen is seen as sovereign, and the state is in service to the citizen. As Stark et al. say, there has been a

> re-working of the traditionally sacrosanct international relations concept of absolute sovereignty. Although the notion of sovereignty has been debated and adjusted over time, it has retained its essential definition in international law, that a state has absolute supremacy over its territory and citizens. [However, under RtoP] sovereignty was re-defined and extended to include the responsibility a state bears towards protecting its own civilians from harm. Furthermore, in cases where a state is unable or unwilling to protect its civilians from mass atrocity crimes, . . . the international community has a responsibility to act swiftly in order to prevent or interdict such crimes. (2011, 4)

The emergence of RtoP stages a new imaginary of the citizen as distinct from the state. At a formal level, RtoP is premised on the assumption that the citizen trumps the authority of a state and provides a foundation for the justification of military intervention by another state actor (International Commission on Intervention and State Sovereignty [ICISS] 2001; UN General Assembly 2005). Put another way, RtoP interventions, like citizen art interventions, interrupt the logic of (status) citizenship by placing the citizen as conceptually on par with a state within a field of action. RtoP, like citizen art interventions, has the characteristic of a dissensual prop, revealing the capacity for new modes of membership to emerge, in principle at least, starting with a notion of the citizen conceived of as separate from the state. I am not suggesting that the idea of RtoP displaces state sovereignty (in fact, quite the opposite, because it relies on states to intervene in other state jurisdictions). I only suggest that RtoP interventions, like citizen art interventions, create a conceptual gap between citizen and state and, in so doing, highlight the potential for new modes of belonging and membership to emerge. Here we see how the idea of citizenship is nebulous and continually open to reformulation.

I have argued that the logic behind RtoP interventions interrupts the notion of status citizenship. However, what I have said may seem to suggest that I am lining up a characterization of RtoP interventions (and by analogy citizen art interventions) as a tool for advancing a notion of cosmopolitan citizenship. However, it does not follow that RtoP actually embodies a cosmopolitan vision of membership. For example, some authors argue that RtoP reaffirms state sovereignty in its emphasis on security over freedom (Dederer 2015; Verellen 2012) and thereby conceptually converts citizens into wards of the state (Cunliffe 2014). In this reading, RtoP is a tool for top-down, state-led action (formulated by political elites rather than through consultation with those affected). Equally, when enacted, some RtoP interventions have been employed negatively for the purposes of regime change (e.g., Iraq, Libya).[33] However, even with these complexities, the fact remains that RtoP has shifted the perspective from state to citizen and, in turn, altered the imaginary of sovereignty and citizenship. As Thomas Verellen says, "Changing positive international law was not their [RtoP's authors] primary objective. Instead, what they wanted to achieve was a *change of perspective*" (2012, 155, my italics). The interventions that take place in the name of RtoP function (either negatively or positively) as tools (i.e., dissensual props) that trouble the notion of state sovereignty and in turn make visible the potential for citizenship to be seen as distinct from the state and, indeed, open to reformulation.[34]

My argument so far has outlined how artists use interventions (either short and disruptive or long-term projects) as tools for laying bare the problems of a status citizenship regime and (re)structuring relationships that alter who is visible as a political agent. I have also suggested that citizen art interventions, in virtue of being dissensual props, expose the nature of citizenship as a perpetually contingent, creative, and generative practice rather than a status sanctioned by the state or a utopian aspiration of universal sentiment. In comparing RtoP with citizen art interventions, I have drawn attention to how these two examples share significant commonalities in the manner in which they both reframe relations and alter our perspective of the citizen and state. This is not to say that there are not important differences between RtoP and citizen art interventions. One obvious difference is the use of military violence to secure protections of citizens within the logic of RtoP. Equally, the protocols of RtoP were devised and drafted by experts (e.g., academics, politicians) primarily based in the West, such as Canada, the United States, and parts of Europe (ICISS 2001) rather than by those who are affected by genocide and war crimes. In this sense, as suggested previously, RtoP is a top-down set of practices, whereas citizen art interventions emerge from the political conditions and complexities that artists are confronted with on the ground, so to speak. Nevertheless, both the architects of RtoP and citizen artists understand that the kind of political doing that is achieved through interventions involves not simply altering the perspective of agents within a field of action but also framing a field of action—that is, the interventions determine what is politically seen and acted on.

In the following chapters I will discuss more complex examples of citizen art projects, such as Tania Bruguera's *Immigrant Movement International* (*IMI*), Jonas Staal's *New World Summit: Rojava*, and three of my own interventions: *Citizen Artist News: The University as a Border Regime*, *Citizen Artist News: Clouded Title*, and *Citizen Artist News: Kinship*. These examples illustrate the scope of citizen art, its value to a deeper discussion about acts of citizenship, and, in turn, the seriousness with which art of this kind carves out new terrain for enacting new modes of nonstatist citizenship.

NOTES

1. See Tania Bruguera (www.taniabruguera.com); Arte Útil (www.arte-util.org); Meschini 2013; Museum of Arte Útil, n.d.

2. "The recent shifts in artistic practice [e.g., socially engaged art practices] have vitalized the concept of cosmopolitanism. What is now at stake is the capacity of art not only to capture a cosmopolitan vision of the world but also to initiate situations in which artists and public participants are engaged in the mediation of new forms of cosmopolitan agency" (Papastergiadis 2012, 11).

3. "The last decades have seen an important change in our perception of art. The focus has shifted from artworks as 'objects' towards the concept of the 'project': a temporal intervention or engagement focusing on research and processes rather than on a final product. The change from [objects to] projects [and] organisations demands more *structural* engagement, more durability and long-term vision[, and] push the

concept of self-governance to another level, both within and outside the art world" (Staal 2015b). See also Wochenklausur 2009.

4. See Graham and Vass 2014; the term "intervention" has "been turned into something of a fetish in artistic circles and institutions." See also Cartiere and Ze-bracki 2016; Harper 1998; Harper and Moyer 2013. Note: there is no consistency in the use of other terms to describe interventions, such as, "tactical media" (Critical Art Ensemble, www.critical-art.net), "guerilla art," or "DIY." See Zeiger 2011 (e.g., a mixture of vocabularies to describe urban interventions). See also Canadian Centre for Architecture 2009.

5. The Arts Council funded a private UK foundation (name unknown) in the 1970s to launch "artists' residencies" modeled on the work of the Artists Placement Group (Connor 2013, 148). See also Slater 2000.

6. See Styhre and Fröberg 2016 re: use of the terms "art interventions" and "artists-in-residence" as synonyms. See also Schnugg 2014 re: the expansion of art-ists' "placements" or "residencies" in Europe in the1990s and 2000s; Berthoin Antal and Nussbaum Bitran 2015 re: use of the term "artistic interventions" to describe this phenomenon; Berthoin Antal 2014; Soila-Wadman and Haselwanter 2014; Wilk 2016; Hewitt 2012.

7. See Gray 1993.

8. The terms "tactical" and "guerilla" art also denote these stuntlike interventions (Thompson 2015).

9. See also H.I.J.O.S. and Grupo de Arte Callejero, which "outed" those com-plicit in the disappearances of citizens in Argentina (during the 1976–1983 military junta led by Jorge Rafael Videla) in a street campaign.

10. Regarding the freighted role of art and its occlusions and elisions of state vio-lence, there have also been demands for the removal of public statues memorializing Confederate soldiers or prominent historical figures who owned slaves (e.g., Thomas Jefferson, George Washington, Andrew Jackson) from the grounds of US universities (Sullivan 2017; Miller 2017) and from public spaces in Washington, DC, and the re-moval of these names from plaques in city parks in Chicago, including the destruction of Mount Rushmore (Payton 2017). See also Monument Lab 2017.

11. See Debord and Wolman 1956.

12. See Locke 1690 re: As citizens, if the state undermines the public good, citi-zens have a right to resist its policies and protest (§§149, 155, 168, 207–10, 220–30, 240–43).

13. Bakhtin 1984: "In the Middle Ages folk humour existed and developed outside of the official sphere of high ideology and literature, but precisely because of its unof-ficial existence, it was marked as exceptional radicalism, freedom, and ruthlessness. Having on the one hand forbidden laughter in every official sphere of life and ideol-ogy, the Middle Ages on the other hand bestowed exceptional privileges of license and lawlessness outside these spheres: in the marketplace, on feast days, in festive recreational literature." See also Hosein 2012.

14. I initiated a collaboration with students Sophia Selby, Rahel Zoller, Nancy Fleischauer, Kristine Bumeister, and Parastow Miri. We researched, designed, and

fabricated the armbands and worked as a group soliciting individual protesters to participate in the *MAE* during the rally.

15. Graeber's assessment is informed by Mikhail Bakhtin's writings on carnival. Bakhtin 1984 suggests that carnival is a bodily expression of the "wholeness of the world." It is a collective reimagining, through enactment, of the social and political ordering of society. The nature of parody in the space of the carnival is an act not of critical distancing but of "the people" being "reborn." As he says, "People were . . . reborn for new, purely human relations. These truly human relations were not only a fruit of the imagination or abstract thought; *they were experienced. . . .* The [parodic] bodily element is deeply positive. It is presented not as a private, egoistic form, severed from other spheres of life, but as something universal, representing all people" (Ibid., my italics).

16. See Hosein 2012 and Graeber 2007 re: the aesthetic experience of sentiment within carnivals and protests and the significance of this for establishing fraternal bonds through preparing materials and organizing events that in turn disturb hierarchies of authority and shape new emblems of identity, agency, and belonging.

17. Stevini 2001.

18. Although the APG makes no reference to contemporaneous sociological trends through the late 1960s and on, there are significant parallels between APG's objectives and the field of ethnomethodology. Garfinkel 1964; see Garfinkel 2014 re: his use of interventionist strategies within his research to disrupt the social habits and practices of individuals in their daily lives.

19. The art projects that Coward generated ranged from writing reports through to producing videos and coauthoring plays. Administrative tasks, such as written reports and "feedback," including Coward's report to the department titled *All Fine & Context & Other Papers* (Coward 1976), were included in the Department of Environment's own report *You and Me Here We Are*. See also the exhibition titled *Roger Coward: You and Me Here We Are* (Eastside Projects 2015).

20. Coward's final report weaves together reflections on art and representation, denoting language and the notion of "relations" as a "medium" of art practice. Coward 1976 states, "It is not only linguistic phenomenon that refer. Everything refers. Any object, thought or feeling has significance only because it refers to others. Because it is in a RELATIONSHIP" (2).

21. See Kaprow 2003; www.suzannelacy.com re: New Genre Public Art.

22. See also Kester 2011, who follows Bourriaud's usage of the phrase "symbolic production," noting, "There is a movement toward participatory, process-based experience and away from a 'textual' mode of production in which the artist fashions an object or event that is subsequently presented to the viewer" (8). He distinguishes between art as "symbolic production" that manifests itself primarily through the fabrication and display of artifacts, where the content in some cases points to some form of representation (or re-presentation) versus art that pivots on "dialogue"—such as interventions, "projects," and the creation of artists' organizations (Ibid.).

23. See Bishop 2004 re: criticism of Bourriaud suggesting that "encounters are more important than the individuals who compose them" (65). Bishop states that this

leads to a shallow assertion that "all relations that permit 'dialogue' are automatically assumed to be democratic and therefore good" (65).

24. See "Nicolas Bourriaud" 1998 re: there is a "current enthusiasm for revisited spaces of conviviality and crucibles where heterogeneous modes of sociability can be worked out. For her exhibition at the Centre pour la Creation Contemporaine, Tours (1993), Angela Bulloch installed a cafe: when sufficient visitors sat down on the chairs, they activated a recording of a piece by Kraftwerk. For her Restaurant show (Paris, October 1993), Georgina Starr described her anxiety about 'dining alone' and produced a text to be handed to diners who came alone to the restaurant. For his part, Ben Kinmont approached randomly-selected people, offered to do their washing up for them and maintained an information network about his work. On a number of occasions Lincoln Tobier set up radio stations in art galleries and invited the public to take part in broadcast discussions."

25. See also Thompson 2012: the concern within contemporary social art practice is not defining whether a thing is an artwork but instead asking, "Is it useful?" (16).

26. Another way to understand art interventions as generative "frictions" and therefore useful tools is in how the status of art can be used to prize open a (public) space of contestation and provide new platforms for public investigation. That is, the political content under discussion in an artists' project (e.g., statelessness, terrorism, migrant rights, etc.) is not always possible under any banner other than "Art." For example, Staal's *New World Summit* hosts assemblies of people who are listed as terrorists; Khalid Jarrar's *State of Palestine* passport stamp undercuts the authority of the Israeli state, and so forth. The designation of (political) interventions as Art makes visible some issues that are normally enclosed or suppressed within formal politics. *New World Summit* would be deeply problematic, if not impossible, if hosted in non-art contexts; it is plausible that Jarrar's actions would attract some form of punishment for producing official state insignia if it were not an art project, and so forth. The status of art affords a degree of permissibility, and, following Rancière again, it can be effective in making visible what has otherwise been elided or, rather, aesthetically (i.e., sensibly) partitioned. "Art can go where politics and academia cannot go; art is a realm where fundamental political discussions can still take place" (Staal 2012, 14).

27. RtoP has yet to be an effective tool for contesting state violence. The Assad regime's actions toward Syrians or Saudi Arabia's brutal involvement in Yemen are just two of RtoP's most recent tests and failures.

28. Within the literature in international relations there is a divergence in opinion regarding the justification for humanitarian intervention (Hehir 2010; MacSweeny, n.d.; Verellen 2012). A division exists between traditional (or historical) conceptions of state sovereignty and the notion of the RtoP. Historically, there is an understanding that states exercise their sovereignty as a kind of "virtual carte blanche [where they] treat citizens however they see fit on the (false) assumption that governments reflect the will of their people" (Bellamy 2012, 39). In this scenario, interference by one state in another state's territory for the purposes of protecting its citizens from harm—genocide, war crimes, ethnic cleansing, or crimes against humanity—is only legal if sanctioned by the United Nations or by invitation from the receiving state. We see examples of this in the US and UK military strikes against Islamic State of

Iraq and the Levant (ISIL). According to a UK government policy paper, the Iraqi government had "requested" that the international community intervene in its fight against ISIL, and the UN sanctioned the military action (United Kingdom Office of the Prime Minister 2014). This sharply contrasts with other cases, such as the Rwandan genocide (1994), which arguably was exacerbated by the absence of humanitarian intervention by the international community (Hehir 2010). These offenses—genocide, war crimes, ethnic cleansing, and crimes against humanity—form the criteria for RtoP interventions and are articulated in the UN General Assembly's 2005 World Summit Outcome document (30). However, these two protocols—intervention authorized by invitation or UN sanction—were radically altered following the violence in the Balkans and especially Kosovo.

29. NATO forces sustained a bombing campaign (by air) for eleven weeks in 1999 without the approval or invitation of the Republic of Kosovo. NATO nor the United States secured UN endorsement (Lyon and Malone 2012). The justification for the violent intervention by the Bill Clinton administration, which led the campaign, was that "the United States had a moral imperative to protect ethnic Albanians" (19).

30. See Evans 2006: Kofi Annan's speech to the UN General Assembly on September 20, 1999, galvanized the UN to act, asking how does the international community legally and legitimately—that is, justifiably—uphold the rights of citizens when faced with genocide and other forms of state violence? This led to the formation of the International Commission on Intervention and State Sovereignty (ICISS), which drafted a set of recommendations for humanitarian intervention titled "The Responsibility to Protect" in 2001.

31. The ICISS first presented its recommendations to the UN in 2001 and at the 2005 World Summit its norms were accepted (with some modifications). Subsequently, the push to translate RtoP into policy—to "operationalize" it—was evident under the leadership of Ban Ki-moon in his report titled "Implementing the Responsibility to Protect: Report of the Secretary-General" (United Nations General Assembly 2009).

32. See Evans 2006: "To be sovereign means both to be responsible to one's own citizens and to the wider international community. The starting point is that any state has a primary responsibility to protect the individuals within in. But that is not the finishing point: where the state fails in that responsibility, through incapacity or ill will, a secondary responsibility to protect falls on the international community, acting primarily through the UN" (709).

33. See Dederer 2015: "[RtoP] calls for outside interference and, thus, disregards the principle of non-intervention, being a fundamental specification of state sovereignty" (157).

34. See the artists' collective called the Centre for Political Beauty (www.political beauty.com), which states that "interventions demonstrate how art can be a fifth state power."

Chapter Four

Enacting New Modes of Citizenship

Solidarities, Assemblies, and Public Thought Experiments

This chapter will discuss three citizen art projects to situate how citizen art constitutes new modes of citizenship. How exactly does citizen art do politics by troubling normative practices of status and cosmopolitan citizenship and, in turn, affirm the idea that citizenship is perpetually nascent and generative rather than a gift of entitlements of the state? If citizenship is a practice and not necessarily a legal status or a utopian universal aspiration, then it is important to examine its manifestations in phenomena such as solidarity (*Immigrant Movement International*) and assemblies (*New World Summit: Rojava*) or by shifting local (political) orientations through, say, public thought experiments (*Citizen Artist News: The University as a Border Regime*, et al.). I will show that through these examples of citizen art projects, we see not only how they shape the aesthetic conditions for social and dialogical contracts but also how the form of citizenship enacted is one of emergence and potentiality: a space of becoming. Engin Isin describes this space of becoming as "incipient citizenship," by which he means that at the interface between individuals and their struggles against or within a polity, there is a moment that evinces a kind of perplexity over "the contested constitution of subjectivity and polities themselves" (Isin and Nyers 2014, 9). As he says, citizenship "involves the art of being with others, negotiating different situations and identities, and articulating ourselves as distinct from, yet similar to, others in our everyday lives" (4). This is important to Isin's argument because citizenship, in its incipient form, is central to the negotiation and framing of (new) rights. "Through these social struggles, citizens develop a sense of their rights as others' obligations and others' rights as their obligations" (4). Citizenship then is "an 'institution' that mediates rights between subjects of politics and the polity to which these subjects belong" (1). Understanding citizenship as an institution (i.e., a social practice) helps us to recognize that within citizen art citizenship manifests as a process of claim making, negotiating, and enacting obligations.

The three art projects[1] that I will focus on in this chapter are Tania Bruguera's *Immigrant Movement International*, Jonas Staal's *New World Summit: Rojava*, and the second of my own practice-based research projects, *Citizen Artist News: The University as a Border Regime* (reserving my third and fourth projects, *Citizen Artist News: Clouded Title* and *Citizen Artist News: Kinship*, for chapters 5 and 6 because they are more comprehensive examples of acts of citizenship that I am responsible for instigating). I will discuss how these projects, on the one hand, challenge to a greater or lesser degree the normative notion of (status and cosmopolitan) citizenship by interrogating three overlapping issues: migration, statelessness, and a border regime. On the other hand, they enact new modes of citizenship in their performance of acts of citizenship. Not only do Staal's, Bruguera's, and my own projects show that outcomes, such as assemblies (*New World Summit: Rojava*), or what Arendt calls "voluntary association" (1972, 96), or dialogical compacts (i.e., what I am describing as [public] thought experiments [*Citizen Artist News*]), or formalized associations that emerge through solidarities (*Immigrant Movement International*), evidence how citizenship is enacted in new and novel ways, but these projects also reconfigure the tools of politics in the act of doing politics through art. Equally significantly, they contest the assumption that the counterpart of a citizen is the immigrant or stateless person. I show how citizen art exposes problematic commonplace binaries of citizen and state, citizen versus foreigner, citizen versus migrant, and citizen versus stateless—namely, the characterization of migrants and stateless peoples as the citizen's "abject other" (Kerber 2009, 76; Schininá 2017). Instead, these citizen art projects expose the problems that are produced—and cannot be resolved—by status citizenship and cosmopolitan imaginaries.[2] They contest normative understandings of citizenship by performing alternative methods and practices of membership. They highlight how, through a "generative friction" (Miessen 2011) produced in the "doing and making" (Rancière 2004)— that is, the aesthetic methods—of their interventions, practices of membership are newly constructed. I will discuss each art project in turn beginning with Bruguera's *Immigrant Movement International*.

IMMIGRANT MOVEMENT INTERNATIONAL

From 2010 to 2015, Tania Bruguera instigated her project Immigrant *Movement International* (*IMI*), an organization housed in New York City's Queens, in an area that is populated by new or recent immigrants to the United States of mixed (ethnic and legal) statuses and levels of need.[3] Bruguera (2011) had attracted a network of collaborators, including arts institutions (Creative Time and Queens Museum), politicians, lawyers, artists, and so forth and, in short, founded an art project that was understood in multiple ways—as a refugee support center, a community center, a legal advice network, a project space, a meeting house, a series of seminars, a school, a space of friendship, and a working hub, all rolled into one (Kershaw 2015). Indeed, *IMI* was a deliberate exercise in shifting perspectives. As Bruguera says, "Our idea is to change the way in which migrants are perceived because they always seem to be portrayed as delinquents" (Castillo 2012). To achieve this, Bruguera applied her ideas of art as a useful tool (Arte Útil), and its capacity to alter perspectives was put into practice by first insisting that its participants were not spectators but "users." As with Roger Coward's intervention (discussed in chapter 3), those directly involved in organizing *IMI*'s activities were conceived of as and given the title of "facilitators." By recasting the roles of *IMI*'s interlocutors, "replacing authors [i.e., artists] with facilitators and spectators [i.e., an audience] with users" (Internationale Sommerakademie für Bildende Kunst 2013, 235), Bruguera reframed the conditions for doing politics and, in turn, performing new modes of *migrant* citizenship. That is, she "approach[ed] migrants as citizens" in their own right (Schwartz 2012, 225) and, in so doing, created a space where migrants themselves were invited to (re)define themselves to others and to collectively "educate their audience." As she says, *IMI* is a space "to imagine social engagement differently and to try to live life that way, instead of accommodating rules. . . . [It is an] educational place where we try to exercise the merging of creative knowledge with practical knowledge in order to generate political knowledge" (Paz 2013).

Bruguera's mandate was not to convert migrants into (status) citizens per se or to induct them into the performance of the habits and manners of US citizens. That is, *IMI* was not a center for teaching migrants how to be US citizens. It was not aimed at reeducating them for the purposes of assimilation (Chen and Bruguera 2012). Instead, it was a complex project that folded together three things:

1. Bruguera's own theoretical framing of Arte Útil: *IMI* itself was an interventionist tool for directly transforming immigrants into political actors. Not only does Bruguera see the capacity for art to effect change, but she also understands very well the immanent nature of new modes of citizenship: "our biggest challenge as artists is to be an active part of the creation of a different society *that is becoming*" (Paz 2013, my italics). It is important to note here that the readiness to experiment, scope out, explore, and expose the complexities of membership, rather than to formulate rules

and procedures—indeed, to recognize the perpetually nascent nature of citizenship—is at the heart of the creative process that drives citizen art interventions generally.

2. Her explicit appeal to "affect" and championing of its centrality in the formation of political agency via day-to-day strategies that, as she says, "turn . . . social affect into political effectiveness" (Paz 2013). Again, the material of *IMI*'s creative practice is not simply a battle for migrants (legal) status but the relationships and the affective bonds that are formed between people in the moment of their "making and doing" (Rancière 2004).

3. *IMI*'s advocacy for the political rights of immigrants on their own terms (e.g., the push for "migrant rights" to be recognized as equivalent to other forms of social rights [women's rights, labor rights, education, health, etc.]) (Castillo 2012). Here we see how Bruguera's project is a daring challenge to a status citizenship regime in its conflation of the language of rights with an appreciation of the "incorrigible" spirit of migrants (De Genova 2010, 101) to be recognized on their own terms.

Bruguera's stated aim, then, was to transform how migrants are perceived from the populist conception of immigrants as "delinquents" or "criminals," and so on, to one where migrants are seen as people who are knowledgeable about the complex conditions of mobility and its corollary, precarious labor. *IMI*'s provocation to "consider immigrants as people we can learn from" (Paz 2013) included demanding respect for and supporting migrants in articulating their collective identity *as migrants*, not only through the activities of *IMI* but also within formal politics in Bruguera's splinter project titled *Migrant People Party* (Castillo 2012), a project that emerged from *IMI*'s headquarters and launched in Mexico City in 2012. It too aimed to encourage people to rethink what it means to act politically as a migrant and what this entails when advocating for migrant rights. *IMI* framed the issue of migrant rights as a set of rights that give credence, status, and political leverage to migrants as migrants—not as migrant citizens aspiring to be absorbed into a state's status citizenship regime but as citizens in their own right. As she says, "What I am looking for is, that migrants, a social group that has no representation of any sort, can have that representation. They are people to whom no laws of any country work, laws from their own countries don't represent them, laws from the country they arrive to don't either and they [countries] do not recognize them as people" (Castillo 2012).

To prepare for, reimagine, and enact a new social and political role of the migrant—that is, to strategize about how to be seen and heard and understood as migrant citizens—and to interrupt popular conceptions of immigrants as marginal or delinquent subjects, *IMI* staged a wide range of workshop activities. Led by those who are immersed in the complexities of being immigrant subjects within a status citizenship regime, *IMI* offered educational advice (e.g., language classes, information about higher education), health and dietary advice, and legal services and also social and cultural events such as dance classes, barbecues, laughter therapy, and so forth (Bruguera 2011). These workshops—the creative making and doing of the *IMI* project—facilitated a community of "users" (Meschini 2013) that afforded opportunities for migrants to shape the politics of daily life in their own image. Users collectively took command of and made visible to themselves and others the issues and concerns of the community as a whole. However, there were also workshops that were more specific to tackling the politics of political representation beyond the immediate domain of the *IMI* headquarters—that is, workshops that were proactive in changing the terms in which immigrants are perceived and described by political organizations and the media. Under the banner "Make a Movement Sunday," workshop projects—such as the "Immigrant Respect Awareness Campaign" (2011), "Open House and Slogan Writing Workshop" (2011), "9/11: The War on Migrants" (2011), "Ghana Think Tank" (2011), "Making Media for the Movement" (2013), and so forth (Immigrant Movement International [https://immigrant-movement.us]; Bruguera 2011)—involved letter-writing campaigns where users sent letters to elected officials asking for immigrants to be respected, trained people to visit detained immigrants in prisons (including making drawings from the descriptions of detainees of their arresting officers), or manufactured signs, buttons, T-shirts, stickers, and so forth, with slogans written by the participants (i.e., users) for dissemination at the street level. Some interventions, such as the "Immigrant Respect Awareness Campaign," were pointed written requests (demands) to politicians to show respect for migrants. These demands used the tools of language (performative utterances; Austin 1975) to impose a kind of contractual obligation on the part of the recipient. That is, to demand respect from a political representative is to assert that politicians, by virtue of their office, represent the presence of migrants too (and not just status citizens) and, therefore, are directly responsible and answerable to immigrants as immigrants. These campaigns highlighted how migrants reside and partake in the culture and, indeed, the economy of place, and because they perform as members of a society on a daily basis, contributing to the economy and culture of a locale, they therefore must not be rendered invisible in public discourses. As Bruguera says, "We need to . . . understand that they [immigrants] are an active and positive part of our society. The temporality of migrants is complex and is generally associated with a type of unstable compromise because one might think 'I'm going to stay a year' and it becomes 5 or 10, or they need to go back. But what happens with all their work and all the help a migrant has accomplished in the host country?" (Castillo 2012). In essence, *IMI* facilitated immigrants in being heard and seen and in directly addressing politicians and publics; the art project made visible and targeted the social and political systems and its agents that (mis)represent migrants as marginal subjects.

IMI had created a self-defining and self-organizing culture where users collectively determined the manner in which they were symbolically represented, both to themselves and to others in the community. However, in practice, immigrants performed as specialists on the subject of migration and their expertise and insights on the conditions, needs, and image of migrants, modeled through the making and doing of the workshops manifested as interruptions to the sedimented norms and practices of status citizenship. *IMI* inverted the status of the migrant subject to one equal to that of other citizens, transforming facilitators and users into migrant citizens—migrants "who [were] asked to act politically" (Kershaw 2015, 13). In this sense, *IMI* was a project that fully embraced the production of a new mode of membership through acts of citizenship. Not only did it expose the complex problems of a statist citizenship regime—a regime that produces the category of migrant—but its members also performed as citizens in their own right. As Bruguera says, "The idea of IMI is to empower immigrants and to educate U.S. residents and citizens. We want immigrants to be seen as political beings" (Paz 2013). In following Isin's insights about acts of citizenship, we see how *IMI*'s members acted out the status of equality by making claims to rights within the domain of the state. *IMI* provided space for individuals to reconceptualize and perform their role and identity as migrant citizens and to carve out their own terrain of membership. Through the implementation of workshops and interventions that test out, (re)imagine, and embody migrant citizenship, the nature of citizenship is revealed to be nascent, generative, and creative rather than a legal status or a utopian aspiration. As Davide Panagia says, "Aesthetic practices that transform perception and sensibility are also political practices of emancipation, solidarity, and participation, and vice versa. For what carries weight in these instances of aesthetic and political simultaneity is the capacity to arrange relations, and therefore worlds, anew regardless of one's assigned ways of being and doing" (2018, 4).

It is important to briefly review the implications of the solidaristic act[4] within Bruguera's project and what this tells us about citizen art enacting new modes of citizenship. Bruguera found ways to facilitate solidarities between people through the creative activities of *IMI*'s new community of people who were deemed to be immigrant strangers and, in so doing, challenged the perception of the immigrant as a stranger (or "criminal" stranger). *IMI*'s newly organized community of immigrants represented themselves as immigrant-citizens, residing in a host "community" of the state (i.e., the United States). However, this larger purported community of the state is, as Jacob Levy suggests,

> more like strangers who find themselves locked in a very large room together than they are like an extended family or voluntary association united in pursuit of a common purpose. . . . They are not what nationalists falsely claim co-nationals to be: members of some pre- or extra-political social whole that can make its will felt through politics, some social soul that wears the state as a body. . . . [F]ellow citizens are in a fundamental sense novel strangers to each other, united only by the shared circumstances of inhabiting a common political jurisdiction, and not by any prior relationship that legitimizes, grounds, underlies, or stands outside of those circumstances. (2015, 2)

In other words, solardaristic affiliations are not a priori foundational properties of a citizenship regime.[5] As Jelena Vasiljević points out, "There is hardly a theory or approach to citizenship that does not presuppose some aspects of solidarity as foundational" (2016, 375). "Solidarity's role is often presupposed, or taken for granted, and rarely thematized as a consistent feature of interpersonal relations that demands its systematic place in citizenship" (376). To be visible—say, in the example of *IMI*—citizenship requires the creation of a deliberate "voluntary association."[6] Solidarity, as instanced here, is an act of citizenship. It is "implicitly levelling . . . and emerges from situations in which people recognize each other as equal. . . . [It is also] defined as an act. . . . To be *in solidarity with* thus implies the sharing of a position or experience with those who need or seek solidarity, and in partaking in their situation" (381).

Most importantly, in the example of *IMI*, we see that solidarity has to be "created, agitated for" and therefore is *"transformative*—capable of challenging and establishing [new] political and social orders" (Vasiljević 2016, 374). In this sense, I suggest that in the formation of artificial communities within citizen art projects, such as Bruguera's, solidarity actively constructs new modes of citizenship—new mini social contracts that shape one's sense of oneself as a citizen and as distinct from the state. To restate this in another way, "solidarity, emancipation and equality aren't concepts, . . . they're *practices*" (Panagia 2018, my italics), and this is more sharply discerned when statehood is understood as "a big happenstance" (Levy 2015, 3). Just because one happens to be residing within a particular political domain, it does not follow that solardaristic practices, even within a state's boundaries (or if "dissenting"), are necessarily expressive of (statist) citizenship. Solidarity and (statist) citizenship are incommensurable (Vasiljević 2016, 380). Citizen art projects (such as Bruguera's) show us not only that acts of citizenship manifest as solidaristic practices but also that, because the nature of citizenship is fluid and perpetually nascent, citizenship has to be constructed to be recognized as citizenship and that construction does not seamlessly align with the state. Citizens are formed in practice, and I suggest that citizen art is one of the modes through which citizenship is not only made visible but also enacted in new and novel ways that do not valorize the state. As Panagia says,

> If we consider [solidarity, emancipation, and equality] practices, then each iteration of the practice is unique precisely because every scene manifests as a specific configuration of forces and objects and persons. That is to say, the construction and reconstruction of the sensible world to which a specific activity and event of assembly-forming belongs means that we can't speak of a general concept of solidarity or equality or emancipation. This is a fundamental point about aesthetic experience: it is born of the particular (not the general) and is resistant to the general application of a concept. Here there are no general concepts of solidarity, emancipation, or equality. There are only scenes whose "conditions are immanent to their being executed." (2018, 4)

The intersection of solidarity, citizenship, and citizen art has not received any critical attention within the limited literature on citizen art. The aim here is to simply alert readers to one of the ways that acts of citizenship manifest within citizen art as solidarity and as a substantively new mode of citizenship and to point out that these acts are not an expression of statist citizenship. There is neither time nor space to examine further complexities of the role that solidarity plays within citizen art and, in turn, citizenship. It certainly merits more attention and analysis and would benefit from emerging literature on how solidarity is a "politically operational concept" (Vasiljević 2016, 374). Key to this would be to do what Jelena Vasiljević suggests and "discuss solidarity from a theoretical point of view and to provide a coherent framework that explains the role of solidarity in constituting the fibre of a political community" (374). It would be productive, too, to examine the role that citizen art plays in providing a coherent framework, where solidarity is understood as creative and "transformative" (374) rather than as an intrinsic component of citizenship and political relations (especially in the context of escalating involvement of individuals in citizen art and activist politics). However, such an inquiry is far beyond the scope of this book. Therefore, the following will turn to a discussion of Jonas Staal's projects to draw out other aspects of doing politics and to show how citizen art opens up yet another way to perceive and practice citizenship.

NEW WORLD SUMMIT: ROJAVA

Jonas Staal's wider project, called *New World Summit* (2012)[7] is a series of interventions that take the form of "alternative parliaments" for and with the participation of those deemed to be stateless, blacklisted ("terrorist") organizations (Staal 2012). The purpose was to formalize a space of public assembly for "organizations that currently find themselves excluded from democracy" (Staal 2012, 14).[8] Staal has hosted a number of *New World Summits* and *New World Embassy* events,[9] with one summit held in northern Syria, in a region called Rojava (2015). I will focus on the projects that involve the people of Rojava (2015–2018) as they exemplify Staal's own ideas about art as "useful" for framing new imaginaries of statelessness, actualized by working with intellectuals and activists in the Kurdish Women's Movement who are proactively shaping and practicing regional "democratic self-governance." Rojava was a newly declared "autonomous" political region (2011) populated by a number of ethnic groups (e.g., Kurdish, Assyrian, Armenian, Arab) engaged in developing and practicing "democratic self-administration"[10] as *stateless*[11] people (Staal 2015a). Staal had collaborated on four projects with the people of Rojava: (1) *New World Summit: Rojava* (2015) in Canton Cizîre, Rojava, (2) a temporary *New World Embassy: Rojava* (2016), housed in Oslo's Town Hall, (3) the design and creation of a new public, open-air parliament for Rojava, located in the Canton Cizîre (completed in 2018), and (4) the installation of a partial replica of the Canton Cizîre parliament in the Van Abbemuseum in Eindhoven, Netherlands, for one year (2018), in collaboration with the Rojavan diasporic community in Europe, in an effort to "activate the parliament continuously" (Van Abbemuseum 2018).

Staal's project is important to my discussion of citizen art in that he and the Democratic Self-Administration of Rojava (DSAR) start from a critique of the political reorganization of the region after World War I and the fall of the Ottoman Empire. They describe how the emergence of the nation-state as a form of political organization disrupted the distribution of power among a plurality of peoples within the region. *New World Summit: Rojava* therefore distinguishes between hegemonic state practices and stateless democratic practices, and this provides us with a potent example of how the form of citizenship performed within citizen art projects (such as Staal's) is not contingent on statist notions of citizenship. What we see instead is a deliberate form of *nonstatist* citizenship enacted within citizen art. The following will outline how Staal's project reveals the "distribution" of who and what is seen as political. I will discuss how it exposes, as Jacques Rancière says, "the conflict about what an 'interest' is [and] the struggle between those who set themselves as able to manage social interests [e.g., the state] and those who are supposed to only be able to reproduce their life [e.g., the stateless]" (2011a, 2). The Rojava example is also most vivid because the activities of the people of this region and their efforts to politically organize themselves as determinedly stateless peoples undergird Staal's own theorizing about the role of art and the development of assemblies as an artistic tool for the performance of new modes of (democratic) *stateless* membership (DSAR and New World Summit 2016, 164). Therefore, I will draw out how Staal's *New World Summit: Rojava* project is twofold in its agency: On the one hand, it parses the notion of the nation-state and citizenship from the perspective of statelessness and, in so doing, further illustrates that the nature of citizenship is perpetually nascent and not necessarily contingent on the existence of a state. On the other hand, through his staging of "assemblies" as an expression of "self-rule," Staal structures the aesthetics and performance of citizenship—indeed, the confluence of action and speech in the shaping of shared (binding) political "interests"—in unprecedented ways. As Hannah Arendt says,

> Action and speech go on between men, as they are directed toward them, and they retain their agent-revealing capacity even if their content is exclusively "objective," concerned with the matters of the world of things in which men move, which physically lies between them and out of which arise their specific, objective, worldly interests. These interests constitute . . . something which *interest*, which lies between people and therefore can relate and bind them together. Most action and speech is concerned with this in-between, which varies with each group of people, so that most words and deeds are *about* some worldly objective reality in addition to being a disclosure of the acting and speaking agent. Since the disclosure of the subject is an integral part of all, even the most "objective" intercourse, the physical, worldly in-between along with its interests is overlaid and, as it were, overgrown with an altogether different in-between which consists of deeds and words and owes its origin exclusively to men's acting and speaking directly *to* one another. (1998, 182)

Hence, the force of Staal's summits is in the use of art to stage political assemblies where those who are excluded from or are deemed to be unworthy of public speech and action can gather and address each other directly, identify shared interests, and articulate statelessness anew. I will first briefly describe the design and format that Staal's assemblies take (and not just those constructed for Rojava) and then discuss how *New World Summit: Rojava* critiques normative notions of the nation-state and, in turn, statist notions of citizenship. I will follow this with an analysis of the use of the assembly as a tool for doing politics and performing acts of citizenship and its significance to citizen art.

The staging for most of the summits (not just for Rojava) involved constructing temporary covered enclosures with circular or rectangular seating plans, elaborate lecterns surrounded by variously arranged and sometimes terraced benches, and the display of national flags (of organizations on international terrorist lists) as decorative features, housed within a public art event (e.g., a biennale) or an existing building dedicated to the display of art (e.g., an art gallery, theater, university) or in the open air (e.g., Canton Cizîre, Rojava). The model for the design of Canton Cizîre's open-air parliament, in particular, is self-consciously an echo of the agora of ancient Greece. As Staal says, "Rojava claims to be recuperating democracy's origins as found in the agora (assembly) of ancient Greece, the space where the theatre of politics began. The circular shape of the parliament derives from its attempts to dislocate power from a clear centre and instead engage in an egalitarian social composition in which the distance between people is equalized" (DSAR and New World Summit 2016, 105). The design of the parliament was also responsive to what had been happening among the people of the region and their nascent organization as stateless-democratic peoples. "In 2012, amidst the civil war in Syria, Kurdish revolutionaries, together with Assyrian, Arab, and other peoples of the region, declared the autonomy of Rojava. This resulted in the foundation of the Democratic Self-Administration of Rojava (DSAR) which practices a form of 'stateless democracy' based on local self-governance, gender equality, and communal economy" (Staal 2015–2018). The design of the parliament therefore collapsed the idea of the agora with direct democratic practices and "communal politics" that valorized the DSAR's feminist and libertarian ideals. The circular open-air building was also decorated with "key terms from the Social Contract" and "fragments of flags of local political and social organizations," bringing together a "spatial manifesto of the Rojava Revolution" and a place in which to enact stateless democracy on a daily basis (Ibid.).

In his analysis of the role and import of the staging of these parliaments, Staal draws attention to the significance of the aesthetic and material supports for the performance of politics and, in turn, its new practices of membership. As he says,

A morphological reading of a parliament . . . shows us the parliament as an arena, as a theatrical space, where power is performed through the specific spatial configuration, a specific number of actors and a composition of symbols, as well as an overall choreography. . . . From a morphological perspective—from a perspective that reads into the form of the parliament—we understand that a square parliament creates a different spatial and social dynamic than a circle, to the point that the form and choreography of the assembly affect the outcome: an open-air parliament might produce a radically different outcome than a covered one: a parliament with benches might produce a radically different outcome than a parliament with chairs. Each spatial configuration, each object, each choreography inscribes a set of ideas into the performance of its actors. So while the nation-state is a construct that demands a specific performance, so do the shapes and forms through which its power is articulated and inscribed upon those speaking its name. Ideology, in other words, has a material reality, which one can understand through morphology—through art. The discipline of the revolutionary practice of stateless democracy thus also affects the possibilities of the discipline of art to engage new, yet unscripted morphologies. (DSAR and New World Summit 2016, 100)

Indeed, the staging of his summits is an avowal of New Worlds—that is to say, newly visible actors within a field of action—and even though the imagery (flags, etc.) is a showy display of ethnically determined national symbols, the summits are not presented as rallies. Nor are they ironic or ostentatious. Instead, the staging of these assemblies, replete with novel architecture and national symbols, is a formal acknowledgment of people who are not recognized on the world stage, and through this we see a disruption to our own orientation as a public audience. In *New World Summit: Berlin* (2012), the participating blacklisted organizations[12] are visually presented as nascent governments and afforded an authority that they do not possess within mainstream or international politics. They are provided with a space in which to perform (and, indeed, defend and express) their claims to political autonomy that determines their statelessness. The summits therefore shape a kind of evolution (or revolution) of stateless political actors through assemblies, where the architectural spaces provide the requisite spectacle for validating the presence, authority, and identity of those assembled.

In keeping with artists such as Bruguera, Staal invokes the idea of the summits as a "useful tool" (DSAR and New World Summit 2016, 104) for facilitating the visibility and audibility of those who are partitioned (Rancière 2004); in addition, the summits embody new approaches to performing politically. The assemblies staged in the Netherlands and Germany appropriate public spaces that are extensions of nation-state (cultural) agendas (museums, galleries, universities, etc.), but they do not valorize the nation-state in their political expression. They "*repartition* the political from the non-political. . . . [They] occur '*out* of place,' *in* a place which was not supposed to be political" (Rancière 2011a, 4). The *New World Summits* appropriate the idea of parliaments but do not reiterate statist ideologies. Instead, these assemblies assume the role of reconfiguring power and, in so doing, illustrate well how art can be a space of action—a means of doing politics that is realized through acts of citizenship. By providing a space for those who would otherwise be excluded from an international political arena, the *New World Summits* create new "forms of life" (Martin 2013, 200) where the actors see themselves as performing as stateless citizens. As an art project, the *New World Summits* stage what otherwise would not be visible or, indeed, possible within the political arena. What we see instead is a new mode of citizenship being actualized in the practice of people assembling as political representatives of stateless states (of being)—that is, affiliations of peoples. These new manifestations of citizenship are not about exercising legal rights as if conferred on status citizens but about new ways to organize and perform politically through alternative public assemblies. The aim of the summits, therefore, is not only to devise ways of recognizing and sanctioning the (political) claims and perspectives of stateless peoples within particular polities through the spectacle of assembled bodies and speech but also, in the case of Rojava's open-air parliament especially, to structure dialogue and shape the aesthetic and material conditions of assemblies through time so as to underpin the performance of politics as "self-administration." This latter point requires further discussion.

New World Summit: Rojava (2015) and *New World Embassy: Rojava* (2016) focused their critiques on the nation-state and drew on the theoretical discussions and practices of stateless governance by the DSAR. That is, the DSAR exercised a scathing and deliberate rejection of the construct of the nation-state as a political and aspirational goal for the stateless people of Rojava, and there is a proactive determination to prevent the idea of a state from taking shape within the politics being developed in the region. This is important to understanding the scope and significance of citizen art projects and their capacity to reveal and problematize the limitations of the nation-state and normative notions of citizenship. The particular analysis of the state that is brought into view and made public through Staal's summit is outlined by the Kurdish Women's Movement. In the late 1990s, they "began to theoretically deconstruct the state" and arrived at the conclusion that the state and democracy are "inherently incompatible" (DSAR and New World Summit 2016, 74). As they say,

None of the tyrannical regimes in the Middle East have ever created solutions; instead of addressing essential issues, they created models that only increased sectarian tensions and laid the basis for the explosion of the entire region.[13] . . . This is colonialism: the forced imposition of borders that do not reflect the realities, loyalties, or identities on the ground, but are based solely on Western (or other nonlocal) interests. . . . Statelessness exposes you to oppression, to denial, to genocide. In a nation-state oriented system, recognition and monopoly of power is reserved for the state and this offers some form of protection. But the point is that the suffering of the stateless results from the same system being based on a nation-state paradigm. . . . Having a state does not mean that your society is liberated, that you will have a just society, or that it will be an ethical society. . . . This shift away from desiring a state was an acknowledgement that the state cannot actually represent one's interests, that the monopoly of power will always be in the hands of a few who can do what they want with you,

specifically because the state is implicated in several international agreements.
. . . That is why the PKK began to understand the importance of rejecting top-down approaches to power and governance. (62, 78)

We see how the principles and practices of the nation-state produce in-justices, inequalities, and ethnic tensions and hatreds among those residing within its boundaries. Equally, it is important to recognize that the nation-state also produces statelessness. The relationship between citizenship and statelessness is a deeply symbiotic one, and current discussions in the litera-ture within citizenship and migration studies see statelessness as a component part of a state's citizenship regime (Mezzadra and Neilson 2008, 2012; De Genova 2009).[14] Statelessness is produced through the managerial technology that develops in the handling of *all* bodies within a territory of a nation-state (including status citizens).[15] Some artists have warned, "When the rights of migrants are denied, the rights of citizens are at risk" (Bruguera quoted in Staal 2013, 82). In my view, the rights of citizens are always at risk,[16] and the denial of migrants' and stateless people's rights simply makes this obvious. By comparison, the DSAT aimed to first reject statist imaginaries and aspirations and instead embody, through practice, a system of devolved governance where villages—society's small cell—through, for instance, local committees, councils, and interest groups, assemble, organize, and represent themselves (in all their ethnic diversity) within a "democratic confederation" (DSAR and New World Summit 2016, 64). "Democratic confederalism is thus not a centralized mechanism of decision making and forming policies, but rather a decentralized form of local self-administration made up of coun-cils, municipalities, and communes. These council's decisions are decentral-ized and are based on self-sustainability" (65). The construct of the state runs counter to these values and objectives and is therefore rejected by the DSAR.

Important to note here is that key to sustaining this system of devolved self-governance and the logical consequences for underpinning experiments with new modes of citizenship is the practice of assembling and engaging in dialogue, as facilitated in this example of a citizen art intervention. We see that assemblies, and not nation-states, are crucial to the performance of citi-zenship. Assemblies that are not oriented to a state enterprise are shown to do the work of facilitating interpersonal "contractual" obligations and duties: They stage a miniature civil society, and they expose the fiction that citizen-ship is contingent on the state. This matters for understanding how the ideas of a stateless democracy, as embodied in Staal's creation and construction of assemblies, not only mobilize new and novel practices of citizenship but also are mobilized by stateless citizens. It is in the act of doing politics within Staal's citizen art project that the principles of self-governance and, in turn, the role of the citizen are actively rescripted. As Hannah Arendt would say,

"What guides the action is not a future aim that is conceived by the imagination and can be seized by the will. The action is guided by something else ... —a principle. The principle inspires the action, but it cannot prescribe the result, as if it were a matter of carrying out a program; it does not manifest itself in any kind of results, but *only in the performance of the action itself*" (2018, 225, my italics).

Arendt's observations help us to see that citizenship, when not conceived as either requiring or being determined by the state, is actually perpetually generative. It manifests in the "action itself," in the act of assembling and speaking and in the context of the pressures and problems that people face, being bound together through "*interest*" (Arendt 1998) and in an active engagement with, in this case, the practice of self-governance. The enactment of new modes of citizenship by the DSAR is given a material form—and creatively transformed—within the assemblies of the *New World Summit: Rojava* and the open-air parliament in Canton Cizîre. And this matters to its participants cognizing and embodying Rojava's stateless self-administration. Indeed, my claim here is that (nonstatist) citizenship, and by extension citizen art in its production of acts of citizenship, *is* a starting point for rescripting genuinely new and alternative modes of doing politics—new modes of political affiliations and membership. When citizen art projects give form to new practices of (nonstatist) citizenship, such as in the summits and open-air parliament staged by Staal, citizen art proves to be responsive, generative, and conceptually and materially productive.

I'd like to add one more observation about the intersection of assemblies, citizen art, and new modes of citizenship. Judith Butler makes an important point about the material supports for action, such as those seen within Staal's assemblies and by extension, within citizen art:

Human action depends upon all sorts of supports—it is always supported action. But in the case of public assemblies, . . . not only is there a struggle over what will be public space, but a struggle as well over those basic ways in which we are, as bodies, supported in the world—a struggle against disenfranchisement, effacement, and abandonment. . . . The material supports for action are not only part of the action, but they are also what is being fought about, especially in those cases when the political struggle is about food, employment, mobility, and access to institutions. To rethink the space of appearance in order to understand the power and effect of public demonstrations for our time, we will need to understand the bodily dimensions of action, what the body requires and the body can do, especially when we must think about bodies together, what holds them there, their conditions of persistence and power. (2011, 1–2)

Each *New World Summit* holds bodies together and structures—and supports—the material conditions that actualize new political actors and, in turn, new modes of citizenship. It is important to appreciate that this is done through the vehicle of citizen art. The summits make visible the "interval" between the "legitimacy of a regime [e.g., a state] called into question" (Butler 2011, 2) and, I would argue, a new regime taking shape. As Butler says, "This time of the interval is the time of the popular will, not a single will, not a unitary will, but one that is characterized by *alliance with the performative power to lay claim to the public*" (2, my italics). The popular will, indeed, the alliance of peoples, is codified through action and assembly—that is, *codified through a citizen art project*. Staal's projects, like that of Tania Bruguera, provide rich frameworks for acts of citizenship within which perceptions are altered and subjects are transformed into visible actors within a field of action. The summits reframe how politics is done and from where new political actors emerge. These citizen art projects trouble the notion of the nation-state as hegemonic and, by extension, normative notions of citizenship. They alter how statelessness is understood, discussed, and mobilized, and they reconfigure the nature and role of the citizen.

CITIZEN ARTIST NEWS:
THE UNIVERSITY AS A BORDER REGIME

This last example of a citizen art intervention is one of my own, *Citizen Artist News: The University as a Border Regime* (2013a; hereafter *CAN: BR*) (see figure 4.1). It was the first of three art interventions in the form of a printed newspaper (the second and third newspaper intervention will be discussed in chapters 5 and 6). This first edition was something of an exploratory exercise in the use of an (archaic) communication medium to contend with the issue of membership and immigration in a moment of the repurposing of the university into a border regime following the ramping up (in 2012 and 2013) of the UK government's requirement for universities to monitor and track their foreign nationals (i.e., international students).[17]

To give some context, the newspaper was produced during my employment as a senior lecturer at the University of the Arts London. On the one hand, I was beginning to glean how one could create the aesthetic and "material supports" (Butler 2011) for doing politics by, in this case, working with the form of a printed newspaper and disseminating it within the spaces of a university. I was interested to explore the potential of this kind of medium for performing an act of citizenship. On the other hand, my interest in combining the form and techniques of journalism with an art intervention was inspired by the phenomenon of citizen journalists (mid-2000s and on) and their capacity to emerge from seemingly nowhere to carve out new spaces for politics. What was impressive

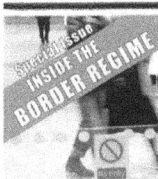

Shirley Douglas
'I never think about my part in the system'
The University of Janus?

☒ the CITIZEN ARTIST NEWS

Special Edition: Commemorating the University's transformation into a Border Regime: 2012-13   citizenartist.org.uk

Studying, working and teaching in a University Border Regime?

A University is assumed to be a place of equality and mobility. However, inside the system, identities vary and barriers and boundaries exist. In this academic year especially, foreign students are heavily monitored by the University on behalf of the Home Office, the costs of fees press up the differences in students' economic status and the spaces and places of an institution are discrete and scrutinised. The year also marks the final phase of the slow and steady economic decoupling of the University from the State and in its wake, the role and purpose of the University has shifted from its Enlightenment objectives (the formation of critical citizens) to a complex commercial enterprise producing 'knowledge capital', the full consequences of which are too immediate to gauge. More surprisingly private changes to the University are the use of its managerial systems as an area of the Immigration Services. As a border regime, the University on the one hand operates as a 'method' where its members (students, staff, administrators etc.) are agents in the production of divisions in status that enact the policing policies of the State and on the other hand, members are subject to the border regime's security rationale and procedures. All of these conditions impact on a member's sense of identity, mobility and belonging.

The concern of this special edition newspaper is to make visible not only how members of the University reproduce the directives of the State's immigration policies, but to indicate how these behaviours supervene on prejudiced and state-bounded conceptions of membership (citizenship) beyond the boundaries of the institution. What is at issue here is revealing the logics, habits and behaviours that are taking shape as the University and to see in this a wider problem: how does the University construct difference and exclusion and how do these discriminations contribute to the repurposing of the citizen-student as servicing the demands of global capital flows? Capital flows that do not in turn contribute to the communities where energies and intelligences combine to create its product. The objective of the newspaper therefore is to first draw out the janus-faced character of the University as, on the one hand, valorising the utopic vision of education as democratic, aspirational and liberatory and on the other, as a space that reinvents discrimination. It is also the aim of this project to problematise the conditions of the University, to make visible the experience of its silent workings as an apparatus of the State, as a space in which polluted objectivities are formed and its use of the logic and language of corporate capitalism.

Daphne Plessner
Affiliated with Goldsmiths College and University of the Arts London

A porter surveils students passing through barriers at one of the main entrances of a university in central London.

The malignant teaching factory

Acknowledgements:
A special thanks to our contributors. Without their participation, this publication would not have been possible. A very special thanks too to Ilix Rogatchevski and Dovile Aleskaute for giving their time so generously to this project. The views expressed in these pages are those of the individual writers and artists.
Daphne Plessner, editor
Ilia Rogatchevski, co-editor
Dovile Aleskaite, co-editor

In a period of little over thirty years, higher education has ventured quite some distance from the old collegiate hierarchical system of privilege, scholarship and content research. It has transformed, by way of Government policy, market demand, commercial opportunity and participant compliance into something quite unrecognisable: a global education industry, intertwined with business and investment, productivity targets, enterprise and creative accounting.

Transitional rather than vocational, forces rather than idea, commission rather than mission, we have seen the exchange of the old gown for the no-gowned compact and a bottom-dollar traffic in innovated investigation (e.g. product trials). Speculative education has replaced the old and frankly merchant idea of speculation as such.

There is nothing redemptive in harking back to the old ways. But it is ...vently that the privatised educational system of today has turned teachers into vendors, vendors into shoppers, researchers into hired mercenaries and senior colleagues into grotesque parodies of corporate greed. Too often otherwise admirable scholars become shiny-suited administrators, hawking student snitches and research contracts round as if they were baubles of divine election and not exactly the last dusty job-lots of a faded glory now peddled out at cut price – everything must go! – discount rates for a sharp-sided emporium of decay. ➤➤ p.6

Figure 4.1. Front page of *Citizen Artist News: The University as a Border Regime.* Launched on May Day (May 1) 2013, London, United Kingdom. *Photo courtesy of F. D. Plessner*

was how citizen journalists operated outside mainstream media networks and yet made visible the issues, concerns, and struggles that percolate within specific locales that otherwise can be elided or obfuscated by state actors and corporate media agencies. I was also attracted to how citizen journalists altered the form and conception of the citizen. In a recent book titled *Citizen Journalism as Conceptual Practice*, Bolette Blaagaard articulates what I was discovering through practice, namely, how to engage in the struggle over what is to be seen in the public space and, in turn, to shape new counterpublics:

> Delinked from a definition determined by professional journalism, the citizen of citizen journalism generates another kind of public, one based on political and cultural habits of meaning and therefore embodied and situated. This kind of definition of the citizen of citizen journalism departs from theorizations that take their starting point in participation and Habermas's public sphere. . . . What is important to the concept of the citizen in citizen journalism . . . is the political engagement and struggle for social change *as well as the embodied experience of a counter-position.* (2018, 43, my italics)

My own intervention was therefore an attempt to further explore how a newspaper, modeled on the actions of citizen journalists, could impinge on the aesthetic and material conditions of the university as it transitioned into a border regime and to do this from the perspective of being deeply entangled in its systems. I wanted to capture and draw attention to the aesthetic (i.e., visual and affective) experience of the silent workings of the university in its perpetual partitioning and bordering of its members.[18]

My aim was to use the newspaper, as an interventionist tool in the hands of a declared citizen artist, to interpose between the seemingly prosaic culture of the university and its new bordering practices by drawing attention to how its individual members were entwined in the daily production and policing of a specific group of its members—international students—in the production of a state's citizenship regime. The newspaper therefore is unique in its aesthetic capture of the moment (2012) when universities became directly responsible for monitoring the physical presence of international students. It predated and, in some way, anticipated the tensions that surrounded immigration and membership in the rise of Brexit and the state's reordering of citizens.[19] The purpose, however, was to make apparent the lived, affective experiences of the members of the university in the moment when the procedures to monitor "foreign" nationals rapidly became instrumentalized within the administrative and pedagogic systems of the institution. My aim was to question this unfolding complexity and trouble the university's logic and rationale through the lens of the aesthetic effects of its bordering regime, to examine how the institution functions as a space where differences and divisions are formed and indeed performed. As Nando Sigona noted in his brief discussion of the impact of immigration policy on citizens, one "side of immigration policy and practice [is] the permeability and historically contingent nature of the boundaries between citizenship and non-citizenship and the concrete ways immigration rules produce and shape not only the position, entitlements and experiences of non-citizens in society, but also the very meaning of what citizenship is and of what being a citizen entails" (2013). The purpose, therefore, of *CAN: BR* was to make visible the silent workings, attitudes, and behaviors and the various managerial systems that prevailed in sustaining the immigration policies of the state. Through its dissemination, the newspaper was a tool to intervene in and indeed interrupt the normalization of the seemingly workaday (but otherwise "malignant" [Hutnyk 2013]) immigration procedures of the university.

To better contextualize the newspaper intervention, the following will briefly detail the internal procedures and administrative systems devised for monitoring the behavior of international students. In servicing what was (in 2012) called the UK Border Agency,[20] teaching staff were required to document and report on international student attendance, and some institutions, such as the one I was working for, had set up an additional layer of administration whereby international students had to sign in at a designated office every week. If faculty did not participate in documenting and reporting[21] on the physical presence of international students and account for their attendance in class, students were then vulnerable to the decisions of the UK Border Agency and under threat of the commencement of deportation procedures. This layer of surveillance was in addition to an elaborate system of screening and application procedures that international students endured to first gain access to universities in the United Kingdom. At the time of this project's development in 2012, John Vine, the then independent chief inspector of borders and immigration, stated, "Tier 4 of the Points Based System (PBS) was introduced in 2008 to strengthen controls over the migration of students from outside the European Economic Area (EEA) to the UK. Strict rules govern what courses can be studied, the educational institutions that a migrant student can attend and the amount of time allowed to study" (2012, 3).[22] Extensive tracking, monitoring, and maintenance of records included review of passports and biometric data, leave stamps or immigration status documents, UK biometric cards, proof of entitlement to study, students' contact detail history (addresses in United Kingdom), copies of the offer to study, clearance certificates for the Academic Technology Approval Scheme (where appropriate), copies/evidence of the documentation required for offer of a place to study (references, certificates, etc.), details of foster carers supplied to the local authority for students younger than eighteen, and so forth.

The point here is that even prior to a student's daily surveillance within the university, numerous government agencies were involved in scrutinizing and surveilling international students, and extensive personal data was collected and stored by the university on behalf of the immigration services.[23] In other words, the administration of a university is deeply entangled in the partitioning of its members from the very start of its recruitment of students.

A central strategy of the newspaper therefore was drawing attention to the "janus-faced" character of the university environment, on the one hand, as a space that propagates the values of equality and mobility and, on the other, as a regime for policing the presence of foreigners, marking out those who do not belong even within its membership—that is, those who are neither equal (are subject to extensive monitoring) nor wholly mobile (are bodily tied to the institution). In this sense, the newspaper intervention drew on contemporary analysis of a state's border regime where the university operates as a "method"[24] (Mezzadra and Neilson 2012) whereby its members (students, staff, administrators, etc.) not only serve as actors in the production of divisions in status that enact the policing policies of the state but are also subject to the state's systems and procedures of securitization. It is the complexity of the tension between the aspirational and idealized values of the university and also one's own role in reproducing social divisions and discriminations that the newspaper was aimed at highlighting and problematizing.

Drawing on what I had learned from *The Mobile Armband Exhibition* intervention and the potential for a citizen art intervention to reframe the aesthetic conditions of an event, and in my capacity as a member of a university who was expected to actively participate in discriminating against its foreign students, I hoped that the act of intervening would go some way to interrupt what was unfolding and being normalized. By disseminating the newspaper within the spaces of various universities, including my own campus, I aimed to involve other teaching and support staff, students, administrators, and so forth, in a public thought experiment and to prompt recognition of the fact that *everyone* was involved in the production of inequalities within the institution. Equally, the intervention was designed to prod at individuals who did not (or would not) recognize this fact. The intervention was therefore an act that not only challenged the university's techniques of bordering and racially categorizing students—by which it was actively redefining who belonged, tacitly contributing to the characterization of foreign students as suspicious and untrustworthy and therefore deserving of close monitoring and policing—but also set out to enfold university members in the dilemma of their own positionality within the very spaces that produce these discriminations.

Fifteen hundred copies were printed and distributed on May 1, 2013, to universities in central London[25] and handed out at select arts organizations (such as the Whitechapel Gallery and the Institute of Contemporary Arts). Copies were also sent to the Department of Education and the Home Office. To convey the seriousness of the political circumstances and to draw readers into the ethical dilemma of being caught within the internal workings of a bordering regime, *CAN: BR* was modeled on the design of a conventional broadsheet newspaper, organized into sections with headings such as International News, National News, Analysis, Opinion, Property, and Lifestyle. Rather than perform an objective analysis of the institution, the newspaper instead highlighted stories of the lived, affective experiences of those who were struggling with the harmful effects of this new regime. All of its elements, such as images, adverts, news items, and so forth, homed in on different aspects of membership and immigration and its complexities and stories by those deemed to be foreign within the spaces of the university. The newspaper's content therefore was an assemblage of views, opinions, and experiences of the university from lecturers, professors, students, alumni, and so forth, regarded as experts by virtue of their direct experience of the university rather than their status as professionals. Every illustration, interview, opinion, reflection, advertisement, and the like had been collated and arranged to build up a multiperspectival reading of the theme. In their encounter with the artifact in the setting of their place of study and work, readers had to puzzle through and experience the implicit contradictions and tensions of the newspaper's thought experiment. For example, authored articles and interviews with specialists in the field of citizenship studies discuss the concept of the citizen and an analysis of "bordering," and these perspectives are juxtaposed with the personal reflections of a lecturer who describes their experience of the use of barriers and security guards within the spaces of their institution, alongside the reflections of an alumnus who critiqued the notion of "foreignness." Material appropriated from online sources, such as anonymously authored texts that give "attendance guidance" to international students and provide lists of immigration rules and legislation, is placed alongside news items that report on international students forming lengthy queues outside police stations, the mapping of "high-risk" nationals, and quotes from students of various nationalities who describe their different treatment within various universities.

As the process of editing the material progressed, the unequal and racialized treatment of students became vividly apparent. Students from Canada and studying at Cambridge, for example, had negligible exposure to policing measures, whereas students from places such as China or Afghanistan studying at the University of the Arts London were subject to weekly checks. Equally, non-national lecturers discussed their struggle with the UK Border

Agency, and this material was placed alongside an interview with a border agent who oversaw case work, next to an advert by an activist group that focused on precarious labor within the university (drawing parallels with migrant labor). Private correspondence, internal notices and memos with bullish language, and oppressive administrative directives evidence the coercive policing of (academic) staff to monitor foreign students. The property pages highlight the ubiquity of security cameras, door-locking mechanisms, warning signage, and turnstiles at entrances of buildings, which inform the control of bodies, the flows and stoppages of people, within the architectural spaces of the university. And the lifestyle and crossword pages point up yet more paradoxes of the university as a border regime, soliciting reader engagement with provocative quizzes and puzzles, "weather" maps, and faux adverts.

All of the newspaper's content was assembled and presented in such a way as to draw attention to aesthetic (affective) dimension and complexities of the politics of membership that the source material had not previously possessed. Articles and images were arranged to draw out and highlight intersecting themes such as the bureaucracy of the state, precarity and mobility of labor, securitization, and the effects of the university's economic conditions. The design of each page was intended to draw readers into an affective experience of and reflection on one's own involvement in constructing the politics of belonging and membership within a university, reminding the reader of the central question: What kind of sociopolitical being is in play here—what kind of "citizen"?

Pages 5 and 14 of the newspaper (figure 4.2) were explicitly designed to challenge the tacit racism that shapes the institutionalized delineation and classification of the foreigner. I will briefly discuss the content of these pages in detail because they were developed through a prior intervention, called the *National Student Surveys*. Two (visual) questionnaires were designed to provoke participants ("home" students) by asking them to complete a quiz about the purported visual appearance of a "foreign" student. Forty-five home students at Central Saint Martins College of Art and Design were approached (March 23, 2013) to complete the task. The questionnaires presented the participants with a dilemma. They were asked to either pick out or describe (i.e., make a drawing of) what a foreign student looked like. However, this task of either rendering the features of a foreign student or selecting one from a set of passport-sized photographs (figure 4.3) involved home students in addressing a set of (tacit) racist assumptions while actively inscribing and classifying who purportedly does and does not belong. It is important to note here that the surveys do not celebrate the language of racism. Instead they draw attention to the vocabulary of foreignness, which was then commonplace within universities and positions those doing the surveys as producers of the institution's classificatory practices in deciding who is foreign. The one survey (figure 4.2) made use of the "evidence" for surveillance—the "proofs of identity"[26]—in the form of passport photographs used when processing the registration of students, which is often assumed to be incontrovertible. In doing this, the survey drew out not only the wider connotations of (visually based) racial prejudices and the assumptions about the fixity of the photographic image and its scope for identifying a person (e.g., as within passport security[27]) but also the assumptions about the veridicality of the passport photograph that play out in society at large. The surveys therefore drew out the problematic of actively classifying who is foreign (or not), distinguishing between the different statuses of "citizens," on the visual evidence of a passport photograph.

By soliciting the involvement of individual home students and instigating a (subtle) moment of disruption in their daily lives within the university, the intervention was a rudimentary act of citizenship. Its aim was to directly discombobulate participants and heighten their awareness and prompt a self-conscious, decisional act. Students had to physically engage with crossing out passport photographs or drawing faces of foreigners (figure 4.3) to affectively enter into the problem of making judgments about who and what is

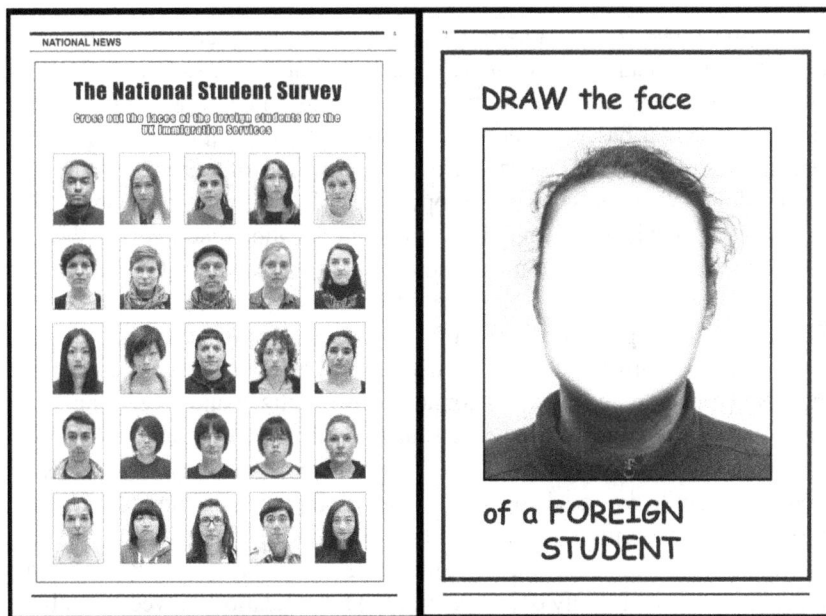

Figure 4.2. *National Student Surveys* **as reproduced on pages 5 and 14 of** *Citizen Artist News: The University as a Border Regime.* **Photo courtesy of F. D. Plessner**

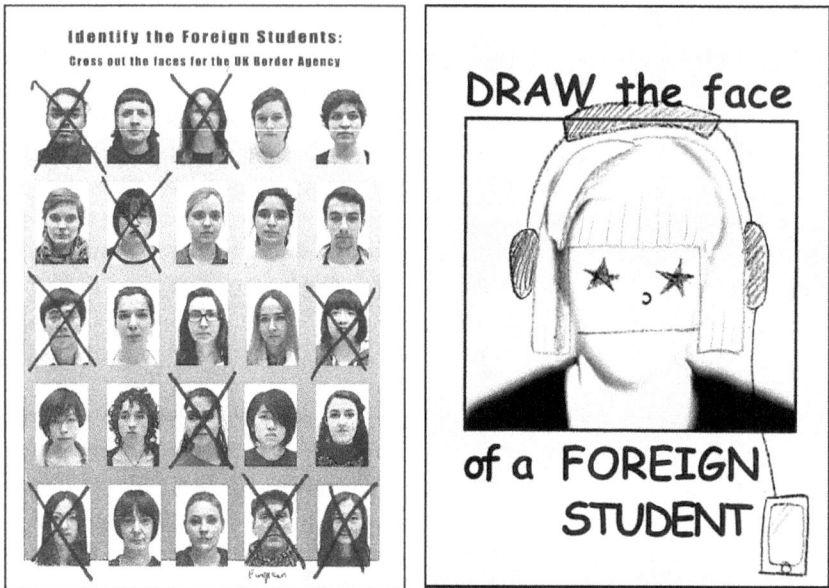

Figure 4.3. Examples of completed *National Student Surveys*, Central St. Martins, University of the Arts London, March 2013. *Photo courtesy of F. D. Plessner*

a foreigner—who is a member of the university or not. Home students had to experience the unanswerable nature of the questionnaires, to live through the absurdity of setting out to make any kind of decision about who may or may not be a foreigner based on mere photographic representations—indeed, representations of their colleagues—or making drawings of their own imaginary assumptions and stereotypes of the appearance of a foreigner. The intervention engaged students in a slow and deliberative provocation that involved them in having to think through and make choices about who and what is foreign and what constitutes a member. The surveys therefore required that they be visual. The point was to pin people down to judging images of others and to have them enact their discriminations by making apparent the tensions between the multiple (visual and conceptual) connotations of citizen and foreign national, status and identity, race and otherness, and membership or nonmembership in the university.[28] This approach to testing political subjectivity via what Rancière has described as a "dissensus" further prompts the problem of the complexity and ambiguities that surround the concept of citizenship. In arguing that citizenship is not simply a set of properties or qualities understood as, say, a legal status (an allegedly objective criteria) but a relation between members, this intervention brought to the fore how the aesthetic dimension of relations can sustain differences and divisions within the arena of the university.

The questionnaires were a medium for a public and dialogical act, but they also turned the dissensual moment inward—to prompt an act of "interiority" ("an inner dialectical logic . . . allowed to think itself out and to become explicit"; Giegerich, n.d.). And this internalization of the dilemmas presented within the questionnaires, in addition to the requirement for individual deliberation (the act of choosing), places the participant at the center of the production of membership. It embeds them in real-world settings and situations and exposes how their own conceptions (and prejudices) of belonging determine the lived experiences of the other. It makes visible, as Rancière (2004) notes, how affective (aesthetic) experience is partitioned and in turn makes apparent one's role in the division of power. The surveys were tools not only for doing politics but also for the politics being done; the troubling of accepted norms and assumptions as they pertain to the classification and intensification of unequal treatment of non-national students and staff within the university was an act of citizenship.

As a performative act, *CAN: BR* raises a question: How exactly is a new mode of citizenship performed in this context, especially when the popular conception of a university, in its current formulation, involves notions of hierarchies of knowledge distribution and centers of excellence (Readings 1996; McGettigan 2013)? Gerald Raunig's (2013) metaphor of a "factory of knowledge" may be useful here in framing the problem anew. His analysis gives us some purchase on what a university is, so as to understand how it can be a space of resistance to statist (and corporatist) enterprises—indeed, how it can produce new modes of membership. This is important for understanding what *CAN: BR* captures as the aesthetic and affective dimension of the university's system of classifying and ordering its members. It also sheds more light on how one might understand this citizen art intervention as an act of citizenship and as a manifestation of incipient citizenship in its active involvement with the university and its systems.

Raunig declares, "What was once the factory is now the university" (2013, 24). By this he means not only that the institution replicates the embodied subservience to a "machine"—the university as an apparatus "supporting authorities" and an "accommodation to subjugation" (2013, 25)—but, importantly, that it is a space in which solidarities and resistance to subservience are realized and take form. He continues to argue that the university is not simply "a site of the transfer of knowledge, but rather . . . a complex space of the overlapping of the most diverse forms of cognitive, affective, subservient labour" (24). He speculates that as a space of "modulation" the university is potentially a site that can be "reterritorialized" into a space of resistance to the production of its own disciplinary regime (23–24) and, in so doing, asks us "to consider the transformations of contemporary modes of production as a condition for the emergence of the modulating university, or more generally the fact that the adaptive capacity of capitalism has taken over precisely the central characteristics of these struggles, in order to flexibly immunize and newly position itself" (25). Although I would agree with Raunig's observation that the university as an institution is responsive to the demands and flows of capital, his argument does not wholly capture the implications of critical discourse and practices among a university's members. This point is better expressed in the work of Jacques Derrida. The following will outline more carefully how one might understand the university as producing a critical space as this bears heavily on how one conceives of the intervention's potentiality for performing new modes of citizenship. It also matters to how one interprets *CAN: BR* as doing politics and as a rudimentary act of citizenship and, in turn, as suggestive of a new mode of citizenship.

Derrida describes the nature of the university in such a way as to see it as not only a space of resistance within its system but also, a larger claim, of independence from the state. As he says, the university is a site of resistance "to the power of the nation state and its phantasm of indivisible sovereignty . . . to corporations and to national and international capital . . . to the powers of the media, ideological, religious, and cultural powers," and so forth (Derrida 2002, 26). Unlike Raunig, who characterizes the university as a modulating space, Derrida suggests that the "unconditional university," as a site of "deconstruction" (i.e., a site of intellectual analysis and hypothesizing without restriction), is not in existence per se, and yet this should be what constitutes its nature. Why? Because for Derrida the unconditional university *stages an "unconditional independence"* (28) *from state and corporate apparatuses*. As he says, "The university claims and ought to be granted in principle, besides what is called academic freedom, an *unconditional* freedom to question and to assert . . . the right to say publicly all that is required by research, knowledge and thought concerning the *truth*" (24). The key point here is that Derrida envisages the university as a sovereign space, as is the state, and he troubles the question of how sovereignty could plausibly be divided between the two (28). To this question he offers a subtle answer: He homes in on how the humanities play a decisive role in foregrounding critical inquiry and in essence capture the necessary preconditions of resistance to state and economic powers, in so far as the humanities represent "the place where the university is exposed to reality, to the forces from without (be they cultural, ideological, political, economic or other)" (55). He continues,

> It is there that the university is in the world that it is attempting to think. On this border, it must therefore negotiate and organise its resistance. And take its responsibilities. Not in order to enclose itself and reconstitute the abstract phantom of sovereignty . . . [b]ut in order to organise an inventive resistance,

through its oeuvre, its work, to all attempts at reappropriation (political, juridical, economic and so forth) to all other figures of sovereignty (55–56).

The push and pull between institutional powers (government authority and the "unconditional independence" of the university) and the role of the university in contesting imaginaries in the ("real") world speak to a democratic ideal, and in turn our role as members of the university and, more widely, as citizens, which Derrida makes visible—an ideal that is "in the world we are attempting to think." Such were the challenges that were in play within the (UK) university that bore heavily on the reality of one's membership and participation and, of course, on the concept and role of a citizen. I would argue too that it is in this context that *CAN: BR* gains real meaning as an act of citizenship: as an act that exposes the aesthetic dimension of the university as it manifests as a border regime, on the one hand, and as a performance of citizenship that does not reiterate or valorize statist notions of membership, on the other.

The *CAN: BR* intervention was not devised to wrong-foot anyone, but by virtue of being a thought experiment, it aimed to take participants through a process that embodied them in recognizing that their own (one's own) membership of the university is a political act that produces the border regime. As an act of citizenship the newspaper made apparent how the university's implementation of bordering involves unequal and differential treatments that are not only obfuscated by the rhetoric of equality but also reproduced or supported in the daily behaviors and actions of its individual members. The intention was to get under the skin, so to speak, and this required that the strategies for engagement be subtle, pointed, and enacted. It also required that material from preliminary interventions that involved collaboration with members of the university (e.g., the *National Student Surveys*, as discussed previously) provided a layering of meaning and content for the newspaper, making apparent intersecting themes of racism, precarious labor, and the language of bordering within its administration. The success of *CAN: BR*, then, lay in its ability not only to tease out and make visible the affective dimension of university membership but also, through its enactment, to call readers to account for one's individual role in the production of a border regime at the moment when the university was in transition. Not only was the newspaper a material support for a subtle form of action (i.e., an act of citizenship), but the performance of citizenship itself also reified a Derridean positionality: The embodiment of a perpetually emergent, nonstatist form of membership, generated through its exposure to and engagement with "the world that it is attempting to think" (Derrida 2002, 55–56).

In sum, the interventions of Bruguera, Staal, and my own *CAN: BR* show that emergent conceptions of citizenship that manifest within citizen art are not expressions of normative notions or practices of citizenship. Nor is citizen art about transcending the problems and conditions of a citizenship regime (say, in virtue of moral imperatives as seen in Martha Nussbaum[29]). Instead, the forms of citizenship that manifests in these citizen art projects are better understood as a process of emergence and potentiality, a space of becoming (Isin and Nielsen 2008; Isin 2012, 2019). I have argued that these citizen art interventions reveal the character of citizenship as a perpetually fluid space of negotiation and reciprocal relations that frame social and dialogical contracts, mini social contracts that impart responsibilities to their interlocutors or forge affiliations between newly visible political actors. They creatively confront the complexities of migration, statelessness, and border regimes while also shaping new modalities of citizenship through acts of citizenship—the act of doing politics.

NOTES

1. These examples are but a small number of citizen art projects that respond to issues of migration and statelessness. See also Schlingensief 2000; Cornerstone Theatre (cornerstonetheater.org); Werthein 2005; Performigrations 2014; Zannos 2014; Geiger-Gerlach 2018; Schneider 1997.

2. See chapter 2 re: Mezzadra, De Genova, et al., show how the state produces statelessness or a metic class, etc., through its status citizenship regime.

3. See also The Silent University (thesilentuniversity.org), whose mandate is "to challenge the idea of silence as a passive state, and explore its powerful potential through performance, writing, and group reflection. These explorations attempt to make apparent the systemic failure and the loss of skills and knowledge experienced through the silencing process of people seeking asylum."

4. See Schwarzenbach (2015): Normative notions of solidarity "tend to refer to class-struggle, to a 'standing-together' in opposition to exploitative practices, whether these are perpetrated by individual capitalists, the political state, or by multi-national corporations. The term's scope is vast, however, *and its meaning unsettled*. In recent scholarship, for instance, the notion of solidarity ranges from indicating the social bond between two or more individuals to a general feeling of empathy or sympathy for others (e.g., for Jean Harvey or Richard Rorty), to group or class cohesion based on the recognition of a common good (William Rehg), to one based on justice (Laurence Blum or Carol Gould); solidarity is even identified with the concept and practice of democracy itself within the modern welfare state (Brunkhorst)" (4, my italics). See also Arendt 1990: "Pity may be the perversion of compassion, but its alternative is solidarity. It is out of pity that men are 'attracted to *les hommes faibles*,' but it is out of solidarity that they establish deliberately and, as it were, dispassionately a community of interest with the oppressed and exploited. . . . For solidarity, because it partakes of reason, and hence of generality, is able to comprehend a multitude conceptually, not only the multitude of a class or a nation or a people, but eventually all mankind. . . .

Terminologically speaking, solidarity is a principle that can inspire and guide action, compassion is one of the passions, and pity is a sentiment" (88–89).

5. See Van der Ploeg and Guérin 2016; Schwarzenbach 2015. Vasiljević 2016 further notes that "many political theories . . . rely on specific visions of solidarity as the cohesive force that turns individuals into members of a society. However, there have been very few attempts, especially in more recent political and social theories, to discuss solidarity from a theoretical point of view and to provide a coherent framework that explains the role of solidarity in constituting the fibre of a political community. . . . [S]ocial theory interpretations of solidarity have predominantly viewed it as a given feature of every group or as the essence of cooperative behaviour. For instance, both mechanical and organic solidarity are assumed in Durkheim's account, emerging from the particular character of individual groups. . . . It is usually also presumed that solidarity takes place between actors who are alike, or, as in rational choice theory, who strive to achieve the same goal. In other words, these accounts do not treat solidarity as created, agitated for, and as *transformative*—capable of challenging and establishing political and social orders" (374).

6. See Arendt 1972 for Arendt's outline of Tocqueville's description: "'As soon as several of the inhabitants of the United States have taken up an opinion or a feeling which they wish to promote in the world,' or have found some fault they wish to correct, 'they look out for mutual assistance, and as soon as they have found one another out, they combine. From that moment, they are no longer isolated men but a power seen from afar, whose actions serve for an example and whose language is listened to'" (95).

7. See also *New World Assembly*, *New World Academy* (2013–2017) and *Artist Organisations International* (Staal 2015b).

8. See also Hank Willis Thomas and Eric Gottesman's *For Freedoms* (2016) (Wikipedia, n.d.c). Unlike Staal, whose project is a weighty critique of the construct of the state, Thomas and Gottesman reinvigorate the US state's values based on Franklin D. Roosevelt's "Four Freedoms" wartime address (freedom of speech and worship and freedom from want and fear). The *For Freedoms* project is intentionally aimed at "using art as a vehicle to build *civic* engagement" (For Freedoms, n.d., my italics), and in doing so, Thomas and Gottesman ape the systems and structures of the nation-state in encouraging "town hall" meetings, producing political advertising, and even reiterating Donald Trump's election slogan "Make America Great Again" (Ibid.; "For Freedoms," n.d.). They finance artists' projects to address civic issues that intersect with the production and role of art. As they say, "For the *For Freedoms 50 State Initiative* in September to November 2018, concurrent decentralized art exhibitions and public events across the country will encourage broad participation in civic discourse and through lifting up a multiplicity of voices, will spark a national dialogue about art, education, advertising and politics" (For Freedoms, n.d., 3). They have also established a Super PAC (political action committee) to generate financing for their project. Super PACs are registered with the Federal Election Commission and permit groups to collect and distribute monies for the purposes of supporting political campaigns. *For Freedoms* is the first "Super PAC where Art Meets Politics" (Novick 2016; Crowdpac, n.d.). However, rather than produce new modes of

citizenship, Thomas and Gottesman emulate the nation-state and civic republican, participatory model of citizenship.

9. See Jonas Staal's *New World Embassy: Azawad* (2014; www.jonasstaal.nl /projects/new-world-embassy-azawad) and *New World Embassy: Rojava* (2016; www.jonasstaal.nl/projects/new-world-embassy-rojava); 7th Berlin Biennale (2012; www.berlinbiennale.de/en/biennalen/22/forget-fear); the Museum de Lakenhal de Veenfabriek, Leiden (2012; www.lakenhal.nl/en); 1st Kochi-Muziris Biennale (2013; https://kochimuzirisbiennale.org); Basis voor Actuele Kunste (BAK) (2014; www .bakonline.org).

10. See Staal 2015a, 2015b: "The Kurdish Women's Movement has played a key role in translating their resistance against state oppression towards a fundamental critique of the nation-state itself, which they regard as a patriarchal construct in service of the global capitalist doctrine. . . . The historic base of the Kurdish Women's Movement can be found in the prominent role of women in the Kurdistan Worker's Party (PKK)" (Staal 2015a, 7). The Kurdish Women's Movement sees the potential for emancipation through nonpatriarchal, *nonstatist* practices. It looks for strategies that do not involve resistance or conflict with a "host" nation but instead ways to operate autonomously. They apply the practice of direct democracy and a more expansive and porous notion of ethnicity (in essence, a critique of their own label as "Kurdish") (Staal 2015a, 2015b).

11. The classification of Kurds as stateless is concurrent with their struggle for autonomy following the colonial remapping of the region of Mesopotamia under the Sykes-Picot Agreement in 1917, the decline of the Ottoman Empire, and the formation of nation-states in the Middle East under Britain and France, including the emergence of the Turkish Republic in 1923 (Staal 2015a, 33). Kurds have dealt with exceptional marginalization of their peoples in not one but four states (e.g., Turkey, Iraq, Syria, and Iran). The PKK is banned in Turkey and labeled a terrorist organization by the Europe Union and the United States (*Times of Israel* 2017; Leduc 2015).

12. Staal (2012) invited "representatives of the Kurdish Women's Movement (affiliated with the PKK), the Basque Independence Movement, the National Liberation Movement of Azawad and the National Democratic Movement of the Philippines, . . . [as well as] lawyers, public prosecutors, judges and governmental advisors involved in [legal] cases after the passing of the Patriot Act in the United States."

13. "People of various religious groups and ethnic groups lived together, with different hierarchies and social orders in place. . . . The world's dominant [nation-state] system is rather primarily based on people forming one collectivity, unity, through monopoly, established and restricted through the terms and borders determined by the nation-state, and having emerged in parallel to the rise of capitalism and the stronger, formal institutionalization of patriarchy. Indeed, the European colonialists forced the concept of the nation-state upon the Middle East, but the notion resonated with certain elites in the region who saw it as an opportunity to assert their power by breaking with former hierarchies and powers. . . . Some of these borders were literally drawn with rulers along colonialist interests, thus blatantly illustrating the arbitrary imposition of imagined constructs like the nation-state, which violate and deny the more fluid and organic realities on the ground" (DSAR and New World Summit 2016, 74).

14. The evidence for this is in the continuing creation of stateless peoples within a state's citizenship regime; it is in the securitization of our mobility, of border crossing (Mezzadra and Neilson 2008, 2012; De Genova 2009), our economic class and status permitting different treatment at the territorial edges of a country; in the data profiles that are captured and inscribed on our bodies and remain with us regardless of where we are located (Rygiel 2010), and so forth. Citizenship and statelessness are not necessarily about a legal "status [per se] but [both are aspects of the] *practice* [of citizenship], made and remade in [the] daily decisions of judges, border guards and prison guards, managers and pimps" (Kerber 2009, 107, my italics).

15. Statelessness is not the absence of citizenship; it is not citizenship's "abject other" (Benhabib and Resnick 2009). The stateless are not at the edges or outside a (status) citizenship regime; nor are the stateless a consequence of the exclusionary management of a state's bureaucracy or a "lack" of legal recognition, under the false assumption that a legal system of rights is the ultimate safeguard and only needs perfecting as suggested by the United Nations High Commission for Refugees (2010a, 2010b, 2011, 2014). Statelessness is the space in which new organizational technologies are explored and devised that then informs the ordering of citizens generally (Rygiel 2010; Mezzadra and Neilson 2008, 2012). It is produced (1) when an individual is deemed "undeportable," that is, situated in a legal limbo; (2) when state borders are redrawn (or newly created), and people are excluded by the new regime (e.g., Europe after World Wars I and II, British and French colonization of the Middle East, the collapse of the Soviet Union in 1989); (3) through administrative bureaucracy of a state (e.g., in twenty-seven countries in the Middle East, North Africa, Asia-Pacific, and sub-Saharan Africa, women cannot transfer citizenship to their children or husbands, and until 1948 British women were stripped of their citizenship if they married a foreign national also in United States [1922] and Japan [1985] [Benhabib and Resnick 2009]); (4) when a state does not acknowledge its minorities (e.g., Roma in Europe; Rohingya in Myanmar, Burma); (5) through nonacknowledgment of migrant labor even after generations of residency (e.g., Nubians in Kenya, Hispanic communities in the United States); (6) when people are born stateless (e.g., children of "illegal" migrants) (e.g., United Kingdom, Ireland); (7) when a state retracts the birthright citizenship of its minorities (e.g., Armenians and Jews during World War II; Kurds in Syria in 1960; Bedoon in Kuwait in 1985; Meshketian Turks in southern Russia).

16. See Arendt 2009 re: "The clearer the proof of [a state's] inability to treat stateless people as legal persons and the greater the extension of arbitrary rule by police decree, the more difficult it is for states to resist the temptation to deprive all citizens of legal status and rule them with an omnipotent police" (290). See also Geuss 2008, 2010: rights are contingent on a policing authority that upholds the law, and this is not always the case within nation-states; nor is it guaranteed. See also Mezzadra and Neilson 2008, 2012; De Genova (2009): statelessness is an integral part of the administration, ordering, and policing of membership and a state's production of inequality.

17. Since 2014, use of the term "foreign national" to describe students from outside the United Kingdom and European Union has diminished. However, in 2012, this vocabulary was used: University and College Union, n.d., 4; University of the Arts London 2012, 7; London School of Economics 2008; *Economist* 2010.

18. The newspaper and preliminary interventions were produced in collaboration with a group of my students (Ilia Rogatchevski, Dovile Alseikiate, Mandy Collett, and Anna Kaufman).

19. Elderly British residents of West Indian descent who arrived as children (1948–1971) were subject to the enforcement of strict rules set out also in 2012 "that required employers, health services and landlords to demand evidence of people's immigration status" (*Al Jazeera* 2018). See Chambers 2018; Sputnik 2018.

20. The then UK Border Agency oversaw all immigration (visas, policing, detention, intelligence, etc.) and held an executive position within government (2009–2013). In 2013, the agency's executive powers were abolished and its work transferred to the Home Office; it was renamed UK Visas and Immigration Enforcement (Wikipedia, n.d.f).

21. Monitoring involved registering students' attendance and passing on information to senior administrators if and when an international student was absent for three classes. Note: if a UK national (i.e., home student) or an EU student was persistently absent, there were no equivalent consequences. In my role as a course director, when there were problems with a home or EU student, the institutional protocol was to help the student in any way to complete their studies (e.g., provide extracurricular support) with no disciplinary procedures (expulsion) as part of the institution's rules or practice.

22. Note: changes to the Tier 4 visa system were made under Home Secretary Sajid Javid (2018). Some restrictions have been eased for eleven countries (Bahrain, Cambodia, China, Dominican Republic, Indonesia, Kuwait, Macau, Maldives, Mexico, Serbia, and Thailand), which have been added to the government's "trusted list" (Waldron and Ali 2018). Tier 4 rules apply to students from these countries; however, they no longer are required to speak English or provide evidence that they can support themselves while in the United Kingdom (Waldron and Ali 2018).

23. The United States made legislative changes (1996) to accommodate an immigration program called the Student and Exchange Visitor Information Service (SEVIS). The program lay dormant until September 2002, following the emphasis on terrorist legislation post 9/11. "SEVIS checks the biographical information of foreign students entering the United States against criminal and terrorist databases. SEVIS participating schools are required to report when a student reports for classes, drops out, or changes a major" (Chishti and Bergeron 2011, 4).

24. See Mezzadra and Nielson 2012: borders are seen as "making a world rather than dividing an already-made world. . . . [I]t is useful, perhaps even necessary, to . . . investigat[e] concrete practices of border crossing that embody the elements of constituent excess present in every scene of border making or border contestation. This is why we focus on the subjective dimensions of migration and the ways in which bodies in motion challenge border regimes across diverse geographical scales. It is also why we emphasize the making and unmaking of social worlds" (60).

25. The University of London (Goldsmiths College; University College London; School of Oriental and African Studies; London School of Economics; Birkbeck College) and the University of the Arts London (London College of Communication and Central St. Martins).

26. See Torpey 2000: the evolution of state-sanctioned identity papers in the modern period goes hand in hand with the characterization of the foreigner as "someone from another country whose trustworthiness is questionable," and this concept of otherness is embedded in the bureaucracy of nation-states as they emerged in Europe, first notably during the French Revolution (30); the foreigner "was perceived more and more *ipso facto* as a suspect" (42).

27. See Torpey 2000 re: the photograph used to verify accompanying descriptors in passports (e.g., name, age, profession, description, domicile, and nationality of the bearer) in countering misidentification among the authorities. The precedent for issuing passports to individuals was due to the historical case of the French king's attempted flight using a servant's travel documents (38).

28. Out of forty-five students, two quickly completed the task, asking if they had answered the questionnaires correctly. We explained that the surveys aren't answerable but instead challenge assumptions about the appearance of people (and, more absurdly, *photographs*) to determine foreignness. Other participants slowly grasped the problem during the act of deliberation (i.e., while crossing out passport photos or drawing facial characteristics), pausing and reflecting on whom they had selected or troubling whom to choose as foreign. Some students asked for advice in making their selection or wanted to be guided, concluding that it was complicated and difficult to make a decision. Others began to discuss the idea of foreignness during the exercise. One student recognized the survey's interrogation of racism from the start, prompting further discussion of the role of students and staff in the workings of the immigration services within the university.

29. See Nussbaum 1994: cosmopolitanism "has the promise of transcending [ethnic, gender, religious, etc.] divisions, because only this stance asks us to give first our allegiance to what is morally good—and that which, being good, [one] can commend as such to all human beings" (2). Nussbaum's discussion details aspirations for world citizenship, and this is not the same as actual bonds between individuals, that is, compared to say, mini social contracts (as outlined in chapter 2), which are not necessarily framed by ethical commitments.

Chapter Five

Altering the Facts on the Ground

Citizen Artist News: Clouded Title

In previous chapters, I discussed in some detail how citizen art projects do politics by exposing the problems created (and sustained) by a state's status citizenship regime. I also outlined how, through acts of citizenship, citizen art performs new modes of citizenship in subtle and nuanced ways. The examples discussed in chapter 4 interrogated a state's citizenship regime through the lens of migration, statelessness, and the practices of bordering citizens and noncitizens alike. By contrast, this chapter and chapter 6 will focus on how two of my own citizen art projects contend with the complex and violent effects of a citizenship regime that was initially devised and, as I will argue, continues to unfold under the hegemony of British-colonial positionalities and problematic local colonial narratives of settler entitlement to appropriated Indigenous lands within the Canadian colonial state. I will more fully explain how citizen art projects can shape new civil spaces for the practice of incipient forms of (nonstatist) citizenship by offering a more fine-grained description of my two most recent interventions: *Citizen Artist News: Clouded Title* (2018) and *Citizen Artist News: Kinship* (2019). These interventions were conceived and disseminated in the context of my returning "home" to a small rural island, called Pender Island, on the southwestern tip of Canada (one of the Gulf Islands in the province of British Columbia) and in response to these lands as the unceded territory of the W̱SÁNEĆ First Nation People.[1] They are therefore produced in response to the continuing conditions of British Canadian colonialism and its persistent efforts to circumscribe and suppress Indigenous people's efforts to live on and govern their lands.[2]

As acts of citizenship, these two interventions therefore have a dual function. First, they respond to the urgent need to contend with the legacy of British Canadian colonialism from *within* the W̱SÁNEĆ First Nation's (unceded) territory, on the understanding that while residing within their terrain, one cannot (and *should not*) ignore how the British Canadian colonial state (overtly and tacitly) sanctions and mandates acts of violence toward First Nations Peoples in the ongoing appropriation and occupation of their lands. Overt acts of state violence are only now coming to public attention in the wake of the Truth and Reconciliation Committee of Canada's 2015 report on residential schools, the 2019 national inquiry into missing and murdered Indigenous women and girls, and the unearthing of mass grave sites of the suspected bodies of schoolchildren located near the sites of residential schools (2021)[3] who were forcibly incarcerated in Canada's residential school system (1840s–1996). By contrast, tacit acts of state violence that are executed through the colonial state's status citizenship regime are not as visible to the general public, or at least are not publicly acknowledged, hence the serious intent of these interventions and the focus of my discussion in the following chapters. Secondly, the interventions have opened the way for important new relationships and (creative and political) collaborations between myself and some members of the W̱SÁNEĆ Nation and others that would not have otherwise occurred, especially as the material conditions of place are shaped—and indeed, sustained—by Canada's silent apartheid.

In this chapter and chapter 6, I therefore discuss how the interventions address this silent apartheid—the epistemic violence—that persists through "settler"[4] assumptions and claims to owning the unceded (is)lands of the W̱SÁNEĆ Nation. This is not to say that the effects of land appropriation are fully articulated and exposed through these citizen art interventions. My discussion can only draw out the connections between the colonial state's rationale for land appropriation and its status citizenship regime as it frames the lived conditions of the specific locale of Pender Island. I will specifically focus on how the privileging of settler-colonial occupation and exploitation of land, at the expense of the W̱SÁNEĆ People, is effected through the Canadian colonial state's status citizenship regime. As indicated previously, I am deeply entangled in these conditions because not only do I currently reside on the island but I grew up here, and various branches of family in-laws (whose ancestors, unlike mine, came from the United Kingdom) have occupied these lands since the commencement of British settlement (1870s). Land ownership is therefore the primary marker of local identity, belonging, and membership and is modeled on and justified in British imaginaries and rationales for claiming other people's lands as one's own. Therefore, a return to my island home is a return to a space that is riddled and layered with real and indeed continuing colonial violence. As Ariella Aïsha Azoulay says, "Violence is what victims and perpetrators have in common, neither can be free of the burden to engage in undoing it. There is no world apart for the victims of violence, and hence, what was done to them is part of the commons. . . .

[U]ndoing Imperialism entails going backward, revisiting violent conjunctures and their effects and giving these situations a second life, *knowing that we live in their wake*" (2019, 148, my italics).

The particular purpose of *CA News: Clouded Title*, therefore, is to begin by going backward and publicly revisiting hegemonic (historical) political narratives of land claims that continue to reify settler-colonial perceptions of belonging and membership and to also expose how local settler narratives and practices of land ownership continue to actively suppress and exclude the W̱SÁNEĆ People's political presence within their own (ceded and unceded) territory. As Mavis Underwood, member of the W̱SÁNEĆ First Nation, says, "Colonization remains a lifelong project for colonizers who maintain an overbearing necessity to change and displace First Peoples from their birthright and connection to their homelands" (2018, 18). This chapter will therefore discuss how *CA News: Clouded Title* set out to make visible to the residents of Pender Island important counternarratives to the history of British Canadian claim making and purported dominion over W̱SÁNEĆ territory, to publicly question whose histories of the land and events in time are recognized, cognized, and acknowledged as realities of (national) origination and belonging. In this example, W̱SÁNEĆ authors make real a deeply submerged but detailed description of the emergence and making of a treaty on parts of their territory in the act of Crown appropriation—a history that conflicts with and is actively suppressed by settler claims to owning land. My discussion will therefore show how the interventions, as acts of citizenship, lay bare how claims to owning W̱SÁNEĆ land are (precariously) contingent on (and dubiously valorized in) the imposition of an 1850s' Crown treaty on parts of W̱SÁNEĆ territory, a treaty that not only (racially) partitions Indigenous and non-Indigenous peoples but also prevents the W̱SÁNEĆ from governing their traditional territory to the present day. I will also describe how the interventions enact recognition of W̱SÁNEĆ presence within their unceded territory, and in countering the erasure and suppression of W̱SÁNEĆ presence and perspectives in the locale, I will show how the interventions open up new pathways and possibilities for nascent modes of (nonstatist) membership to take shape. However, a more comprehensive discussion of the aesthetic effects of these two interventions will be discussed in the conclusion.

These interventions, like my previous art project *Citizen Artist News: The University as a Border Regime* (2013), also took the form of a printed newspaper. In line with what Bolette Blaagaard observes of citizen journalists, these newspaper interventions are rooted in a "process of becoming [a new kind of] citizen—that is, politically engaged and invested through the creative force of expression . . . [that] functions on a deeply personal and affective level while acknowledging that [one is] always already enmeshed in a wider language, history, politics and life" (2018, 109). By directly targeting local settler-residents in speech and action, the interventions recast the island as a *W̱SÁNEĆ community* and the W̱SÁNEĆ Peoples' presence "as an idea of steady, solid simultaneity through time" (Anderson 2006, 62). It is important to stress again that these citizen art interventions are a tool for not only doing politics but also enacting new and nascent modes of citizenship, starting with public recognition of the W̱SÁNEĆ People as at the center of the local political community and revisiting, as Azoulay says, inescapable, historical "violent conjunctures and their effects" (2019, 148). In such a way, these newspaper interventions carve out new intellectual and affective terrain for exploring and enacting new orientations to place. They take on the important task of breaking new ground, so to speak, for doing politics within the local community and as specifically *within* W̱SÁNEĆ territory, rather than within a purportedly settled and widely celebrated British colony. I should say too that in assembling materials for *Citizen Artist News: Clouded Title*, I was fortunate to meet with and discuss the source material and its claims on a regular basis with Earl Claxton Jr., an elder of the W̱SÁNEĆ First Nation. Not only is he cited within the pages of the newspapers, but his contribution deepened my appreciation of the "voices" of W̱SÁNEĆ authors in relating W̱SÁNEĆ histories and understandings of place.

Germane to this discussion, then, is understanding the differing conceptions and nature of relations to land within the local settler-colonial community and the W̱SÁNEĆ First Nation. My discussion will therefore include distinguishing between settler-colonial and W̱SÁNEĆ aesthetic conceptions of land that underpin widely contrasting orientations to belonging and membership as they manifest today. It will also draw out more expansive conceptions of political membership that become visible through W̱SÁNEĆ descriptions of kinship relations to nonhuman actors—relationships that sidestep normative notions and practices of status citizenship. *CA News: Kinship* focused specifically on challenging colonial understandings of membership as solely human. Launched eighteen months after *CA News: Clouded Title*, it was an important extension to that project in that residents of the island were invited to again contend with their (British) colonial subjecthood and orientation to the (is)land in light of a legal principle in W̱SÁNEĆ law. I will discuss this point at length herein and chapter 6.

One last note before turning to a description of *CA News: Clouded Title*: Throughout my discussion, I invite reflection on the complexities and potentialities of what Engin Isin describes as the "incipient" nature of citizenship (Isin and Nielsen 2008; Isin 2012) for framing new modes of belonging and membership. I believe it is appropriate to suggest that there are modes of nonstatist citizenship in play within First Nations communities, given that they are self-described as "nations,"[5] denoting their formal organization as political units with (various and plural) systems of governance (i.e., various because not all First Nations are similarly organized), but nevertheless incipient (i.e., perpetually emergent) because they are founded on (1) dynamic and evolving (kinship) relations to human and nonhuman beings and ancestors, (2) reciprocal responsibilities and duties to the (is)lands as nonhuman beings (in the case of the W̱SÁNEĆ in particular), and (3) membership as actively performed.[6] That is, kin relations (to human and nonhuman beings), which are subtended by histories of place "produced through discussion, debate, and enactment, through social interactions that perpetuate and create the past, through the living and the present," show that membership is brokered through community "recognition" and active relations with humans and nonhumans alike (Simpson 2014, 43). In describing specifically Mohawk approaches to membership, Audra Simpson (2014) points out that even though some people may claim identity and lineage derived from place, they may not be recognized by the community and therefore not acknowledged as members. The recognition and acknowledgment of the W̱SÁNEĆ, as enacted through these citizen art interventions, takes on new meaning and, as an act of citizenship, engages directly with nonstatist practices of citizenship as produced and contingent on relations and public acknowledgment between peoples (and nonhuman beings, in principle). Membership has to be performed: It is *active* rather than a static designation of status conferred by the state or legitimated by the purported ownership of land. Again, this point will be fully discussed.

The following will first describe the mode and manner of *CA News: Clouded Title* as an art intervention. I will then outline some of the main themes of the newspaper to draw out how appropriated land and Canada's status citizenship regime are entangled. Woven through my discussion will be a brief outline of related aspects of Canadian and Indigenous politics to give context to the challenges that the intervention presented to the local residents of Pender Island. I will reserve, for the conclusion, a fuller discussion of how both of the interventions were designed to circumvent established networks of communication, local gatekeepers, and locally organized and ordered political pathways within the island community (what Jacques Rancière would call the "police order," as discussed in chapter 2). In the conclusion, I will also describe how Pender Island residents, some members of the W̱SÁNEĆ community, and others further afield responded to the interventions. I will also discuss more fully the aesthetics of the interventions and their effects and how, as acts of citizenship, they have forged new paths for doing politics as a mode of nonstatist citizenship.

CITIZEN ARTIST NEWS: CLOUDED TITLE

On April 3, 2018, I launched *Clouded Title* (see figure 5.1). From a printing of 1,100 copies, 820 copies were posted to individual residents' homes on Pender Island (a settler population then of approximately twenty-six hundred people) via Canada Post.[7] The launch also involved a one-day art and research workshop on Pender Island, devised and co-organized with fellow artist Emily Artinian,[8] which invited island residents to engage in the topic of appropriated (is)lands. The title of the newspaper refers to a term in US property law and was intended to bring to light the core problem of claiming to own unceded W̱SÁNEĆ lands. "Cloud on title" refers to "any document, claim, unreleased lien or encumbrance that might invalidate or impair the title to real property or make a title doubtful" (Wikipedia, n.d.b), and use of this term aimed to focus the attention of island residents on the proverbial elephant in the room. In 2018, the issue of possessing unceded W̱SÁNEĆ lands was not openly or publicly discussed at the local level on Pender Island.[9] What existed was a small, newly formed reading group organized through the local Anglican church, which gathered to reflect on the contents of *Honoring the Truth, Reconciling for the Future: Final Report of the Truth and Reconciliation Commission of Canada* (Truth and Reconciliation Commission of Canada 2015). This reading circle was organized to facilitate reflection on the consequences of the containment and abuse of First Nations Peoples, as related specifically to the residential school system. However, at the time, there was significant silence regarding W̱SÁNEĆ rights and title and no real reckoning for the violence that was and is exercised through the British, now Canadian, colonial state, especially not as pertains to local habits and practices. The extent of local acknowledgment of Pender Island as within the unceded territory of the W̱SÁNEĆ People was instead publicly expressed though a one-day event that included a pit cook (provided by members of the W̱SÁNEĆ First Nation at the invitation of island organizers) and an installation of a sign depicting the W̱SÁNEĆ thirteen-moon calendar in front of a decommissioned Anglican church. These public markers of "reconciliation" were both launched on the occasion of a national celebration of Canada's confederation (Canada 150, July 1, 2017). Despite the value of these modest grassroots efforts, neither of these events addressed or educated on the specific details of Crown appropriation or ongoing injustices rooted in British Canadian colonial occupation of the island locale. In fact, they actively deflected attention away from discussion of the dubious acquisition of specifically Pender Island "property," initially sanctioned under British Rule, which, ironically, was being celebrated and normalized at a national level. Hence, the title of the intervention signals its central purpose: to begin a rigorous process of *actual*

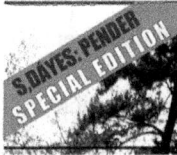

Citizen Artist News: Clouded Title

examining Indigenous and non-Indigenous perspectives   spring edition: 2018   citizenartist.org.uk

Reconsidering place: thinking through notions of 'ownership' in the Douglas Treaty

This newspaper is an invitation to enter into an experiment – a thought experiment – to explore the different orientations of settler and indigenous conceptions of inhabiting 'land'. It is focused on a local example and takes as its starting point an examination of the notion of 'ownership' in the context of the Douglas Treaty and contrasts this with a W̱SÁNEĆ (Saanich) Nation creation story, as a way of illuminating some of the complexities of differing conceptions of place that in turn, frame relations between communities.

Since 2013 (when I returned to Canada), I have witnessed non-Indigenous Canadians endeavouring to understand the complexities of their own reality as inhabitants of indigenous lands. In light of the publication of the *Final Report: Truth and Reconciliation Commission of Canada*, it has also become increasingly evident that colonialism persists and sustains fictions of entitlement and possession. Who we are as 'Canadians' and how we behave as a 'community' is deeply entangled with western (British colonial) ideas of ourselves as 'owners'. Happily though, there is growing awareness on the island that Pender is within the traditional territory of W̱SÁNEĆ people and this has led to grass roots activities such as a Reading Circle, the erection of a monument on South Pender and some celebratory social events, the latter two in collaboration with primarily members of the SȾÁ,UTW̱ (Tsawout) Nation. These are heartening examples and it is hoped that this publication will help to further enrich discussions of the implications of one's occupancy of the island, in the context of the treaty, by providing a point of entry to the complications of this intellectual and material terrain.

As a proviso, this publication does not represent the W̱SÁNEĆ Nation nor residents of Pender Island. It speaks for neither community. Instead, it is an assemblage of published material from W̱SÁNEĆ and other indigenous and non-indigenous writers, accompanied by sections of commentary intended to draw out some of the intricacies of the language of the treaty, to illustrate (and examine) differing notions and practices of 'ownership'. Readers will find that there is no singular explanation and barring some suggestions, no solutions to its problems are posed. To expect answers or directives is to miss the point of the publication. The aim is to evaluate the implications of living on lands that are clouded in title.

I am immensely grateful to Earl Claxton Jr (SȾÁ,UTW̱ Nation) for his gracious conversation, patience and guidance in discussing this material. I would also like to thank Emily Artinian of Street/Road Artists Space for her enthusiasm, stimulating conversations and commitment and with whom this project forms part of a larger collaborative art and research project called 'Clouded Title'. I also thank Robb Zuk for his kind and generous help in the preparation of this document. I follow the example of authors such the late Dave Elliot Sr. (W̱JOȽEȽP Nation), Robert YELḰÁTTE Clifford (SȾÁ,UTW̱ Nation) and Raymond Frogner in the use of SENĆOŦEN spellings (pronounced Sun-cho-thun) i.e., the W̱SÁNEĆ language. The material presented relies on quotes from assembled literature and responsibility for any errors is entirely my own.

Fawn Daphne Plessner
S.DAYES/Pender Island

Introduction to what's at issue:

It is widely assumed that Pender Island was 'purchased' from First Nations under the Douglas Treaty. It is also currently understood that 'the Tsawout, Tsartlip, Pauquachin and Tseycum First Nations [...] have land and harvesting rights to Pender under the 1852 Douglas Treaty' (Pender Islands Museum, n.d.). Equally, it is known that 'there is an indian reserve at Hay Point on South Pender Island, which is home to members of the Tsawout and Tseycum First Nations. Carbon dating of artifacts in small middens near Belden Cove identify an Indian village site that has been more or less continuously inhabited for five millennia. The Poets Cove Resort was built on an ancient First Nations village site' (Wikipedia, n.d.). However, cutting across these claims is 'the provincial government's 2007 settlement with the Tsawwassen First Nation [that] includes hunting and fishing rights on and around Pender Island—an arrangement to which the Sencot'en Alliance objected, saying those rights are theirs under the 1852 Douglas Treaty' (Wikipedia, n.d.). Also, it has been said that 'The Saanich people have never surrendered title to the Gulf Islands and we also feel that our territory expands across the U.S.A. border" (Claxton, 2007). That is, most of the W̱SÁNEĆ traditional territory has never been ceded. But what exactly does all of this mean? What is the Douglas Treaty and how is it to be interpreted given that it is a document that embodies scarred histories, disputed claims and differing world views?

To date, there is little public awareness of what the Douglas Treaty is and there is no comprehensive or thoughtful public discussion in the Media, let alone evidence of a lived appreciation of one's individual role in its enactment. By its very nature, a treaty imparts responsibilities and duties to the other party -- and not just at a governmental level -- but there is no transparent understanding of one's obligations in this relationship with the W̱SÁNEĆ people. Nor is there any public knowledge of the experiences and perspectives of the W̱SÁNEĆ Nation in the history of the treaty's making. The pervasive silence that surrounds this topic sustains public ignorance of the important details that bear on our economic, social, political, environmental and ethical responsibilities in this relationship.

The following discussion therefore is an introduction to how 'land' and 'ownership' are differently regarded as evidenced in published commentaries on the Douglas Treaty and a W̱SÁNEĆ creation story. What follows is not a complete exposition. Instead, this newspaper aims to simply draw out some dimensions of the treaty that frame and indeed, underpin understandings of belonging and claims to 'ownership' by contrasting it with a discussion of relationality in W̱SÁNEĆ cosmology and culture. As islanders, we are bound together in a relationship with the SȾÁ,UTW̱ (Tsawout), W̱JOȽEȽP (Tsartlip), BOḰEĆEN (Pauquachin) and W̱SÍḴEM (Tseycum) First Nations bands in virtue of our presence on their territory and under treaty. That is to say, as residents we live here with members of the W̱SÁNEĆ Nation even though our colonial history has created the conditions of an apartheid. It is my hope therefore that the following exposition provides a starting point for the recognition of the deeper, more nuanced, W̱SÁNEĆ perspectives or claims to place as illustrated in the literature and the importance of interrogating the persistent British colonial assumptions about inhabiting these lands.

Figure 5.1.   Front page of *Citizen Artist News: Clouded Title*. Launched on Pender Island, British Columbia, Canada, April 14, 2018. *Photo courtesy of F. D. Plessner*

recognition by first disrupting local British Canadian colonial assumptions about owning lands that are, in fact, clouded in title.

The tone of the newspaper's address was personal and specific to island residents: It invited islanders to participate in a public thought experiment—that is, to actively engage in comparing two historical legal documents (origin stories) that are foundational to divergent embodiments of belonging and membership. I chose the text of the "Douglas Treaty: North Saanich"[10] (1852, hereafter referred to as the Douglas Treaty; see appendix A) because it was fundamental to the establishment of the British, now Canadian, colonial state and is specific to the state's claim to govern the W̱SÁNEĆ People and their lands. I also chose a transcription of a W̱SÁNEĆ origin story by legal scholar Robert YELḰÁTﬢE Clifford (W̱SÁNEĆ First Nation) that speaks to a core principle in W̱SÁNEĆ law about interdependent responsibilities of human and nonhuman actors such as the islands (see appendix B). In the introductory paragraphs of the newspaper, I state,

> This newspaper is an invitation to enter into an experiment—a thought experiment—to explore the different orientations of settler and Indigenous conceptions of inhabiting "land." It is focused on a local example and takes as its starting point an examination of the notion of "ownership" in the context of the Douglas Treaty and contrasts this with a W̱SÁNEĆ (Saanich) Nation creation story, as a way of illuminating some of the complexities of differing conceptions of place that in turn, frame relations between communities. . . . Who we are as "Canadians" and how we behave as a "community" is deeply entangled with western (British colonial) ideas of ourselves as "owners." . . . It is hoped that this publication will help to further enrich discussions of the implications of one's occupancy of the island . . . by providing a point of entry to the complications of this intellectual and material terrain (Plessner 2018, 1).

This public thought experiment challenged all of the island's residents to (1) grasp the fact that the island is within the *unceded* territory of the W̱SÁNEĆ People—a fact not widely known or recognized as having real meaning or significance among a majority of island residents; (2) actively review the originary act of Crown appropriation via the treaty and thus grapple with the violent history and problematics of claiming unceded W̱SÁNEĆ lands as one's own; and (3) comprehend that every island resident plays a part in the continuance of colonial violence by not recognizing the legitimacy and entitlement of the W̱SÁNEĆ to govern their territory. It also required residents to contend with W̱SÁNEĆ laws and ethics and an expanded notion of political membership (I will discuss this further herein and in chapter 6).

To structure this community-based act of reckoning, the text of the treaty and the W̱SÁNEĆ cosmological story were displayed on the adjacent pages 2 and 3 of the newspaper (see figure 5.2). These texts were superimposed on a staged image of a Royal Canadian Mounted Police officer and First Nations chief shaking hands (I will return to this point). On page 2, the full text of the Douglas Treaty describes the alleged transfer of W̱SÁNEĆ lands and title to James Douglas, chief factor of the Hudson Bay Company, representing the British Crown (1852). To highlight the profound differences between British Canadian colonial and W̱SÁNEĆ imaginaries of belonging, membership, and governance, the W̱SÁNEĆ story of X̱ÁLS, retold by Robert Clifford, is displayed on page 3. Clifford describes how the Transformer (Creator) not only changed some of the W̱SÁNEĆ People into islands (thus creating nonhuman ancestral kin to the W̱SÁNEĆ People today) but also ascribed reciprocal obligations and duties of care (stewardship) and life support to the two parties as a founding compact between humans and nonhuman beings (islands). As Clifford says, the story of X̱ÁLS "is not only *about* land but deeply *informed* by the land as a system of reciprocal relations and obligations" (2016b, 774)—that is, not only as a system of mini social contracts that determines social and cultural membership (i.e., who is encompassed by this ancestral kinship story) but also as a set of concepts, principles, and practices that

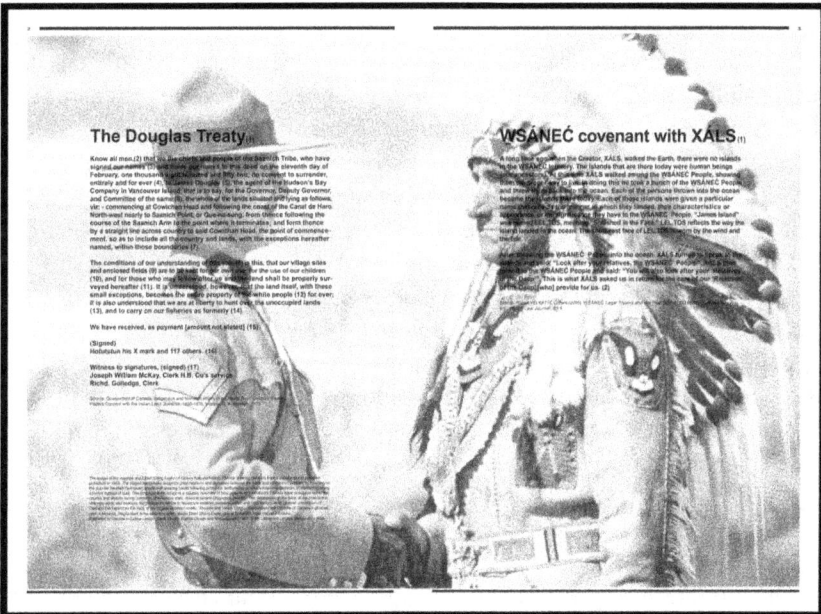

Figure 5.2. **Pages 2 and 3 of** *Citizen Artist News: Clouded Title,* **2018. The text of the Douglas Treaty North Saanich (left) and the** W̱SÁNEĆ **cosmological story of a legal compact between humans and islands (right), superimposed on an image of a staged handshake between an officer of the Royal Canadian Mounted Police (left) and a First Nation chief (right).** *Photo courtesy of F. D. Plessner*

expand the domain of legal and political membership (i.e., inclusion of the lives of animals and nonanimal beings, such as islands etc., within the politics of the community and at the center of governance). The notion of a reciprocal political relationship is rooted in the knowledge that the lives of other beings are central to the continuance and survival of humans. I will discuss this point further in chapter 6. For now, the aim here is to illustrate the tension between the two worldviews as presented to island residents in the newspaper and to draw out the wider implications of claiming land as one's own.

The texts of the treaty and Clifford's story of XÁLS were accompanied by extensive and detailed footnotes that interrogated and critiqued specific phrases and claims in each text. Importantly, most of the footnotes accompanying the treaty were an assemblage of counterclaims from W̱SÁNEĆ (and other Indigenous) authors to evidence the conflicting history of the treaty's making and to make vividly apparent the legacy of elisions and dubious legal claims that form the foundation of the state's current dominion over W̱SÁNEĆ land. This included citing W̱SÁNEĆ descriptions of the treaty as a peace treaty and not a sale of land (to be discussed). The footnotes accompanying the story of XÁLS were a detailed exposition on the legal, spiritual, ethical, and cultural compact between the W̱SÁNEĆ and nonhuman ancestral "kin" (Clifford 2016a, 2016b) to make apparent the W̱SÁNEĆ People's own (legal) foundations for membership and governance as centered on reciprocal responsibilities (Plessner 2018, 9). This was done to introduce residents to an important subtext of these interventions: The notion that political membership can manifest and be practiced in profoundly different ways from that of the Canadian state's status citizenship regime.

It is important to also understand that the contents of *CA News: Clouded Title* drew attention to many other facets of colonial violence that are enfolded in the interpretation of the Douglas Treaty as a legitimation of state (i.e., Crown) ownership of W̱SÁNEĆ land. Due to limitations of space, I must put aside discussion of the newspaper's contents that elaborate on these conflicting interpretations. However, the following is a brief list of the issues discussed in the newspaper that intersect with the problematics of claiming to own (ceded and) unceded lands:

- Detailing to whom the treaty is meant to apply (footnotes 1 and 4 in the newspaper)
- The purported "legal" framework under the imperial laws of the Doctrine of Discovery (footnotes 2 and 13)
- Controversy about W̱SÁNEĆ signatories having to sign an X on a blank piece of paper, etc. (footnotes 3 and 4)

- Conflicting historical descriptions of the purpose of the treaty (as a peace treaty versus a sale of land) and, in turn, the dubious assertion that the W̱SÁNEĆ consented to such a "sale" of land (footnotes 3, 4, and 8)
- Contrasting notions of land borders, boundaries, and enclosures in the politics of surveying versus wayfinding (footnote 7, 9, and 116)
- Biographical information about the agents of the Crown and the treaty's signatories and the egregious behavior and self-interest of Crown agents as beneficiaries of the landgrab (footnotes 5, 6, 16, and 17)
- The racialization and classification of the W̱SÁNEĆ as "Indians" versus "white" (meaning specifically British) people (discussed further), which led to restrictions placed on the W̱SÁNEĆ to "use" land for "hunting and fishing" only, with the Crown purportedly securing land title (footnotes 10, 11, and 14)

All of the footnotes therefore problematized and, indeed, contemporized the realities of living on and claiming ownership of lands that are steeped in violence.

To further illustrate the role and significance of the art intervention as a tool for doing politics, I will describe the aesthetics of the newspaper—the design of its key pages. Folded into this discussion is my use of journalistic techniques as an artistic medium for troubling commonplace settler-colonial imaginaries about ownership, belonging, and membership. As Alfredo Cramerotti suggests, "The artist who uses the tools of investigative journalism in their [art]work adopts techniques like archive and field research, interviewing, surveys; they also employ specific narrative and display formats such as documentary style, graphic visualization, text-based reportage and photo reportage . . . as a subversive but effective and meaningful agent of reality" (2009, 22). As "a meaningful agent" uncovering a suppressed reality, *CA News: Clouded Title* brought to light the published accounts of W̱SÁNEĆ authors to show how the claims of the Douglas Treaty and the state's status citizenship regime are deeply entwined in the continuance of colonial land appropriation. As suggested, these two modes of state technology—the treaty and Canada's status citizenship regime—not only politically (and racially) segregate those residing within a terrain but are also state mechanisms for preventing First Nations from governing their lands. I will discuss this point at length because it is fundamental to my wider discussion of not only how this citizen art intervention does politics by "rupturing the given" (Rancière 2010)—that is, the aesthetic and material conditions of the locale—but also how it performs as a nonstatist mode of membership at a local level. As I have argued in previous chapters, citizen art interventions deliberately aim to reframe the aesthetic and material conditions of civic or civil spaces in which acts of citizenship take effect. This intervention and *CA News: Kinship* (to be discussed in chapter 6) are no different.

To make obvious the contrasting interpretations of the treaty as, on the one hand, a peace treaty and, on the other, a purported sale of land, the two texts are superimposed on an image from a 1955 postcard (see figure 5.3) of a Royal Mounted Canadian Police officer and an "Indian" chief (Chief Sitting Eagle) shaking hands. Their clasped hands—a gesture freighted with meanings of settlement, contractual agreements, or peaceable relations—are positioned on the center seam of the newspaper so as to visually underpin the central problem posed in the newspaper: how to address the legacy and persistence of colonial violence and land appropriation inscribed in state narratives of purported assent to the sale and control of lands. It is important to note that the postcard was also selected because it was produced during the peak of extensive violence toward Indigenous people across Canada (residential schools, incarceration on reserves; Truth and Reconciliation Report of Canada 2015) and speaks to the hypocrisy of the Canadian state and the colonial legacy of whitewashing and propagandizing.

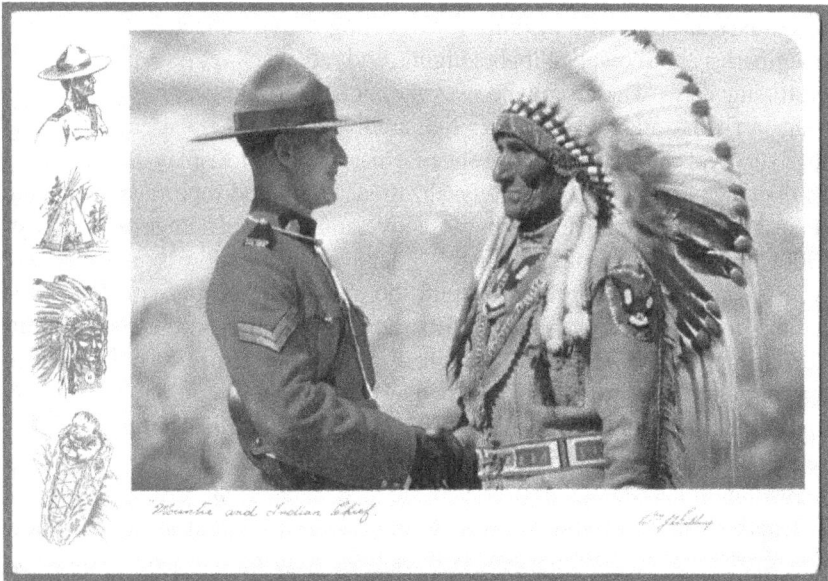

Figure 5.3. The original postcard image used for pages 2 and 3 of *Citizen Artist News: Clouded Title*, published in 1955 at the height of widespread state-sanctioned violence (residential schools, etc.) perpetrated against First Nations and other Indigenous Peoples in Canada. *Photo courtesy of Smith Lithography Co. Ltd, Vancouver.*

By superimposing the text of the treaty and the story of XÁLS on this image of staged clement relations, the newspaper co-opts and critiques the state narrative of colonial police/state benevolence. These pages are therefore to be read critically in their reminder to readers that a treaty is a social, ethical, legal, and political promise that, like the handshake within the pages of the newspaper, can and has come apart. The design of these two pages therefore makes real the core disputes about the meaning of the Douglas Treaty that continue to antagonize relations today: the state continues to insist that the treaty is a transfer of land title (Miller 2007), and the W̱SÁNEĆ people understand it as a peace treaty—a settlement for harm done by Douglas and his men on their territory[11] and a set of promises for compensation and future peaceful conduct. Through the eyes of the W̱SÁNEĆ, we also learn that the treaty is perpetually relational, a set of ongoing undertakings and promises, meant to be based on annual review and discussion—a dialogue—and assurances to live well (Miller 2007) and remain self-sufficient (*Supreme Court of British Columbia v. Tsawout First Nation* 2018, 5). In footnote 3 of the newspaper, I quote J. R. Miller's analysis to emphasize the significance of relationality within W̱SÁNEĆ political agreements:

> [First Nations] take the position that the treaties were not just contracts, and disagree that the full meaning of the treaties is found in the government's published version. . . . [Instead,] First Nations approached treaty making *in search of connection with the incoming people and the crown.* They were looking for *assurances of friendship* and *future support* that would guarantee their survival. For them, the meaning of the treaties is found in the *relationship* established rather than any specific clause, and the overall significance of treaties to them is that *they were promised* help to live well. (Plessner 2018, 4, my italics)

To underscore the contested textual and legal interpretations of the treaty and to make clear the British Canadian state's (unscrupulous) practices, the placement of the story of XÁLS adjacent to the text of the treaty facilitated cross-readings of the two stories and further evidenced the implausibility—indeed, the absurdity—of the assertion that the W̱SÁNEĆ entered into a sale of land. As indicated previously, the story of XÁLS expresses a core covenant in W̱SÁNEĆ law, a compact that is foundational and binding, determining one's orientation to the (is)lands as vibrant forms of more-than-human life—a "being"—that one is intrinsically connected to through time, by virtue of kinship and ancestry and, indeed, the practicalities of sustaining of one's own life (Clifford 2016a, 2016b; Tsawout First Nation, n.d.). The newspaper therefore foregrounded that the idea of selling the world to which one belongs—indeed, one's own (ancestral and more-than-human) kin relative—would have been conceptually and morally impossible for the W̱SÁNEĆ People. It would have been beyond their ken. The newspaper's thought experiment therefore compelled island residents to reflect on the layered and complex problems of colonial appropriation of land and its recurring violence as a basis for settler belonging and membership. It also challenged the logic of political membership as limited to human beings. The newspaper therefore enfolded residents in a public act of being "outed" when presuming dominion over W̱SÁNEĆ lands and the concurrent problem of centering (political) membership only on human life. By drawing attention to the misuse and (willful) abuse of formal agreements at a state level, which in practice actually aggravate any real or just settlement between peoples, the newspaper shows that at a formal level of the state, promises have been broken and ignored. I would argue too that the "sharp dealing" of the Crown (*Supreme Court of British Columbia v. Tsawout First Nation* 2018, 9) has been achieved without recompense because the promises of the peace treaty are not embodied in the practices, understandings, and daily lives of the people who reside within the domain of W̱SÁNEĆ Nation territory. There is no open public dialogue or widespread understanding among island residents and the W̱SÁNEĆ People, a legacy rooted in the early attitudes and practices of (British) settlers and the state, the partitioning of peoples through Canada's status citizenship regime (to be discussed further), and the persistence of glossed narratives of settler entitlements to appropriated W̱SÁNEĆ lands. As Taiaiake Alfred says, "Settler society must be forced into a reckoning with its past, its present, its future, and itself. White people who are not yet decolonized must come to admit that they were and are wrong" (2005, 113). I would add that this also applies to all non-Indigenous people who are black and "of color," because no one is an innocent bystander when possessing Canadian citizenship and residing on lands that are clouded in title.

There is a certain urgency, then, for these citizen art interventions to open up a space of dialogue and to publicly acknowledge the reality of W̱SÁNEĆ perspectives within their territory. Public recognition requires making visible to island residents the specific and conflicting histories and realities of the locale. Tracing out a critique by W̱SÁNEĆ and other First Nations authors of some of the core political claims of the state was therefore key to troubling problematic assumptions about settler belonging and membership that are assumed and performed within the local community. This was also key to the art intervention's "reterritorializing" of the aesthetic and material conditions of the public space. By using the tools and strategies of (investigative) journalism, and by selecting, assembling, and recirculating published commentaries by W̱SÁNEĆ and other First Nations authors, the pages of the newspaper forged a "phenomenological space" for a new public—a counterpublic—to emerge (Blaagaard 2018, 46). And this counterpublic is founded on actively acknowledging and foregrounding the W̱SÁNEĆ as a political presence within their wider territory. To further contextualize the social and political significance of this citizen art intervention for doing politics and, in turn, its value as an act of citizenship, the following will outline two examples of the legacy of colonial readings of the Douglas Treaty that continue to play out today.

First, the State's (legal) interpretation of the treaty as a purported sale of land is seen in a recent *Notice of Civil Claim* (*Supreme Court of British Columbia v. Tsawout First Nation* 2018) issued by Tsawout First Nation to the attorney general of Canada, Her Majesty the Queen in right of the province of British Columbia, and J. I. Properties. Tsawout First Nation is seeking reparation for the sharp dealing of the Crown and its appropriation of reserve lands, specifically an island called L̵EL,TOS (in the SENĆOŦEN language) but otherwise known as James Island, named for its first claimant, Governor James Douglas, which was initially part of the reserve lands of Tsawout First Nation. That is, it was among lands deemed to have been set aside[12] for the W̱SÁNEĆ but subsequently purloined by Douglas as his private property, *after* the (alleged) signing[13] of the Douglas Treaty (*Supreme Court of British Columbia v. Tsawout First Nation* 2018, 3). Tsawout Nation's civil claim states, "Among the purposes of the Imperial Crown and the Colony of Vancouver Island in entering into Treaty, and in *promising* to confirm the Indians in the occupation of, and to set aside, village sites and enclosed fields was to provide for *peace and order* on Vancouver Island, to enable settlers to occupy lands *purportedly* acquired pursuant to the Treaty without fear of reprisals from Aboriginals in the area" (*Supreme Court of British Columbia v. Tsawout First Nation* 2018, 9, my italics). Equally, the civil claim states, "A further purpose was to provide for *peace and friendship* of the ancestors of the Plaintiff [Tsawout First Nation] and to provide sufficient land, village sites and access to resources so that the Plaintiff would remain self-sufficient" (Plessner 2018, 5, my italics).

Here we see the full import of the divergent interpretations of the treaty. Reading it as a peace treaty, we see that its purpose and the Crown's responsibility—its promise to the W̱SÁNEĆ—was to ensure the continuance of W̱SÁNEĆ well-being, social and political culture, and economy, ensuring that Douglas and the early settlers would restrain themselves from perpetrating further violence, "without fear of reprisals from the Aboriginals in the area" (*Supreme Court of British Columbia v. Tsawout First Nation* 2018, 5). Importantly, the emphasis on peace and friendship—the affective and aesthetic dimension of this political relationship—is acknowledged here as not only the conditions for cohabitation but also central to the well-being of the W̱SÁNEĆ People, facilitating their remaining self-sufficient. Peace and friendship were conceptualized, at least fleetingly, as a potential foundation for a new, emergent, and legally binding membership based on fraternity between newcomers and the W̱SÁNEĆ people. This reading illustrates an important aspect of the nascent character of citizenship and the significance of the newspaper intervention as an act of citizenship (Isin and Nielsen 2008; Isin 2012). That is, not only does the newspaper intervention disrupt the status quo but it also serves as a space of "connectivity" (Blaagaard 2018, 46). By connecting historical narratives to present-day conditions, in raising the specter of past voices in relation to current concerns, the intervention speaks to the perpetually emergent character of citizenship as a performed act. In essence, the intervention is an act of restitution and forges a new basis for relations between island residents and the W̱SÁNEĆ by "going backward, revisiting violent conjunctures and their effects and giving these situations as second life" (Azoulay 2019, 149)—that is, it offers a second chance for settlers to take responsibility for the embodiment and silencing of colonial violence, executed by the British, now Canadian state. By homing in on the problem of colonial narratives of entitlement to lands within the language of the treaty, the intervention directly addresses this epistemic violence of place. Equally, the fact that relations and peaceable friendships can be formed or destroyed but nevertheless negotiated between peoples in a terrain shows that the behaviors and relations between people in a region not only shape the character of citizenship but can be and have been skewed, as I will explain, by the abstract principles, laws, and procedures of the state's status citizenship regime, which privileges the interests of the Crown and in turn the island's settler inhabitants.[14]

To further illustrate the scope and depth of the art intervention in challenging asymmetrical readings of the Douglas Treaty, my second example will discuss how the newspaper further troubled the ongoing violence of land appropriation, reinforced by the practice of the state's status citizenship regime. I will discuss how the criteria and differentials in people's citizenship status continue to legally segregate and suppress W̱SÁNEĆ political presence within their wider traditional territory. I argue here that the aesthetic and material conditions of the settler community—its silent apartheid—are a manifestation of the classification and management of people's legal identities and are integral to colonial dominion over Indigenous people's lands. I will quote sections of the annotated notes in *Clouded Title* to highlight the intervention's role in making visible how the imposition of treaties instituted the categorization of First Nations Peoples as "status Indians," who, unlike the Metis and Inuit, are specifically an "administered people" (Cairns 2000, 21).

Footnote 2 of the newspaper examines the opening phrase of the Douglas Treaty: "Know all men." This phrase is "an invocation to an international audience that frames the Crown's purported 'legal' claim to appropriated lands in the context of the Imperial laws of the Doctrine of Discovery" (Plessner 2018, 3). I cite Raymond Frogner's (2010) explanation as follows:

> "All men" brings Aboriginal peoples into the jurisdiction of international law where unique cultural orders [i.e., the laws of the W̱SÁNEĆ, are made to be] susceptible to common [law] rules of land title and governance. But incorporating Aboriginal peoples into the legal domain of international law is not the same thing as recognizing their rights. Within the interpretative framework of English common law, land title and possession demanded evidence of settlement and improvement. By this standard, the Colonial Office recognized that the Aboriginal peoples of Vancouver Island . . . held an . . . inchoate form of "qualified Dominium" (Frogner 2010, 62). However, *the claim to ownership of underlying title, within the exploits of the Crown, is declared without "direct reference to the original possessors of the land.* The notification at once declares the document's addressee [the W̱SÁNEĆ] and asserts English sovereignty [over the 'ownership' of lands. At the same time it codifies] settlement for colonial land acquisition" (2010, 63) and erases recognition of W̱SÁNEĆ law within the international forum. (Plessner 2018, 4)

In the act of claiming dominion over land within an international forum of imperial powers, the British Crown also effected the conditions for status citizenship in terms of *jus soli* (from the Latin meaning literally "law relating to the soil [of one's country]"; Oxford Reference, n.d.). I will discuss this point at length because it bears heavily on understanding the deep tension that exists between the colonial state and indigenous conceptions and practices of membership. It is also important for appreciating how the art intervention disrupts normative claims of Canadian status citizenship undergirded by purported treatied ownership of Indigenous lands. For example, formal membership for non-Indigenous people in Canada is (primarily) legitimized via one's place of birth—*on the land*—hence, the metaphor of "soil" as captured in the phrase jus soli.[15] "Indians" by contrast, are allotted status as "Indians" in respect of *jus sanguinis* ("the principle that the nationality of children is the same as that of their parents, irrespective of their place of birth"; Oxford Reference, n.d.). This exposes an implicit paradox existent in Canada today. Non-Indigenous "Canadians" (the wide array of migrant peoples, both present and past) are granted status as citizens by the state in virtue of living on the soil (through birth or naturalization). By contrast, under the terms of the Indian Act, the federal government determines who can be considered a *legal* "Indian"[16] in virtue of a blood quantum[17] and "registered under the Indian Act on the Indian Register—a central registry maintained by Indian and Northern Affairs Canada (INAC). Status Indians are issued a status card that contains information about their identity, their band, and their registration number"

(First Nations Study Program 2009). Additionally, Indians have been and continue to be regarded as "wards of state."[18] Hence, "the Indian Act is a form of *apartheid law*" (First Nations Study Program 2009, my italics).

The central problem (an acutely injurious one, too) is that First Nations Peoples, as discussed previously, are deeply entangled with the land through kin relations that entail reciprocal responsibilities rooted in cosmological histories but, because only recognized by the state via their blood stock, are *legally* severed from the land—the very source of their identity. Indeed, at a local level, the imposition of a membership regime based on blood stock strips the W̱SÁNEĆ of the ethicopolitical and legal authority to exercise their responsibilities and duties of care for the (is)lands and other nonhuman beings within their territory. The results of Canada's segregationist regime are palpable in the fact that there is no W̱SÁNEĆ governance of or for the island (or, indeed, over other parts of the community's ceded and unceded territory). It is important to point out here too that there is no conceptual space within the categories of jus soli or jus sanguinis to capture W̱SÁNEĆ practices of membership that emerge from a deep integration of culture, identity, ancestry, human and non-human kinship relationships (including but not restricted to "blood stock"), law, and governance—and, indeed, the protocols and practices of community "recognition" (Simpson 2014), already discussed at length.

To further trouble local fictions of entitlement to own or use unceded W̱SÁNEĆ territory (Pender Island), the newspaper also highlighted how the federal government's "management" of the legal identity of Indians is shown to have more pernicious consequences for the rights of First Nations Peoples to the occupation and benefits of their reserve lands. For example, footnote 10 of the newspaper critiques the treaty's clause referring to the use of reserve lands in perpetuity: "kept for our own [i.e., W̱SÁNEĆ] use, for the use of our children" (Plessner 2018, 5). At face value this is meant to secure rights to the small parcels of reserved lands (colloquially called reservations or reserves) that were designated (purportedly under the treaty) for the descendants of the W̱SÁNEĆ. But how are those descendants formally recognized by the state today? Unfortunately, the classification of individual Indians, that is, the identification of who can be an Indian, continues to be controlled by the federal government. The registration of status Indians directly corresponds to an individual's entitlement to reserve lands—that is, who can claim rights to reserve lands under the terms of the Indian Act and Section 91.24 of the Constitution of Canada. The following quote from footnote 10 of the newspaper explains this point in more detail:

> The Indian Act has regulatory power over all facets of Indian life and provides the federal government with a major concentration of authority and social control over Indians—i.e., those that are identified [by the federal government] as

Indians. To decide Indian status, [the] Registrar in Ottawa . . . determines who is and who is not and Indian, based on [Department of Indigenous and Northern Affairs Canada] policies and legislation. The Registrar, accordingly, adds or takes people off the list called the Indian Register. The issue is not who is *actually* an Indian, but who is entitled to be *registered* as an Indian *according to the Indian Act*. The Registrar also decides who is not entitled to be registered in the Indian Register (National Centre for First Nations Governance, n.d., 3, my italics) (Plessner 2018, 6).[19]

The history of the state's system of registration of status Indians under the Indian Act has proven to be implicitly prejudiced and injurious, with previous legislation stripping the status of Indian from women who had either married those classified as non-Indians or "married out" (another ethnicity) and eliminating passage of the status to their children (Underwood 2018). The Canadian state also stripped status from any Indians who left the reserve without permission from the local agent of the Indian Office (Claxton 2017) or who lived abroad for more than five years (Indigenous and Northern Affairs 2010) and anyone who

became a lawyer, doctor or clergyman [or] received a degree from a university, or joined the military. If you lost your status you lost the right to live on the reserve [i.e., one is legally barred from one's own home, family and culture] and any benefits that might be associated with it. The Federal Government viewed [what it called] enfranchisement as a way of "civilizing" and *assimilating* the Indian (National Centre for First Nations Governance, n.d., 4, my italics; Plessner 2018, 6).[20]

And deep injustices continue to this day. With the implementation of Bill-C31 (in 1985), the Mulroney government instituted a new classificatory system that divides Indians into two categories: status "Indians" (6[1]) and "half-Indians" (6[2]), with the result that "there is a population growing on reserves that have no status as a result of Section 6(2)" (National Centre for First Nations Governance, n.d., 10). Half-Indians are in some cases, but not exclusively, those who are of mixed race. They also might be the children of those who were stripped of their legal status due to all of what has been listed previously and more, such as forced adoption (the "Sixties Scoop"[21]). The classification of half-Indians also effects those who were born, for example, on a reserve in the United States whose territory is severed by the US–Canadian border (as, for example, W̱SÁNEĆ Nation traditional territory) and are not recognized as First Nations Peoples in Canada.

What complicates this new division of 6(1) and 6(2) is the ability to pass along status. Should a status Indian under subsection 6(2) have children with a non-status person, their children are ineligible for Indian status. This is some-times called the "second generation cutoff." A person accorded status under subsection 6(1) does not face this penalty. Interestingly, should two 6(2) status Indians marry and have children, their child will become 6(1). This perpetuates the discriminatory measures of the Indian Act before Bill C-31, as certain In-dians face penalties for "marrying out," or marrying (and subsequently having children with) a non-status person. While Bill C-31 made it impossible for the government to remove one's status, the government has simply created a new mechanism to serve this same purpose. The government's original objective of eventually removing Indian status entirely is still served; Bill C-31 simply deferred it a generation. (First Nations Study Program 2009)

Those dispossessed of their status who maintain "ties to their ancestral homelands, cultures and histories, may find themselves excluded from land claims, treaties, and other similar agreements" (First Nations Study Program 2009). It has been pointed out that "these individuals will have no political rights as either band members or status Indians. They will live on the reserve but will become 'ghost people' people with no rights" (National Centre for First Nations Governance, n.d., 10). Mavis Underwood describes the impact of the state's protracted interference with indigenous systems of member-ship on the lives of W̱SÁNEĆ women. I quote her at length to draw atten-tion to the lived complexity—and, indeed, a local example of—the affective (aesthetic) dimension of a colonial state's citizenship regime and its effects in undermining First Nations women and skewing relations between people living within W̱SÁNEĆ territory. We see in Underwood's discussion just how markedly different and, indeed, unjust W̱SÁNEĆ women's experiences of membership are from those of non-Indigenous women and "citizens."

Imagine the experience of being devalued by your own kin because Indian Act policy is applied to an assessment of your bloodline and through the interpre-tation of policy you did not qualify for Indian status? Many Saltwater People [i.e., W̱SÁNEĆ people] who lived actively on the land and waters of the Gulf and San Juan Islands were too busy making a daily living to "come in off the water" at the demand of an Indian Agent for enumeration. Those who did not obey the call for enumeration suddenly became non-entities in their homelands as Indian agents no longer defined them as Indian but instead branded them as "disenfranchised" or "non-status."

No more evident is the attitude toward women expressed than in the manifes-tation of the Indian Act in the occasions of a status male marrying a non-Native woman. Prior to 1985 the act of marriage resulted in full status entitlement to the non-Native wife and their children. This same grace did not apply when a Na-tive woman married a non-Native man, the Native woman would lose all status entitlements for herself and her children. Even though Bill C-31 was introduced in an effort to correct inequity in true Indian Act fashion circumstances became even more convoluted. To counter this affront many Indian women recalled how frequently they would make decisions to live common-law.

As land became premium and identity became highly politicized, status entitlement became a heavy consideration when pondering matrimony. Some families without status were not only disenfranchised but they also lost rights to hereditary titles, lands, and were evicted from homelands by Indian agents. Many First Nations women enacted their own remedy and chose common-law relationships or relationships of convenience, they selectively mated choosing to preserve the status they had rather than risk losing not only status but their residence if a relationship broke down.

The decision known as *McIvor v. Canada* (2009) was intended to eliminate discrimination against the children and wives of non-status Indians through amendment to Section 6 of the Indian Act. As many First Nations now enact their own Membership Laws there may be contentious circumstances that still may prevent or delay status entitlement or membership. Membership in First Nations remains a point of controversy. The decisions, or the lack of decisions, practice a selective racism that creates outsiders within the community. Those on the outside feel the difference and repercussions of being denied membership for themselves and for their families not only as denied services but also as ill-treatment, indifference, or physical threat. (Underwood 2018, 14)

To have no status is the same as losing one's land and the material and cultural benefits of the land. The state's management and framework of the register has, perhaps deliberately, accelerated the disenfranchisement of First Nations and their rights to reserve lands.[22] "Even if a band controls its membership list . . . *Indian Affairs maintains control over who is registered as an Indian*" (National Centre for First Nations Governance, n.d., 11, my italics). Not only does this racialized system of classification disenfranchise those who are actual Indians, but it further shows how actual membership—of families and kin groups, including intermarriages or, indeed, the possibility of formally incorporating nonhuman beings, say, into the category of legal persons—is undermined by the state system of management of Indigenous people's legal body.[23] The problem is rooted in the limitations of the European Enlightenment and common-law notions of citizenship that presuppose that the colonial state is (1) able to recognize and grasp First Nations affiliations and membership networks, when in fact this is beyond the ken of such a regime, and (2) entitled to define and manage the legal identity and status of Indians, when in fact its practices are imposed on the political organization of First Nations communities.

Within the newspaper intervention, the discussion of the failure of the state's classificatory regime—categorizing individuals as either status Indians or status citizens—captures and reflects the complexity of lived membership today. "Indians" and Canadians are thus "bordered" by and through the practices of the state's management of bodies, with the former being highly visible and embedded within the state's apparatus but also regulated to become invisible through the continuing colonial project of dispossession and assimilation. By evidencing the techniques of the state's status citizenship regime and its discrimination against First Nations Peoples and by troubling and challenging settler-Canadian assumptions of belonging and entitlement, the newspaper also demonstrates how one's membership status—one's privileged political status—is aligned with and consolidates the ongoing act of appropriation, rendering resident-citizens complicit in the suppression of W̱SÁNEĆ presence and governance within the locale. It becomes apparent then that in designating First Nations Peoples as status Indians, the state's citizenship regime structures the bordering of peoples within a region. Canada's status citizenship regime also skews First Nations' practice of more dynamic modes of membership that can be realized through their own laws and acts of recognition or formally extended to nonhuman beings.

To review: The newspaper intervention made visible the facts on the ground via the assemblage of W̱SÁNEĆ writings and perspectives that are otherwise suppressed or obfuscated or treated as peripheral to the concerns of residents of Pender Island. In recirculating W̱SÁNEĆ counternarratives, the intervention alerted island residents to the problems and contradictions that are elided in settler claims to ownership of land, sanctioned by the Crown and constituting the foundation of the state and, thereby, troubled the normalization of statist articulations of belonging and membership that sustain and entrench the silent apartheid that persists in the lived conditions of the island. It therefore directly challenged assumptions about who "we" are and what "we" claim to be. The intervention also exposed how the state's management of First Nations legal identities as status Indians exacerbates the partitioning of peoples and is coterminous with the appropriation of First Nations lands.

The intervention also performed an act of citizenship by challenging local settler narratives of a virtuous (British) colonial history by publicly inviting residents to question their assumptions of ownership and belonging within the specifics of local W̱SÁNEĆ counternarratives of Crown (treatied) appropriation and the state's sharp dealing. It also tacitly imposed an obligation on residents to at least recognize and, in turn, acknowledge the implicit epistemic violence of claim making, occupation, and possession in their residing on the unceded territory of the W̱SÁNEĆ People. By targeting the homes of island residents and recirculating the assemblage of (previously) published W̱SÁNEĆ descriptions of the meaning and purpose of the treaty as a peace treaty, and by drawing attention to a W̱SÁNEĆ cosmological story of the origin of the islands as ancestral kin with whom one is entangled in a reciprocal relationship of caretaking (a core principle in W̱SÁNEĆ law), the intervention itself publicly performed an act of recognition of W̱SÁNEĆ presence and prerogative within their unceded territory. In tasking residents to learn about and then grapple with a critique of the Douglas Treaty through the lens of W̱SÁNEĆ and other First Nations authors, the newspaper brought to light how colonial interpretations of the treaty continue to reinforce and, indeed, antagonize foundational political, cultural, and ethical differences between Indigenous and non-Indigenous peoples living in this region. I have argued that scoping out the possibilities for new relationships and new modes of membership pivots on revisiting local and national colonial narratives that suppress the differential effects of the state's partitioning of people, its subtle but persistent violences, and its system of classification by drawing attention to the problems of the "fantasy" of ownership of lands (Mackey 2016) subtended by the capture of legal identities. The intervention therefore effected a twofold "dissensus" (Rancière 2010) within the local community: On the one hand, in challenging colonial logics of land appropriation, as discussed previously, the intervention called into question the foundation on which claims to belonging and (state) membership depend. On the other hand, it introduced residents to a more complex conception and practice of political membership, based on responsibilities and duties to nonhuman beings (such as the islands and other beings) as kin.

Still wanting is a more robust description of the radical implications of W̱SÁNEĆ conceptions of nonhuman kinship relations for doing politics. Seeing land as a kin relative expands the basis on which political actors are cognized and included within a membership regime. Introducing island residents to this more nuanced conception of more-than-human beings as part of the political domain was the point and purpose of my second intervention, *Citizen Artist News: Kinship*, which will be examined in detail in chapter 6.

NOTES

1. The W̱SÁNEĆ (Saanich) First Nation is a collective name for four bands located at four different village sites on the North Saanich Peninsula on Vancouver Island, British Columbia, Canada: SȾÁ,UTW̱ (Tsawout) First Nation, W̱JOȽEȽP (Tsartlip) First Nation, BOḴEĆEN (Pauquachin) First Nation, and W̱SIḴEM (Tseycum) First Nation.

2. My discussion of colonialism is limited to only a few of its conditions as they pertain to issues of membership and the appropriation of lands. I reference only British Canadian colonial practices and not French Canadian or other modes of colonization in the world. This is to home in on the legacy (and continuance) of British colonial orientations within (provincial and federal) state administrations, expressions, and practices (including legal and judicial infrastructures) that are privileged as the

social, political, and cultural "norm" within the local community of Pender Island in the province of British Columbia.

3. See Hopper 2013b: "Since, May, more than 1,308 suspected graves have been uncovered near the sites of former residential schools: 215 in Kamloops, B.C., 182 in Cranbrook, B.C., 715 in Marieval, Sask., and more than 160 found on Penelakut Island, B.C."

4. The term "settler" does not denote a coherent category. The terms "settler-colonial" and "settler" as used within this book follow the work of Alfred (2005) to denote an *orientation*—"a social construct" (2005, 110), rather than a designation of race (e.g., white people) or specific ethnicities, even though the term flattens the complexities of ethnic and migrational histories and legacies of racism in the formation of the Canadian state, which is modeled on the British subject as the norm.

5. See Chatterjee 1993: colonial nationalisms that emerge in places such as Asia and Africa "are posited *not* on an identity [with European models of nationalism] but rather on a *difference* with the 'modular' forms of the national society propagated with the modern West" (5, my italics). Chatterjee describes the nature of nationalism in places such as India as "dividing the world of social institutions and practices into two domains—the material and the spiritual. The material is the domain of the 'outside,' of the economy and state craft, of science and technology, a domain where the West has proved its superiority and the East had succumbed. The Spiritual, on the other hand, is an 'inner' domain bearing the 'essential' marks of cultural identity. The greater the success in imitating Western skills in the material domain, . . . the greater the need to preserve the distinctness of one's spiritual culture. This formula is . . . a fundamental feature of anti-colonial nationalisms" (6). Chatterjee's characterization of anticolonial nationalism brings to light the "inner" affective and aesthetic dimension of membership and belonging and how it frames a political domain.

6. Within First Nations communities, membership and systems of governance differ widely, including the use of the term "citizen." The term "citizen" is not common or universally adopted; nor does it carry the same meaning as status citizenship. For example, not only does the Fort Nelson First Nation (2004) use the term "citizen" to describe members who meet the requirements of being a status Indian (i.e., a criterion set out by the Indian Act), but members need to satisfy an additional criterion of being a traditional citizen (i.e., a person who has familial or blood ties to members who *were or are known* to the nation). Hence, the term "citizen" can denote a nation's traditional political practices of membership through "recognition" of and by the community.

7. Copies were also distributed through Tsawout First Nation Band Office, posted to some members of Parliament and leaders of the Green Party, and dispatched through a newsstand in the local supermarket.

8. Emily Artinian, artist and founder of Street Road Artists' Space (streetroad.org), co-organized the workshop and exhibition at Pender Island's community hall. The event included a pop-up art exhibition featuring the work of ten participating artists (see Street Road 2018) and two speaker events: (1) a panel discussion with Mavis Underwood (council member, Tsawout First Nation Band Council), Earl Claxton (Elder, Tsawout First Nation), and David Boyd, (UN special rapporteur on human rights and the environment, University of British Columbia law professor) discussing differing

conceptions of "land" and "ownership" and legal developments in the rights of non-human beings (land, rivers, animals, etc.), and (2) a live (phone-in) interview with Robert Clifford (Tsawout First Nation) discussing his scholarly work in W̱SÁNEĆ law as a sui generis system of principles, understood as operating independently of Canadian common law. See Street Road 2018.

9. Some discussion was emerging at a national level in 2017; see Shahzad 2017; Kapler 2017.

10. From 1850 to 1854, large parts of First Peoples territories, now known as Vancouver Island, were claimed by James Douglas on behalf of the British Crown. There are fourteen treaties in total, known collectively as the Douglas Treaties. The North Saanich treaty is specific to one small part of W̱SÁNEĆ (Saanich) Nation territory, creating the reserve lands of SȾÁ,UTW̱, W̱JOȽEȽP, BOḰEĆEN, and W̱SIḴEM First Nations.

11. Following the murder of a young messenger boy from Tsawout Nation by James Douglas's men, in addition to the felling and theft of trees in Cadboro Bay, Songhees territory, the treaty signaled agreement not to enter into war with Douglas and the settlers (Claxton 2017; Elliott 1990; Sources of the Douglas Treaties, n.d., #10, #13, #14, #16).

12. See Plessner 2018, note 9, re: "the containment of the W̱SÁNEĆ to their 'village sites' and 'enclosed fields,' currently understood as the reservations located on the Saanich peninsula. . . . As a result of inconsistent surveys of lands that were executed in the interests of the Crown and its settlers, there is continuing disagreement over what constitutes the domain of the reserve lands under the *Douglas Treaty: North Saanich*. . . . The vague language of the Douglas Treaty and the presumption of Crown title, continues to cast a long shadow over contemporary practices of partitioning terrain. Until only recently has Goldstream No. 13 reserve (located 18 kilometres from Victoria) [been returned to the W̱SÁNEĆ. . . .] It was improperly reduced in 1962 by approximately 10 acres from its original size. . . . Chief Bruce Underwood states: 'This historic settlement and return of the land has been a critical part of our discussions for the betterment for future generations. . . . Our leaders are pleased the wrongdoings of this mis-survey to our Nations' land is now being corrected' (BC Gov News 2013, n.p.)" (5).

13. See Plessner 2018, note 3: "The W̱SÁNEĆ were asked to sign a blank piece of paper and the text was added *after* members of the W̱SÁNEĆ had been required to mark an X (Claxton 2017; Sources of the Douglas Treaties, n.d. see #9). . . . Whatever may be said or written at the time [the W̱SÁNEĆ] believed that the document was a *peace* treaty. There had been trouble over logging and over the shooting of a young Indian lad, and when Douglas produced piles of blankets and asked them to put 'X's' on a piece of paper, they thought they were being asked, under sign of the Christian cross, to accept compensation for not making war (Sources of the Douglas Treaties, n.d.; see #10 and #14)" (4). The legitimacy of signatures is also controversial because of language barriers, with few Hudson's Bay Company employees understanding the Salish language (SENĆOŦEN) and few local Indigenous people understanding English (Governor's Letters, http://govlet.ca/en/index.php; Elliott 1990; Sources of the Douglas Treaties, n.d., #10–#14). Some W̱SÁNEĆ spoke Chinook, the local native

trading language on the West Coast, as did J. W. MacKay, Hudson's Bay Company secretary to Douglas and signing witness on the document. However, "Chinook *does not possess the vocabulary for land sale*" (Frogner 2010, 65, my italics). Also, there is controversy regarding the authenticity of the X marks: "Look at the X's yourself and you'll see they're all alike, probably written by the same hand. They actually didn't know those were their names and many of those names are not even accurate. They are not known to Saanich People" (Elliott 1990; Sources of the Douglas Treaties, n.d. see #16).

14. See Plessner 2018, 7n14: the W̱SÁNEĆ continue to struggle to protect their "right to hunt and fish as formerly." In 1916, they were banned from using their traditional fishing technology, which undermined W̱SÁNEĆ access and control over their fishing economy (Elliott 1990). The provincial government instead licensed a British company (J. H. Todd and Sons) to commercially fish in W̱SÁNEĆ (and other First Nation) territories (Elliott 1990). Todd and Sons subsequently became B. C. Packers, one of Canada's largest marine extraction industries and processers (closing in 1997 due to overfishing). "Sharp dealings" continue: Tsawout Nation took the BC government to court on many occasions to assert their fishing rights on reserve lands; see *Claxton v. Saanichton Marina and the Queen* (1989); *Regina v. Bartleman* (1984); *Regina v. Morris* (2006). Anecdotal evidence from members of Tsawout Nation holds that fishing licenses to access designated reserve waters continue to be given to non-Indigenous commercial fishermen, who then further deplete the now scant fish stock.

15. Johann Kaspar Bluntschli (2000), a nineteenth-century political theorist, defined the state through the metaphor of soil: "A permanent relation of the people to the soil is necessary for the continuance of the State. The State requires its territory: nation and country go together. Nomadic peoples, although they have chiefs to command them and law to govern them, have not yet reached the full condition of States until they have a fixed abode. . . . Another characteristic of the State is the unity of the whole, the cohesion of the nation. Internally there may indeed be different divisions with considerable independence of their own. . . . But unless the community forms a coherent whole in its internal organization, or can appear and act as a unit in external relations, there is no State" (25). Reference to governance, "soil," and rightful occupation is seen in the findings of Louise Mandell, an Indigenous lawyer who, in 1981, was an active member of the Union of BC Indian Chiefs. At the Thirteenth Annual General Assembly (October 20–30, 1981), she relates the outcomes of a historical court case in the United States, in the aftermath of Britain's "winning the fight between other European Nations over the Dominion of Canada[. W]hat Britain won, as a matter of law, was the right to acquire Indian people's land *when Indian people consented to give it to them. They didn't win the land* . . . [and this was] affirmed as early as 1830 [by the Court]. The Court said . . . talking about the Indians, they were admitted to be *the rightful occupants of the soil* with legal as well as the just right to retain possession of it and to use it according to their own discretion" (UBCIC 1981, 10, my italics).

16. In 1960 status Indians were given the right to vote (Cairns 2000; Indigenous Foundations, n.d.). Prior to this *and in continuance*, all decisions on behalf of First Nations are managed through the federal government, beginning at Confederation

(1867) via the British North America Act (1867) and then articulated in more oppressive detail in the Indian Act (commencing in 1876). The state assumes control over all aspects of the lives of status Indians and First Nation bands such as their status, lands, health care, education, wills, resources, band administration, and so forth (Cairns 2000; First Nations Study Program 2009). "Since the publication of the legal opinion on federal and provincial jurisdiction over Indians in the Hawthorn Report in 1966 the trend . . . has been to view 'Indians' as a 'double aspect' constitutional subject matter and to extend various provincial services to them on the basis that they are provincial citizens as well as a federal subject matter and the possessors of special constitutional status" (Giokas 1995, 7). Participation in voting, however, does not denote equality between status Indians and citizens. The rights of status Indians are substantially curtailed regarding owning lands because technically reserves lands are owned by the Crown under the jurisdiction of the federal government. Status Indians residing on reserves have to seek permission from "the Minister of Aboriginal Affairs and the Band government to guarantee mortgages" (Lebourdais 2013). "It is nearly impossible for a First Nation's woman to qualify for an independent mortgage to obtain housing on reserve. Mortgage loans may require a co-signer from Indian Affairs who provides a ministerial guarantee of a mortgage loan to ensure that the bank may foreclose if there is default on the mortgage. Alternatively, the bank may accept a legal agreement in the form of a Band Council Resolution signed off by Chief and Council of the First Nation describing accommodation of foreclosure/seizure process if there is a mortgage default. These conditions may apply even if there is substantive income that would financially qualify the woman off-reserve" (Underwood 2018, 16). Some First Nations are seeking changes in legislation to allow for reserve lands to be translated into private property (private ownership). Chief Michael Lebourdais (2013) of Whispering Pines/Clinton Indian Band states, "Not owning our land has been an economic catastrophe. We have little of the equity in our homes that is needed to build wealth, gain access to credit and start businesses. We don't have wealth to bequeath to the next generation so it can do better than us." This viewpoint is not widely shared, and the idea of private property has been criticized. In 2010, "the Assembly of First Nations passed a resolution stating bluntly that 'fee simple title,' the landholding inaugurated by the Nisga'a [People under their recent treaty agreements with the federal government], will lead ultimately to the individual privatization of indigenous collective lands and resources and impose the colonizer's model on our Peoples. . . . Fears of private ownership of Indigenous land are certainly not without precedent. . . . In 1887 the United States imposed the Dawes Act; a homestead-style system that essentially liquidated all collective Indigenous land and forced Indians to settle on privately owned, European-style farm plots. The act was premised on the so-called 'civilizing power' of private property, but within 30 years, all it had done was shatter traditional governance structures and help to hand more than two-thirds of all native land . . . to white settlers. Today, the Dawes Act is seen as a social catastrophe in league with Canada's Indian Residential Schools" (Hopper 2013a).

17. "The ascendant Imperial and colonial authorities [within Canada] applied a policy of recognition based on [allegedly 'objective'] factors such as blood quantum or kinship as determined through the male line, thereby denying to Aboriginal nations

their former capacity to self-define" (Giokas 1995, 157). Recognition "focuses on individuals and not members of a group"; for instance, bands are also understood as groups of "individuals."

18. "Status Indians are wards of the Canadian Federal Government, . . . a paternalistic legal relationship that illustrates the historical Imperial notion that Aboriginal peoples are 'children' requiring control and direction to bring them into more 'civilized' colonial ways of life. As an 1876 Department of Indian Affairs report explains: 'Our Indian legislation generally rests on the principle, that the aborigines are to be kept in a condition of tutelage and treated as wards or children of the State. . . . [T]he true interests of the aborigines and of the State alike require that every effort should be made to aid the Red man in lifting himself out of his condition of tutelage and dependence, and that is clearly our wisdom and our duty, through education and every other means, to prepare him for a higher civilization by encouraging him to assume the privileges and responsibilities of full citizenship.' . . . In keeping with paternalistic policies towards Aboriginal peoples, the Canadian federal government assumed fiscal responsibility for Indians in order to support the colonial structures it imposed on Aboriginal peoples through the Indian Act, such as band administration, education, and health care" (First Nations Study Program 2009).

19. "In 1985, an amendment to the Indian Act separated Indian status from band membership. Bands were granted the right to develop their own membership codes, and thereby determine who can participate in band politics and society, as well as who can access band resources such as band property. Bands, however, did not have control over who gained or lost status. This power was retained by the federal government. While band membership frequently accompanies Indian status, it is possible to have Indian status without having band membership, or vice versa" (First Nations Study Program 2009).

20. Assimilationist policies were first articulated under British rule. For instance, statesman Duncan Campbell Scott (deputy superintendent of the Department of Indian Affairs, 1913–1932), in mandating a bill for compulsory incarceration of Indian children in residential schools, stated, "'I want to get rid of the Indian problem. I do not think as a matter of fact, that the country ought to continuously protect a class of people who are able to stand alone. . . . Our objective is to continue until there is not a single Indian in Canada that has not been absorbed into the body politic and there is no Indian question, and no Indian Department, that is the whole object of this Bill.' The First Peoples, despite many agreements with the Crown [namely, the Royal Proclamation of 1763] that guaranteed their independence, were to be eradicated as distinct nations and cultures" (Facing History and Ourselves, n.d.). The issue of assimilation continues to frustrate; see Coulthard 2014.

21. See Underwood 2018: "The . . . 'sixties scoop' refers to prevalent social work practice in the 1960s that resulted in the apprehension of First Nations' children for 'cultural deprivation,' poverty, or neglect. Cultural deprivation referred to the inability of First Nations parents to provide an enriched life that mimicked the amenities and values of dominant white society. The standards of culture were established often through the entry of First Nations' children into public schools and by the observation of children by federal public health nurses who served reserve-based communities.

They often had strong influence in assessing families and often described the differences as value judgements. The realm of their experiences often failed to recognize First Nations history and culture and failed to recognize the breadth of First Nations family support. Child apprehension in the 1960's often resulted in a permanent disconnection from family and community of origin as the children were rapidly absorbed by the system and placed for adoption" (15).

22. "Many people view Indian status as an assimilative tool, a mechanism for the Canadian government to eventually 'legislate out' Indian identity. The Canadian government has historically acknowledged its unique relationship with, and hence obligation to, First Nations, and therefore the government created a definition of 'Indian' in order to administer services and resources to the appropriate people (namely, Aboriginal peoples). However, in using legislation to determine who qualifies for 'Indian Status' and the rights conferred with that status, some have argued that it creates a conflict of interest [e.g.,] . . . it is in the government's interest to reduce the numbers of eligible Indians and therefore ease [its associated] responsibilities and expenditures" (First Nations Study Program 2009).

23. Attempts had been made to abolish the classification of status Indians by the federal government in a "Statement of the Government on Indian Policy" (1969, aka the White Paper). It aimed to relinquish all previous legal documents pertaining to Indigenous people, including the Indian Act and Treaties and to "assimilate all 'Indians' fully into the Canadian state" (Canadian Encyclopedia, n.d.). Understandably, this was resisted by First Nations in view of the fact that Indian status "forced the government to legally acknowledge [its] obligations to Aboriginal peoples. Aboriginal leaders were concerned that to abolish status would absolve the government of its commitments [under the 1763 royal proclamation, to recognize Indian nations' sovereignty and right to their own lands unless ceded under the consent of that nation]. Further, to propose abolishing status infers that the eventual assimilation of Aboriginal peoples into the mainstream Canadian society is inevitable" (First Nations Study Program 2009). See also Louise Mandell: "The Trudeau proposal [the White Paper] is attempting to sever the relationships that the Indian people have with the Crown; to say it more clearly, to make it impossible for those obligations which the Crown has undertaken to the Indian Nations ever to be fulfilled. . . . [W]hat it proposes to do is place the Indian people in a state where they legally do not have any rights within the Constitution of Canada" (UBCIC, 1981, 7).

Chapter Six

Expanding Membership

Citizen Artist News: Kinship

In chapter 5, I discussed how *Citizen Artist News: Clouded Title* carved out a new civil space on Pender Island for doing politics in its performance as an act of citizenship (Isin and Nielsen 2008; Isin 2012). Not only did the intervention pointedly challenge local settler-residents to examine their assumptions of (purported) ownership of unceded lands, which in turn undergirds local colonial narratives and sentiments of belonging and membership, but also the intervention was a determined political act in its public acknowledgment of the W̱SÁNEĆ People as central to the politics of the island. That is, the intervention deliberately interrupted the silent apartheid that dominates the politics and culture of the locale and that persists in the normalization of colonial occupation. Woven into this act of public recognition was the opening up of a space to explore important aspects of W̱SÁNEĆ beliefs, laws, systems of governance, and relations to place as founded on reciprocal responsibilities to more-than-human beings. Residents were introduced to W̱SÁNEĆ authors who described W̱SÁNEĆ law and governance of their lands as founded on ethical responsibilities to human and nonhuman kin (Clifford 2011, 2016a, 2016b, 2019; Tsawout First Nation 2015, n.d.). Ethicopolitical and legal responsibilities and duties to more-than-human beings are strikingly distinct from the colonial state's exercise of a legal system rooted in the notion of ownership of property (as evidenced in the Douglas Treaty discussed in chapter 5). Indeed, the colonial legal construct of "people" and "property" as at the foundation of law comes under some scrutiny. W̱SÁNEĆ core values and principles of law upend normative colonial imaginaries on two levels: First, they challenge the notion of kinship as signifying only human relationships, and second, they trouble assumptions about the cogency of political membership as relating only to humans.

The practice of centering law and governance on obligations to more-than-human beings regarded as kin is radically provocative and conceptually expands the scope and conditions of political membership in important ways. This chapter will therefore first describe and then discuss *Citizen Artist News: Kinship* (see figure 6.1), my second citizen art intervention, also specific to Pender Island, that set out to trouble colonial logics and practices. At a local level, there is widespread ignorance (or dismissal) of the (is)lands as even unceded W̱SÁNEĆ territory, let alone more fine-grained W̱SÁNEĆ perspectives on human-nonhuman kinship relations and what this entails for living within W̱SÁNEĆ territory. Therefore, the core of my discussion will illustrate the differing aesthetic orientations to (is)lands within W̱SÁNEĆ and (British) colonial culture to show that aesthetics is central to the doing of politics within these citizen art interventions. I will show that the notion of more-than-human beings (such as, say, islands, trees, fish, etc.) conceived of as resources is indicative of exploitative colonial imaginaries that, although widespread and pervasive, are also (mistakenly) assumed to be normative and universal rather than simply expressive of an orientation.[1] The following will therefore focus on how aesthetic orientations to land (as an inert substance or as kin) are explored through this and the previous newspaper intervention to further trouble the politics of place. I will discuss how *CA News: Kinship* agitated in its examination of nonhuman kin relations, and I will reserve a wider review of these citizen art interventions as acts of citizenship and their enactment of new modes of (nonstatist) citizenship primarily for the conclusion, where I will outline the effects of these interventions.

Before turning to my discussion of *CA News: Kinship*, it is important to briefly note that Donna Haraway has done some work on examining the idea of nonhuman beings as "kin" in her book *Staying with the Trouble: Making Kin in the Chthulucene* (2016) and a short article called "Anthropocene, Capitalocene, Plantationocene, Chthulucene: Making Kin" (2015). In both texts, she emphasizes the connections between different species and relations of interdependence in the struggle for life in a world that she sees as dying. As she says, "no species, not even our own arrogant one pretending to be good individuals in so-called modern Western scripts, acts alone" (Haraway 2015, 159). Much of her writing is a kind of rallying call to seek ways for "multispecies flourishing . . . and to join forces to reconstitute refuges" (120), starting with expanding the category of kin to include relations to other beings. As she says, "My purpose is to make 'kin' mean something other/more than entities tied by ancestry or genealogy" (Haraway 2015, 161). Although I share her sentiments and concur that there is an urgent need for people to think anew about human-nonhuman relationships and ways of being in the world and that "it matters which stories tell stories, which concepts think concepts . . . which figures figure figures, which systems systematize

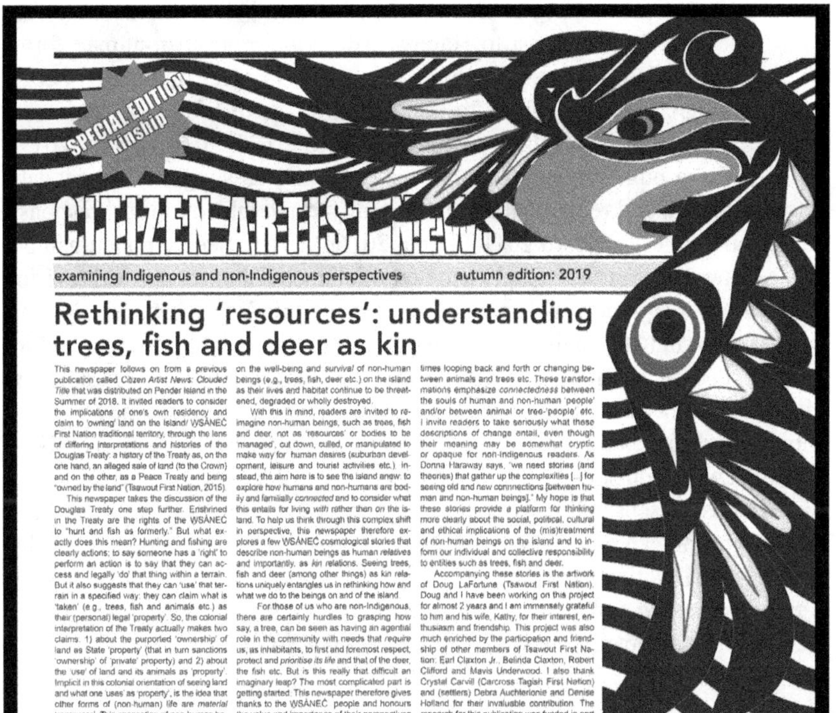

SPECIAL EDITION kinship

CITIZEN ARTIST NEWS

examining Indigenous and non-Indigenous perspectives autumn edition: 2019

Rethinking 'resources': understanding trees, fish and deer as kin

This newspaper follows on from a previous publication called *Citizen Artist News: Clouded Title* that was distributed on Pender Island in the Summer of 2018. It invited readers to consider the implications of one's own residency and claim to 'owning' land on the Island/ W̱SÁNEĆ First Nation traditional territory, through the lens of differing interpretations and histories of the Douglas Treaty: a history of the Treaty as, on the one hand, an alleged sale of land (to the Crown) and on the other, as a Peace Treaty and being "owned by the land" (Tsawout First Nation, 2015).

This newspaper takes the discussion of the Douglas Treaty one step further. Enshrined in the Treaty are the rights of the W̱SÁNEĆ to "hunt and fish as formerly." But what exactly does this mean? Hunting and fishing are clearly actions; to say someone has a 'right' to perform an action is to say that they can access and legally 'do' that thing within a terrain. But it also suggests that they can 'use' that terrain in a specified way: they can claim what is 'taken' (e.g., trees, fish and animals etc.) as their (personal) legal 'property'. So, the colonial interpretation of the Treaty actually makes two claims: 1) about the purported 'ownership' of land as State 'property' (that in turn sanctions 'ownership' of 'private' property) and 2) about the 'use' of land and its animals as 'property'. Implicit in this colonial orientation of seeing land and what one 'uses' as 'property', is the idea that other forms of (non-human) life are *material 'resources'*. This conception of non-human beings as material 'resources' and as bodies to be 'managed' (reproduced or killed etc.) for human 'use', desire and/or industry, profoundly shapes (indeed, skews) how we live with non-human beings on a daily basis. It also deeply impacts on the well-being and *survival* of non-human beings (e.g., trees, fish, deer etc.) on the island as their lives and habitat continue to be threatened, degraded or wholly destroyed.

With this in mind, readers are invited to re-imagine non-human beings, such as trees, fish and deer, not as 'resources' or bodies to be 'managed', cut down, culled, or manipulated to make way for human desires (suburban development, leisure and tourist activities etc.). Instead, the aim here is to see the island anew: to explore how humans and non-humans are bodily and familially *connected* and to consider what this entails for living *with* rather than *on* the island. To help us think through this complex shift in perspective, this *newspaper* therefore explores a few W̱SÁNEĆ cosmological stories that describe non-human beings as human *relatives* and importantly, as *kin relations*. Seeing trees, fish and deer (among other things) as kin *relations* uniquely entangles us in rethinking how and what we do to the beings on and of the island.

For those of us who are non-Indigenous, there are certainly hurdles to grasping how say, a tree, can be seen as having an agential role in the community with needs that *require* us, as inhabitants, to first and foremost respect, protect and *prioritise its life* and that of the deer, the fish etc. But is this really that difficult an imaginary leap? The most complicated part is getting started. This newspaper therefore gives thanks to the W̱SÁNEĆ people and honours the value and importance of their perspectives and understandings of kin and ancestral relations to islands, trees, fish and deer.

Central to W̱SÁNEĆ stories is the notion of transformation of one bodily form to another, from human to non-human body and sometimes looping back and forth or changing between animals and trees etc. These transformations emphasize *connectedness* between the souls of human and non-human 'people' and/or between animal or tree-'people' etc. I invite readers to take seriously what these descriptions of change entail, even though their meaning may be somewhat cryptic or opaque for non-Indigenous readers. As Donna Haraway says, "we need stories (and theories) that gather up the complexities [...] for seeing old and new connections [between human and non-human beings]." My hope is that these stories provide a platform for thinking more clearly about the social, political, cultural and ethical implications of the (mis)treatment of non-human beings on the island and to inform our individual and collective responsibility to entities such as trees, fish and deer.

Accompanying these stories is the artwork of Doug LaFortune (Tsawout First Nation). Doug and I have been working on this project for almost 2 years and I am immensely grateful to him and his wife, Kathy, for their interest, enthusiasm and friendship. This project was also much enriched by the participation and friendship of other members of Tsawout First Nation: Earl Claxton Jr., Belinda Claxton, Robert Clifford and Mavis Underwood. I also thank Crystal Carvill (Carcross Tagish First Nation) and (settlers) Debra Auchterlonie and Denise Holland for their invaluable contribution. The research for this publication was funded in part by the Canada Council for the Arts. I thank them for their support and hope that as members of the Island community, you too will enjoy sharing in this discussion.

Fawn Daphne Plessner

Overcoming more than a 'species barrier'

The notion of kinship, as indicated above, is a foundational concept and a cornerstone of how Indigenous and non-Indigenous communities differently view land and other forms of non-human life. But what does this entail for those of us who live on Pender Island and within W̱SÁNEĆ territory? Seeing trees, fish and deer as kin has deep and important implications for understanding (political) membership of the island's community. *Who* is counted as living on the island? *Who* exactly is *entitled to have their needs recognized and their lives sustained?* Should human desire (dream and holiday homes, tourist and recreational activities etc.) be privileged over the lives and well-being of this wider group of beings, the meagre few who have so far survived the rapid and relatively recent increase of human presence and suburban development here?

Exploring W̱SÁNEĆ conceptions of kinship and rethinking membership of a community, in addition to assessing one's ethical and political obligations to non-human beings, is the point of this publication. It is aimed at making visible and taking responsibility for how settler colonial desires and practices continually disenfranchise W̱SÁNEĆ perspectives by not making way for more complex and nuanced understandings of human and non-human relationships. As residents within W̱SÁNEĆ territory, being responsible to the W̱SÁNEĆ people, and also non-human beings, matters if there is to be any honest and purposeful engagement with reconciliation. It is also of vital importance for the well-being and survival of all the non-human inhabitants of the island. Numerous species of animals have disappeared from this island in the last 40 years. Trees, fish and deer have declined in health and number by the rapid increase of human activity and exploitation. Non-human beings have had to endure considerable violence to their environ and lives as a consequence of the infrastructural decision-making of recent decades that has prioritized the expansion of the built environment.

The real story of Pender Island starts with trees. The following passage is from the writings of Dave Elliott Sr., a W̱SÁNEĆ Nation Elder, Historian and Linguist (1910 - 1985). He tells of the first moments of British colonization, the felling of trees and the exploitation of 'resources'. This passage begins this newspaper's exploration of the idea of 'resources' versus 'kin' and the implications for living within W̱SÁNEĆ territory.

"There are many, many things that have brought us to where we are – broken promises discrimination, legislation. Just take the Saanich Peninsula; the Saanich Peninsula was the homeland of the Saanich People for who knows how long. [...] When James Douglas moved himself and his people into Victoria Harbour he moved right in with the Songhees people, the LEQENEN [sic]. He made that the headquarters of the Hudson Bay Company. Then after some time they began to claim the land, they began to exploit the land. One of the things they were doing was logging this beautiful stand of [trees] in Cadboro Bay area. [These trees were] tall and slim going straight up, no limbs 'til almost way up to the top, maybe sixty, seventy, eighty, one hundred feet high. A beautiful stand of timber in great demand for ship's masts. This is why they [Douglas's men] were there. Of course you know all shipping those days was by sail. This is why masts were in such demand. They were taking them away by the shipload for the purpose of using them for masts."

(Elliott, D. 1983, *Saltwater People*)

Citizen Artist News is an art project led by Fawn Daphne Plessner (artist/editor) in collaboration with Doug LaFortune (artist) and Denise Holland (artist/co-editor).
For more information:
citizenartist.org.uk
fdplessner@shaw.ca

Canada Council for the Arts

Figure 6.1. Front page of *Citizen Artist News: Kinship*. Launched on Pender Island, British Columbia, Canada, September 30, 2019. *Photo courtesy of F. D. Plessner* systems" (Haraway 2016, 101), her discussion of kinship with nonhuman beings is not as penetrating as that expressed within W̱SÁNEĆ culture. That is, the W̱SÁNEĆ, in contrast to Haraway, describe more-than-human forms of life (e.g., "islands") specifically as ancestors; in turn, notions of bodily and genealogical connectedness to nonhuman forms of life are at the center of a storied lineage of kinship relations (Clifford 2011, 2016a, 2016b, 2019). Equally, these human-nonhuman kin relations are, as suggested previously, active, agential, and reciprocal and importantly entail ethicopolitical responsibilities and duties (Clifford 2011, 2016a, 2016b, 2019). Seeing nonhuman beings as kin relatives is not simply a matter of conceptual or categorical revision (albeit a necessary one), as Haraway suggests; within W̱SÁNEĆ descriptions, we learn that human-nonhuman kin relations are an aesthetic, bodied, and indeed spirited connection that is an implicitly ethical and political relationship. Missing in Haraway's writing is an appreciation of the a priori binds between humans and more-than-humans (expressed through genealogy in W̱SÁNEĆ culture) and a consideration of what this entails for who and what is then cognized as present within a terrain and, indeed, seen as deserving of political recognition generally. I will discuss these points more fully and argue that the W̱SÁNEĆ notion of kinship relations to other forms of life puts us on the path to expanding and enacting important new modes of (nonstatist) political membership, especially for those of us living within W̱SÁNEĆ territory.

CITIZEN ARTIST NEWS: KINSHIP

This newspaper intervention was created in collaboration with the artist Doug LaFortune and his wife, Kathy, both of whom are members of Tsawout First Nation Band (W̱SÁNEĆ First Nation).[2] Our aim was to explore the aesthetics of trees, fish, and deer as a way of celebrating W̱SÁNEĆ nonhuman kinship relations while also navigating the more problematic colonial conception of land and its animals as resources. To give some local context, the Douglas Treaty: North Saanich is supposed to guarantee the rights of the W̱SÁNEĆ First Nation People to "hunt and fish as formerly" (Government of Canada Indigenous and Northern Affairs, n.d.). This is generally understood as the right to access and "use" the resources of the land and sea.[3] However, this emphasis on use of land and its animals as resources closes down W̱SÁNEĆ descriptions of especially the aesthetic dimension of nonhuman kin relations. I will expand on this point fully herein. For now, and from my perspective as a resident on W̱SÁNEĆ territory, the colonial impulse to use land has manifested as rampant urbanization of Pender Island in recent decades. The human population and, indeed, the built environment have increased approximately twelvefold in only forty years. In this short period, the forest, shoreline, and ocean have been extensively degraded, and there have been widespread animal extinctions. These two observations—treatied conceptions of resources and the widespread destruction of the island and its animals to make way for suburban "development" (e.g., an "ecocide")[4]—prompted a set of questions about the aesthetics and politics of multiplicitous settler relationships to forests, seas, and animal lives. How has the widespread and accelerated annihilation of animals, the polluting of oceans, and the felling of forests become normalized and entwined with acts of British, now Canadian colonial land appropriation, identity, and desire? How do settler-colonial logics of use of resources, underpinned by an asymmetrical reading of the Douglas Treaty, manifest within local treatments of land and attitudes to possessing "property"? *CA News: Kinship* set out to creatively respond to the aesthetic and affective experiences of land as, on the one hand, nonhuman kin and, on the other, as resources (commodities).

After two years of discussion and research with Doug and Kathy LaFortune and other members of Tsawout First Nation (Earl Claxton Jr., Mavis Underwood, Robert Clifford, Belinda Claxton, and settlers Debra Auchterlonie and Denise Holland), LaFortune and I developed the newspaper, which brought together his illustrations and an assemblage of W̱SÁNEĆ origin stories and posters, an information panel mapping alternate meanings of the image of the beaver (a Canadian symbol of "industry"), and an interview with Robert Clifford (to be discussed further). In short, this intervention was an elaborately illustrated newspaper intended to entice residents to engage with its more demanding contents. It was launched eighteen months after *Clouded Title* and extended the meaning and performance of these citizen art projects through time. Twenty-two hundred copies were printed and once again initially distributed by post to all homes on Pender Island, the mayor's office, members of the provincial legislature, and leaders of the Green Party who represent the islands. Copies were also made available at a newsstand at the local supermarket and distributed through the W̱SÁNEĆ School Board offices, the Tsawout First Nation Band office, and the First Peoples House at the University of Victoria.

The intervention used the same strategy as *Clouded Title*, directly soliciting Pender Island residents to enter into a public thought experiment. It asked residents to actively engage with W̱SÁNEĆ interlocutors but, this time, to grapple with the import of being in a *relationship* with more-than-human beings based on reciprocal responsibilities and duties to (is)lands and animals as vibrant forms of agential life (rather than on human dominion and management of "land" and its animals). On the front page of the newspaper, I drew out the problem in the following way:

The notion of kinship is a foundational concept and a cornerstone of how Indigenous and non-Indigenous communities differently view land and others
forms of non-human life. But what does this entail for those of us who live on
Pender Island and within W̱SÁNEĆ territory? Seeing trees, fish and deer as kin
has deep and important implications for understanding (political) membership
of the island's community. *Who* is counted as living on the island? *Who* exactly
is *entitled to have their needs recognized and their lives sustained?* (Plessner
2019, 1)

As a second act of citizenship, the intention was to challenge settler logics
and treatments of land (as a malleable substance) by examining how kinship
relations to the (is)land and other beings are at the center of W̱SÁNEĆ law and
governance. I wanted residents to consider, at the very least, how the island,
forests, fish, deer, and so forth, are currently used (sanitized, fenced, curated,
cultivated, harmed, etc.) and, in turn, how an expanded form of membership
presses residents to recognize the island's more-than-human residents as at
the center of the political community in real and material ways. At the heart
of the intervention was an interview, conducted by me, with Robert Clifford,
whose research in W̱SÁNEĆ law was first introduced to residents in *Clouded
Title*.[5] We focused our discussion on only two stories. The first was that of
XÁLS the Creator (aka Transformer), who, in transforming some W̱SÁNEĆ
human ancestors into islands, had thereby established a covenant between the
W̱SÁNEĆ People and the islands as kin. As Clifford says, this story "relates
to one of our laws about how to care for those islands and how those islands
are to care for us—[the islands] provide a way of life for us—and so there is
a mutual relationship and responsibility" (Plessner 2019, 2). The second story
tells of the transformation of a young W̱SÁNEĆ man into a deer (SMÍEȽ,
pronounced "smeye-eth"). This story of bodily transformation not only implicitly rejects the conceptual boundary between man and animal but also is
signified in the use of name SMÍEȽ as the name for deer in the SENĆOŦEN
language. Equally important is that the transformation of SMÍEȽ (man) into
SMÍEȽ (deer) is believed to have taken place at a specific location within
W̱SÁNEĆ territory. This information was included in the newspaper so as
to draw attention to the reality and seriousness of W̱SÁNEĆ beliefs, culture,
and politics regarding these lands. Clifford drew out an interpretation of the
story of SMÍEȽ as a reminder that life forms not only change through time,
manifesting as difference, but are also relationally dynamic and materially
and spiritually interconnected and therefore require ongoing attention and review, depending on need. We learn that within W̱SÁNEĆ law it is understood
that human-nonhuman relationships are inherently reciprocal and temporal
and necessitate ongoing awareness, respect, and attention. W̱SÁNEĆ laws
and governance, then, are understood as implicitly relational, spirited, and

dialogical and widely differ from codified directives (case law) founded on notions of ownership of land where more-than-human beings are seen as resources or property. In the interview Clifford elaborates on the centrality of this cosmological story as an educational and orientational tool for cognizing not only the principle of ethicopolitical reciprocal responsibilities to other beings within W̱SÁNEĆ law but the fact that these storied laws are actions (i.e., implicit duties that require one to act). As he says,

> If we asked ourselves, "what do these stories do?" I think that what these stories are always doing is pointing us beyond the story in itself to a particular relationship, relationships that we always need to embody, engage with and continually work through. . . . These stories acculturate you to a relationship with islands (and deer etc.). And then *the actual learning really comes from the doing side of things*. That is, these stories are not simply a set of "ideas". I mean obviously you have to understand it in your mind as well, but you don't just know it in your mind—that is not what it's about. It's about knowing it on a deeper level as well, . . . internalizing it and allowing that to shape the way that you act on a day to day basis, how you enter into relationships with other things and how you orient yourself (Plessner 2019, 8).

The intervention therefore called upon residents (1) to reimagine their relationship to the island and see it as an agential being with needs and abilities, in addition to seeing it and all other more-than-human residents as kin relations; (2) to critique hegemonic (colonial) attitudes and treatments of land as material substances and in turn resources" (3) to question again their understanding of ownership of land that is codified and legitimated (in common law) through "use" of land; and (4) to begin the process of thinking through how nonhuman beings can be members of the political community, at least in principle.

In troubling sedimented assumptions about political membership as solely human, this intervention was again an act of citizenship in that it publicly problematized normative assumptions about relations to place. Specifically, in directly addressing residents, it asked them to "orient" themselves to an understanding of the island as not simply a collection of rocks and soil and trees or a bit of property that they own but as a nonhuman being and ancestral kin of the W̱SÁNEĆ People. The intervention thereby carved out a space for new relationships with members of the W̱SÁNEĆ community, based on reorienting oneself to their laws from *within* their unceded territory. In this way, the intervention embodies and practices a new mode of (nonstatist) membership that is immanent. As an act of citizenship it too shapes "how you enter into relationships with other things and how you orient yourself" (Plessner 2019, 8, quoting Clifford). That is, not only is the newspaper intervention a witness to W̱SÁNEĆ positionality, but also, as a performative act, it is responsive to the tacit but otherwise binding demands on those of us living within their territory to uphold and enact their laws. As Clifford says within the pages of the newspaper, "Our laws . . . require us to act and to protect our homelands and the other beings that are within it, the islands, the salmon, the whales, the water, and much, much more. . . . It is a positive obligation within our W̱SÁNEĆ Law" (Plessner 2019, 2). This obligation to act (i.e., reorient oneself and behave differently) is precisely what the interventions embody. They therefore introduced and extended W̱SÁNEĆ ethicopolitical responsibilities to island residents not only by drawing them into my conversation with Clifford but also through retellings of cosmological stories (transcribed from some of my interviews with elders or selected from publications) to gain an affective appreciation of trees, fish, deer, islands, and so forth, as agential bodies that are "ends in themselves"—that is, entitled to live their lives in the ways that they need to live (Korsgaard 2018) and "free from harm" (Plessner 2019, 2, quoting Clifford).

I reasoned that by homing in on the notion of kinship, island residents might grasp the moral import of Clifford's conversation and check (i.e., review) their own sentiments of owning land and belonging to the island against the reframing of the island and other more-than-human beings as co-residents entitled to live their lives unharmed by settler practices. However, my wider aim was to challenge assumptions about political membership as solely human, and this required wedging open commonplace notions of land as a resource. It also required that the newspaper refer back to the first intervention, so as to pick up on the problems of proprietorial attitudes and behaviors that are rooted in assumptions about owning land, as well as to further expose the normalization of British imperial orientations and practices that not only harm (and have destroyed) the lives of nonhuman beings on the island but also continue to undermine W̱SÁNEĆ positionalities. On the front page of *CA News: Kinship*, I titled the problem "Rethinking 'Resources': Understanding Trees, Fish and Deer as Kin" and framed it in the following way:

> This newspaper follows on from a previous publication called *Citizen Artist News: Clouded Title* that was distributed on Pender Island in the summer of 2018. . . . It takes the discussion of the Douglas Treaty one step further. Enshrined in the Treaty are the rights of the W̱SÁNEĆ to "hunt and fish as formerly." But what exactly does this mean? Hunting and fishing are clearly actions; to say someone has a "right" to perform an action is to say that they can access and legally "do" that thing within a terrain. But it also suggests that they can "use" that terrain in a specified way: they can claim what is "taken" (e.g., trees, fish and animals etc.) as their (personal) legal "property." So, the colonial interpretation of the Treaty actually makes two claims: (1) about the purported

"ownership" of land as State "property" (that in turn sanctions "ownership" of "private" property) and (2) about the "use" of land and its animals as "property." Implicit in this colonial orientation of seeing land and what one "uses" as "property," is the idea that other forms of (non-human) life are *material "resources."* This conception of non-human beings as material "resources" and as bodies to be "managed" (reproduced or killed etc.) for human "use," desire and/or industry, profoundly shapes (indeed, skews) how we live with non-human beings on a daily basis. It also deeply impacts on the well-being and *survival* of non-human beings (e.g., trees, fish, deer etc.) on the island as their lives and habitat continue to be threatened, degraded or wholly destroyed. With this in mind, readers are invited to reimagine non-human beings, such as islands, trees, fish and deer, not as "resources" or bodies to be "managed," cut down, culled, or manipulated to make way for human desires (suburban development, leisure and tourist activities etc.). Instead, the aim here is to see the island anew: to explore how humans and non-humans are bodily and familially *connected* and to consider what this entails for living *with* rather than *on* the island. To help us think through this complex shift in perspective, the newspaper therefore explores a few WSÁNEĆ cosmological stories that describe non-human beings as human *relatives* and importantly, as *kin* relations. Seeing islands, trees, fish and deer (among other things) as relatives uniquely entangles us in rethinking how and what we do to the beings on and of the island. (Plessner 2019, 1)

This opened the way for a discussion with Clifford about how the cosmological stories draw out the nature of human-nonhuman relations as an aesthetic relationship (i.e., involving sensed and affective experiences) and what this entails for conceptualizing more-than-human entities as members of the political community. In my view, these transformation stories show island residents that "bodily changes . . . [inform the] scope of kinship relations [to nonhuman beings . . . and thereby] truly *embody* relations to place" (Plessner 2019, 3). I go on to say, "I do not see these stories as simply stories but as important aesthetic experiences" (3). The intervention therefore had a deliberate subversive dimension to it in that, as a tool for doing politics, it highlighted the sophistication of WSÁNEĆ perspectives on kinship and made apparent the ethical and political demands that flow from regarding the island and other beings as kin, thereby tacitly charging island residents with a responsibility to care for the (is)land. For island residents who thought carefully about Clifford's discussion, the profoundly different aesthetic orientations to land in play here would also have become apparent. It is necessary to explain this in more detail and demonstrate how *CA News: Kinship* was a critique of the roots of British colonial notions of land use, first introduced in *Clouded Title*. The following will therefore give an overview of the whole discussion to show how this second citizen art intervention does politics in challenging residents to consider the aesthetics of colonial dominion, expressed through suburban cultivation (lawns, fences, etc.), "cleaning" and grooming of the land, farming, and so forth. This was done to draw attention to the visuality of the material conditions of the island as a particular British colonial setting and to evidence how (British) colonial aesthetic tastes and treatments of land continue to shape the material conditions of the affective and performative dimension of belonging and membership.

In *Clouded Title*, I went to some length to outline the Lockean argument for the appropriation of First Peoples' lands based on use of land via one's labor. I will discuss this in some detail to show how citizen art interventions mapped some of the convergences between colonial ways of "seeing" land as a resource to be "used" and the resultant problematic outcomes.

> In his chapter on property (*Second Treatise*, Ch. 5, ss 25–51, 123–26) Locke offers a narrative on how one can "rightfully" claim a "thing" to be the property of an individual. He argues that "there must of necessity be a means *to appropriate*" what one removes from the commons (the commons, as he describes it, is the Earth and all that it offers that was given to all human beings by God). To *justify* what one has taken that is not, in and of itself, one's own, Locke constructs an argument that builds on the premise that one "owns" one's own body. From this he infers that "the *Labour* of his Body and the *Work* of his Hands, we may say, are properly his." That is, because one owns one's own body it follows logically that one owns whatever results from the "work of one's hands," i.e., one's labour. He then claims that whatever one removes from the State of Nature and has "mixed his *Labour* with" has, by extension, made (i.e., produced) the thing that was taken into his own and consequently, "owns" (has a "right" to) that "property." (Plessner 2018, 7)

In contrast to W̱SÁNEĆ descriptions of islands as ancestral kin, these bodily activities of "working" and "mixing" land with one's hands (removing it from the commons) and laboring with the materials of the earth, tilling soil, and so forth, reveal an important dimension of colonial aesthetic, sensory experiences of land (the esthesis of physical labor). The tacit assumption within John Locke's argument is that the "right of 'mixing' soil (earth)" prevails and is metaphorically instantiated here through an individual's (agrarian) manipulation and "improvement" of "earth"/nature (understood as a *moral* improvement, according to Mackey 2016). However, what stands out in Locke's argument but is not discussed (either in Locke or in authors such as Mackey 2016), is the aesthetic (i.e., visual, sensory, and affective) dimension of this act of mixing the earth that also signals possession and entitlement. I make it clear within the contents of *Clouded Title* that settler attitudes to owning land are rooted in a problematic presupposition in Locke's argument: that one has to manipulate the earth's materials with one's body and, indeed, *embody* the land for the claim of possession to be valid and to *legitimize* one's presence and membership within the suprastructure of the state.

It is important to draw attention to these slippages in the Lockean narrative here to emphasize the import of the *CA News: Kinship* intervention as a political tool for exposing how settler aesthetics (sensory and sentient experience) entrenches self-justifying sentiments of claiming (unceded) lands as one's own. In the newspaper, I show how "improving" land (Locke 1823, §32) dubiously frames assumptions about rights to the possession and dominion over land as one's private property. Mapping the slippery inferences in Locke's argument further troubles residents' affective attachment to their own *private* property, expressed and justified through the manipulation and curation of land (treated as a malleable substance). These aesthetic practices are not simply constitutive of claim making but also determine how a terrain looks, further inscribing beliefs about entitlement to land, especially among island settlers of British ancestry who dominate the social, political, and cultural life of the island and, in turn, the visual display of colonial habitation (e.g., suburban features such as hedges, lawns and fences, cultivated gardens, introduction of invasive species of plants from the United Kingdom, farmlands, and so forth).

Author Eva Mackey valuably adds to an understanding of the implications of British Canadian colonial treatments of land by drawing attention to the cultural specificity of British moralistic attitudes toward agrarian practices that, in turn, inform racist perceptions of Indigenous people encoded in the Canadian state. This is important for seeing the real force of the *CA News: Kinship* intervention and its challenge to the aesthetic culture of the island, dominated as it is by British colonial imaginaries. She argues that British Canadian treatments of land carry a moral imperative that manifests in attitudes to land as requiring "improvement" (Mackey 2016). As she says, "God, in Locke's voice, mandates that improving, productive labour is the key to entitlement to property. So mandated, colonizers felt the entitlement, even the duty, to appropriate, enclose, develop, and 'subdue' the (purportedly) vacant lands of America that were regarded as lying to waste by the inhabitants, who were seen as 'actively neglecting' the land" (50). She notes that "British colonizers conceptualized and legitimized their colonial process through images of 'planting' . . . [and agrarian techniques of] 'husbandry' [in comparison to] Spanish colonizers' images of 'conquest'" (50). The English in particular "engaged in 'turf and twig' ceremonies that stemmed from sixteenth century gardening rhetoric, land ownership practices and fertility rituals" (51). This manifested in marking individual territory through "building a dwelling, planting a hedge around fields [i.e., fencing], or an activity demonstrating use of (or intent to use., i.e., clearing) the land. . . . [These] markers . . . signified private ownership of land . . . and private property" (51). According to

Mackey, these practices of enclosure and planting, based on "subduing" and "replenishing" the soil, are specific to British agriculture and are strikingly at odds with not only other modes of colonial subjugation by other imperial powers (e.g., Spain and France) but also clearly indigenous orientations to land. However, as I suggested previously, claim making, as enacted through planting and bordering a terrain (e.g., hedges, lawns, fences), is also a formal, visual, aesthetic display of British colonization, widely practiced in the treatment of property on Pender Island. The aesthetic display of colonial habitation is another example of the "distribution of the sensible" (Rancière 2004, 2011b) in that British colonial ways of *seeing* and *curating* land are explicitly privileged. One can come to understand how, as discussed previously and throughout *CA News: Kinship*, the perception of land as a vibrant, nonhuman being with agency is so profoundly antithetical to the materialism of British settlers. As Mackey says,

> Colonizers saw such outsiders to the improvement process as less than human beings. Native Americans, having "failed to subdue the earth" and having "given themselves up to nature, and to passivity" . . . became, conceptually and legally, "wandering nomads" [on seemingly vacant lands]. . . . In this way, culturally specific ideas about property, labour, personhood and morality . . . [created] differential categories of social being, cultural belonging and political authority. Ideas about property and rights, tied as they were to notions of "improving labour," were used by these colonizers to entitle themselves to appropriate the land and continue to define Indigenous peoples as savages. In other words, Indigenous peoples were defined as savages because they did not know how to own land in a possessively individualistic way that European [and specifically British] colonizers defined as proper. As such, their inability (or unwillingness) to control land was interpreted to mean that they needed to be under the control of colonizing, sovereign, settler subjects. Ultimately then, ideas about property and personhood were (and continue to be) intimately connected, as legitimating strategies for ongoing colonization. (53)

I would add that although Mackey (and Locke) had not emphasized the aesthetic dimension of the improvement of land or the affective and sensory experiences of even tilling soil, aesthetic (sensory) experiences of place nevertheless underpin the emotional dimension of claiming land as "one's own property." These aesthetic sensibilities also tacitly reinforce the primacy of the colonial state. Indeed, a lacuna at the heart of Locke's argument has implications for the (assumed) validity of status citizenship that flows from aesthetic orientations to land. I would argue that the entwining of the aesthetic (sensory and affective) experience of manipulating earth/soil and bodily labor with possessing property (including what Mackey describes as the valorization of agrarian labor as the basis for colonial imaginaries of socially located, individual personhood[6]) suggests that membership—its perpetually incipient character—is formed through and founded on affective experiences and the aesthetic discernment of people living within a terrain. In weighing up these differences, the subtext of *CA News: Kinship* shows that colonial orientations to land—especially the aesthetic underpinnings of belonging, membership, and statehood—are *not* more coherent than ancestral kinship relations to (is)lands, as seen in the W̱SÁNEĆ creation stories discussed. These newspaper interventions therefore do politics by pushing back on colonial norms and rhetoric by demonstrating that W̱SÁNEĆ kinship relations are a cogent foundation for engagement with the (is)lands (and other nonhuman beings) as members of the political community as well as for sovereignty and governance.

Indeed, the centrality of aesthetic experiences of (is)lands and waterways is discussed in Tsawout First Nation's (2015) critique of the Kinder Morgan Pipeline Trans Mountain Expansion. Their analysis of the potential harm of the industrialization of their waterways details not only significant damage to their fishing and harvesting grounds and the forms of life that exist within them (this also in practice further undermines the terms of the Douglas Treaty and W̱SÁNEĆ rights to "hunt and fish as formerly"; Plessner 2018, 2) but also negativly impacts on the "aesthetic, visual, and sensory experiences of harvesting"—the basis of relations to land in all its vibrant, animate forms (Tsawout First Nation 2015, 10, 125). As Clifford says in *CA News: Kinship*, human-nonhuman relationships pivot on "the intentions one brings to say, harvesting, but part of those intentions . . . influence the being that you are in a relationship with [i.e.,] it might be that [a] plant or animal knows that you can be harmful to the relationship" (Plessner 2019, 8). In other words, awareness of and respect for sentient experiences of other beings establishes (reciprocal) relationships with more-than-humans as agential members of a community. Equally important are references to the spiritual dimension of connectedness to the water, (is)lands, and other nonhuman beings and animals that also yields an aesthetic experience of place that is relational and predicates a form of political membership that is responsive and responsible. "The same land has spiritual power distributed throughout in a variety of ways. This power could be quested for and obtained. The acquisition of this power often resulted in the accumulation of more food, which was therefore sacred. The acquisition of food had a spiritual side to it, which could not be easily separated from its practical side" (Tsawout First Nation 2015, 34). In other words, "First Ancestors and other powerful beings are inscribed in the landscape through legends that describe the creation of the landscape's features by the mythic acts of a powerful Transformer (sometimes glossed in English . . . as the Creator) and through the powers of these ancestors and other beings of the spirit world that continue to be recalled and experienced in these places" (Plessner 2018, 4).

I draw attention to these differing aesthetic dimensions of relations to land to demonstrate the constraints of a (status) citizenship regime: It is not necessarily abstract legal rights and principles that animate the experience of belonging and membership but the aesthetic experiences of people either laboring over and curating the landscape, (allegedly) "improving" the earth beneath their feet, or by comparison, one's corelational and embodied kinship with (is)lands and nonhuman and animal beings, indeed, glossed as being "owned by the land" (Tsawout First Nation 2015, 23), that speaks to the nature of citizenship as perpetually formed and reformed through aesthetic engagements with place. This is where we see how the politics of aesthetics play out within a locale. Rancière's discussion of the distribution of the sensible is again valuable here. In addition to the partitioning of peoples through the practices of the state's status citizenship regime (as discussed at length in chapter 5), aesthetic treatments of land also frame who and what is visible within a political arena. My point here is that the tangible effects of Canada's silent apartheid also manifest through colonial aesthetic treatments of land within the rubric of the nation-state. Indeed, colonial orientations to land *dominate* the material culture of a locale and the visuality of a civic space. By contrast, Indigenous presence on the land and within a territory is not reducible to materialist assumptions about demonstrable use and dominion *over* land, nor is it inscribed through grooming, curating, or landscaping and so on, as an expression of moral righteousness (Mackey). Instead, the W̱SÁNEĆ describe their habitation and, in turn, civic spaces as implicitly *relational* and constituted of collective kinship "knots," or groupings, where a seasonal, temporal, and mobile system of stewardship predominates in relation to specific sites of familial, economic (livelihood), and spiritual activity. Indeed, specific roles and responsibilities of harvesting, fishing, and so forth, of individual families not only are foundational to the servicing of the community as whole but also constitute the basis of W̱SÁNEĆ markers of presence and place (Tsawout First Nation 2015; Elliott 1990; Paul et al. 1995; Claxton 2003). As Nick Claxton, a member of the W̱SÁNEĆ Nation, says of reef-net fishing sites in particular, "The relationship between families and their reef-net sites is better understood as families *belonging* to their sites" (Tsawout First Nation 2015, 37). However, this description of belonging is not simply a material reality in the way that settler inhabitants of, say, Pender Island might claim to belong to such and such a place in virtue of one's family's ownership of property or having "improved" the land through farming or suburban or other forms of land development. Instead, the kind of belonging that informs and marks out the political and, indeed, the territorial space of the W̱SÁNEĆ is described as gifts of the ancestors and spirits. In the example of reef-net sites, not only do individual family groups inherit rights and responsibilities to (care for) specific fishing sites (called A SWÁLET in SENĆOŦEN; Elliott 1990), but "spirits and their corresponding powers and abilities could also be inherited. . . . [A] fisherman with [an inherited] spirit that bestowed an ability to fish, might not only pass down his spirit and a corresponding prowess related to fishing within his family, but, thereby his role and function within the community too" (Tsawout Nation 2015, 35). Thus, there is "a pattern of roles performed exclusively by members of specific families. . . . [F]or generations one family has held an exclusive responsibility for providing marine foods for Tsawout community functions, another for providing ducks for longhouse ceremonies, and another for tending the fires in the longhouse," and so forth (35). W̱SÁNEĆ political organization and presence through time within a terrain is performed not through altering or cultivating land but through modes of conduct that include enacting responsibilities within the human and more-than-human community. In the newspaper, I draw attention to the nuances of kinship relations and territorial rights and responsibilities by quoting Brian Thom (2009).

> Relations with these ancestral figures requires reciprocity, sharing and respect for other persons, both human and non-human, who are associated with place. They reinforce kin-based property relations, when the land at once belongs to the ancestors who dwell there, and to those living today who encounter the ancestors. The kin-based properties in this land-tenure system map out on the land in complex, multi-faceted ways. Not every named place is owned by kin groups. Ancestors may be associated with lands in numerous locations and individuals associating with these ancestors may enjoy property rights in a number of places. These associations with ancestors reveal a network of places in the region that an individual may access by virtue of their genealogy (Thom 2009, 185–186). (Plessner 2018, 5)

W̱SÁNEĆ relations to land, the reciprocal responsibilities that are entailed by the layered and nuanced relationships to place, and the laws and governance that are entwined with aesthetic, spirit, and ancestral relations to non-human and animal beings are profoundly distinct from colonial imaginaries and the regimes of the Crown, Canadian courts, and the common law. The aesthetic dimension of relations to land and what it can mean for better understanding the affective, perceptive, and substantive foundations of belonging and membership are closed down in colonial logics (as evident in Locke's argument) by an insistence on and, indeed, a valorization of proprietorship and exploitation. Conversely, W̱SÁNEĆ perspectives, even though much disrupted by the effects of colonialism, involve an interweaving of aesthetic and spiritual experiences of place, captured in cosmological stories that inform protocols and organizational roles and structure membership, law, and governance. Political membership therefore is characteristically generative, dynamic, and dialogical and expanded to include all forms of life, *in practice*. It is determined through ongoing aesthetic relations with land as kin, under-pinned by ethicopolitical compacts of reciprocal duties. Importantly, too, it is open to new and changing relationships to bodies of all kind, rather than contingent on statuses determined by dominion over bounded jurisdictions or bordered terrain.

In sum: Scoping out the possibilities for new relationships, new under-standings, and new modes of membership is a pressing matter in the context of residing on the lands of First Nations Peoples. I have argued that these citizen art interventions are responsive to the differential effects of the state's subtle but persistent violences, its partitioning of people, not just in the ad-ministration of its status citizenship regime but also in the distribution of the sensible (Rancière 2004)—that is, the aesthetic ordering and organization of a locale. I have argued that these interventions do politics and forge new modes of an incipient (nonstatist) citizenship by drawing out W̱SÁNEĆ perspectives that are otherwise obfuscated, marginalized, or invisible to (specifically) residents of Pender Island and within W̱SÁNEĆ territory. The newspapers instead position W̱SÁNEĆ voices as central to the realities of place and trouble assumptions about who "we" are and what "we" claim to be as members of a political community. *CA News: Kinship* therefore effected a rudimentary Copernican turn—that is, a shift in perspective—with regard to the scope and significance of political membership as extended to nonhuman actors. On an island that is dominated by (British) colonial material practices and imaginaries as normative, the intervention pushed back by foregrounding W̱SÁNEĆ conceptions and relations to the non-human world as at the center of the political community. It performed an act of citizenship in that it pub-licly acknowledged the prerogative of W̱SÁNEĆ values and law from within the community's wider territory and on the island. By detailing some of the problems and troubling hegemonic colonial rhetoric and aesthetic treatments of land, both of these citizen art interventions carve out a new civil space for the enactment of new practices of (nonstatist) membership. They not only present a robust critique of status citizenship but also practice a new mode of citizenship, one that takes seriously the binding commitment to observe the laws of the W̱SÁNEĆ People, who in turn extend political membership to other living beings as "coresidents" of the island. What remains to be discussed are the effects that these interventions had on island residents and how they have facilitated new relationships of trust and friendship with some members of the W̱SÁNEĆ Nation. The conclusion will offer a brief overview of the consequences of these two interventions and a general overview of how citizen art interventions more generally do politics in compelling and innova-tive ways and are worthy markers of new and nascent modes of membership.

NOTES

1. For evidence of the consequences of Canadian colonial orientations with regard to treatments of land, see also the work of First Nation media outlets, such as *Unreserved, Investigates, The Indigenous Café, Nation to Nation: Think Indigenous, Living Indigenous Media*, and *Indigenous Rights Movement and Aboriginal Peoples Television Network*. Also see intellectuals such as Taiaiake Alfred (2005) and activist organizations such as RAVEN Trust (https://raventrust.com).

2. Research for the newspaper was supported by a grant from the Canada Council for the Arts (Research to Creation Grant 2017).

3. Nick Claxton has argued that the treaty not only guarantees "use" but, importantly, entitles the W̱SÁNEĆ to "protect" lands and sea from "harm" (Tsawout First Nation, n.d.).

4. The term "ecocide" is under some scrutiny within legal circles (see Stop Ecocide International, n.d.) and is generally defined as the "the destruction of large areas of the natural environment as a consequence of human action" (https://www.merriam -webster.com/dictionary/ecocide).

5. Robert Clifford also presented his work to an audience during the Clouded Title Art & Research workshop held on Pender Island, April 2018. See also chapter 5, note 8, for further detail about the *Clouded Title* event.

6. According to Mackey (2016), "personhood" is "the process of how, and through what specific ideas and frameworks, socially located peoples and societies are accorded (or not) categories of social recognition, inclusion, citizenship and rights" (49).

Conclusion

In previous chapters I have described and discussed the double aspect of citizen art projects that, on the one hand, bring into view the problems and pitfalls of status citizenship regimes and the limitations of cosmopolitan imaginaries and, on the other hand, perform an incipient form of (nonstatist) citizenship through doing politics. In chapters 5 and 6, I offered a detailed explanation of two of my most recent interventions, describing how they carved out a new civil space for doing politics in such a way that confronts the silent apartheid that persists within the rural locale of Pender Island—that is, a silent apartheid that is consequent on the epistemic, material, institutional, and historical violence of occupying the unceded lands of the W̱SÁNEĆ First Nation People. I have discussed the interventions as tools for making visible and troubling British Canadian colonial habits, practices, and assumptions within the small island community, knowing that (1) the issue of the ownership of appropriated land is normalized in the manifestation and internalization of British imperial narratives of Crown entitlement to (dubiously) treated and unceded lands and (2) this also informs how political membership (status citizenship) is cognized as a solely human affair in contrast to local W̱SÁNEĆ cosmologies, laws, and principles of governance centered on reciprocal relations to human and nonhuman beings alike (Clifford 2011, 2016a, 2016b, 2019; Tsawout First Nation 2015, n.d.). I have not yet described or discussed in much detail, however, the effects that these interventions had within the locale. This conclusion will therefore provide a final reflection on the affects and effects of the interventions in the manner in which they were performed as acts of citizenship. I will also describe these aesthetic experiences as signs, or rather indicators, of a nascent mode of (nonstatist) citizenship that is only emerging in the wake of their actions.

It is necessary to first say that *Citizen Artist News: Clouded Title* and *Citizen Artist News: Kinship* do not stage transactional relationships between me as editor/artist and residents as readers. Nor do I assess the interventions in terms of any quantitative methods that might measure how the objectives of the interventions obtained, and so forth. The purpose of this analysis is not to chart the various registers of understanding and the like, as one might if this were an exercise in mapping "results." Instead, I will describe the comments, exchanges, conversations, anecdotal stories, hostilities and silences, indirect actions, and new relationships that unfolded following the interventions. That is, I will describe the aesthetic and affective dimension of the political doing that was reflected back at me, on the understanding that there are nuanced and multifaceted outcomes. The aim here is to bring the aesthetic dimension of the interventions, their effects and affects, "into view as a scene of immanent force" (Stewart 2007, 1). As Kathleen Stewart says,

> Ordinary affects are the varied, surging capacities to affect and be affected that give everyday life the quality of continual motion of relations, scenes, contingencies, and emergences . . . [T]hey happen in impulses, sensations, expectations, daydreams, encounters, and habits of relating, in strategies and their failures, in forms of persuasion, contagion, and compulsion, in modes of attention, attachment, and agency, and in publics and social worlds of all kinds that catch people up in something that feels like *some*thing. (2)

With this in mind, this chapter will describe how and why the newspapers were designed and disseminated in the way that they were and the effects that they had in provoking residents and facilitating new relationships among me, some members of the W̱SÁNEĆ First Nation, and some of the island residents and beyond. Woven into this description is a discussion of the implications of the interventions as acts of citizenship. It is important to say again too that these interventions as acts are not singular events per se. As noted in previous chapters, the interventions were launched eighteen months apart and were intended to build on one another, so their effects, although multiple and various, continue to surface in unanticipated ways, even during the writing of this book. Equally, as creative tools, the interventions are not closed off in their execution and not only have established a foundation for forthcoming (newspaper) interventions but also have been folded into a current art project, the Tree Museum (www.tree-museum.com), that expands on the political doing that is so vital to exploring and enacting new modes of citizenship within the locale. However, for the purposes of brevity, the following discussion will limit its summary to a discussion of the two newspaper interventions so as to focus on what has been learned through their practice. I will also discuss each one in turn so as to convey how these acts of citizenship continue to expose and disrupt settler-colonial norms and practices through time.

In my unmediated (or, rather, self-media) address, indeed request, to take part in a public thought experiment, the interventions certainly made demands on island residents to engage in an act of thinking anew about who lives within the unceded territory of the W̱SÁNEĆ People and how. By soliciting residents to act (i.e., to fulfill the invitation that was directed at them), I gambled that the interventions would enclose residents in a kind of mini social contract akin to a performative utterance (Austin 1975), and this did happen. The interventions established an unarticulated, but nevertheless important, performative, tacit contract between me and island residents, prompting and concentrating a moment of public attention on the reality of occupying unceded lands and making claims to belonging and being a member of "here." The interventions thereby transformed the field of political action. The fact that the newspapers were produced by me (one individual artist and fellow resident), rather than a local councilor, community organizer, or organization, upended assumed positions of authority and local political hierarchies (to be discussed further). Equally disruptive was the fact that the contents of the newspapers did not present my own opinions or views, even though the editing was clearly biased in my selection of the writings of W̱SÁNEĆ (and other First Nations) authors and included my own voice in interviews with elders and experts. However, in *Clouded Title* this partiality (of mine as the editor/artist) was tempered by the newspaper as conveying "news." News, here, was instead a recirculation of the facts of research in the assemblage of quotations of local W̱SÁNEĆ and other First Nations (academic) authors so as to verify and evidence the telling of an alternative political history of the locale. I stress here again that the newspaper did not represent the W̱SÁNEĆ People but recirculated what had already been said by numerous authors but had not been heard, let alone heeded, within the local community of Pender Island. The myriad citations and quotations had the effect of breaking the "self-evidence" of local settler "doxa" (Bourdieu 2008, 278). It also did what Pierre Bourdieu (2008) had himself experimented with in his own interventions: He presented "research" or "expertise" (in my case, the work of W̱SÁNEĆ and other Indigenous authors) within a popular medium rather than remaining restricted to academic spaces of discourse.[1] By comparison, these interventions hijacked the newsprint medium and the conventional aesthetic display of objective stories for the purposes of presenting a detailed, extensive, and complex exposé on the internal workings of the nascent colonial state in the making of a treaty that, as I have argued in previous chapters, continues to skew local settler and W̱SÁNEĆ relationships and understandings of the island as the unceded territory of the W̱SÁNEĆ People.

As a political act then, these citizen art newspapers "make visible what was hidden in the customary perceptions of the social world" (273), as well as the material world, at a local and personal level.

The newspapers also proved to be an effective tool for doing politics in the manner of their dissemination. As mentioned in chapters 5 and 6, printed copies of: *Clouded Title* and *Kinship* were delivered by post to the private homes of permanent residents (i.e., people who live year-round) on the small island of Pender (approximately 820 homes in total in 2017–2018) and were also made available at a newsstand in the local supermarket (a hub of island life). It was important to the execution of these interventions that copies were sent to individual resident's homes for several reasons. First, I wanted people to handle the newspapers as tangible objects in the spaces of their homes. Although the newspapers reference the design of a broadsheet newspaper, they nevertheless do not look like an ordinary newspaper. Each is unique, and in my estimation the aesthetic experience of the objects (handling them, viewing their specialist design, seeing them in relation to other objects, in short, their formal and sensed aesthetic features) also informs how the artifacts are cognized as an intervention within the private spaces and lives of people. As an object, each newspaper demanded attention. They had to be touched, opened, looked at, puzzled over, read or not read, kept or thrown away—that is, they required some form of cognizance and discrimination. Second, I wanted to take advantage of the postal services as a novel infrastructure for communicating with residents. I ventured that in being delivered to their own homes, the oddness of this solicitation would also create an element of surprise and focus the attention of at least some residents. I gambled that this might entice people to then engage with the newspapers' informationally rich, complex, and provocative contents.

Third, I needed to intervene in the conversations that were in circulation through the social and cultural gatherings that had been orchestrated by some of the island's residents (a church group and a historical society), who had staged events on the subject of reconciliation following the publication of the report of the Truth and Reconciliation Commission (TRC) (as described in chapter 5). These discussions among local residents focused on grappling with the TRC's potent description of state and settler crimes perpetrated through the residential school system. However, these discourses lacked an examination of specifically British settler occupation (going back to the first Scottish and English farmers and the lack of disclosure about how they acquired their property) as a source of epistemic violence that continues to be performed and inscribed within local colonial fictions of belonging and entitlement. That is, no one directed attention to their own (family's) appropriation of land or acknowledged that the state's policing of First Nations

Peoples (e.g., residential schools, incarceration on reserves) facilitated their claims to purportedly owning unceded land. Nor did residents question the construction of a local history of British colonization as a purportedly benign act of occupation, narrated as a virtuous moment in a "Canadian" origin story. Hence, the epistemic violence of place was being reinscribed in the moment of these local emotional adjustments to the TRC's report.

The first intervention, *Clouded Title*, therefore commenced a challenge to the comfort and satisfaction of residents in performing themselves as good citizens with statuses subtended by the ownership of appropriated land. *Kinship* followed up on and extended this challenge. I need to expand on this point at some length so as to draw out the full import of what is in play here regarding the aesthetic and affective culture of the island and the intensity of its British colonial underpinnings. One striking feature of local (and indeed regional) sociopolitical culture is the propensity of people to frame their public behaviors as showing them to be "good" Canadians. There is, without doubt, a deeply engrained impulse not only to personalize but also to moralize about one's (public) actions as always rooted in being "good." In my own experience, I have always found this oddly perverse, and throughout my life this frequent turn to announce one's sense of personal goodness has caused me untold moments of frustration when initiating conversationally critical work to unpack the legacy of violence here. It is a standard response to any attempt to assess the ubiquity of British colonial markers of presence inscribed on the (is)land locally and in the province of British Columbia (e.g., place names, monuments, state insignias, aesthetic treatments of land) as a material infrastructure or to point out the dominance of actors of Scotts, English, Welsh, or Scotts-Irish ethnicity in local and provincial government or in managerial roles in educational spaces, industry, and property development, or to question the possession of large landholdings on the island by early British settlers, and so forth. I now see this propensity to moralize as part of the legacy of the British imperial project and its disciplinary regime. The way in which Canadians recoil from discussions about the violence of specifically British colonialism, I would argue, is an expression of an individual's British-colonial subjecthood. It is not, as other authors would claim, an expression of "white fragility" (Robinson 2020, 19). Claims to be good, in my observation, are (usually) uttered by people whose ethnicity is rooted in the United Kingdom (Scotts, English, Welsh, Scotts-Irish, or a mixture thereof). Such claims are a way of saying that one has been good at (i.e., obedient to) being disciplined and modeled as a British Canadian colonial subject. I say this too because of the lack of cognizance of the tacit and disciplinary ethnic micro-racisms that persist in interpersonal exchanges and the prevalence of reductive political vocabularies that obfuscate, suppress, or wholly erase the complexities of peoples' ethnic histories, if rooted elsewhere than the United Kingdom, and what this entails regarding the assimilation of divergent (including nonimperial) orientations. That is, family histories of migration as aspirational, or economically gainful, or motivated by flight from other arenas and moments of state violence—which then sometimes involved further punishment under British rule within Canada (e.g., being interned in camps, forbidden from speaking their language in schools, barred from voting) and assimilation through anglicization, and so forth—are concealed in the disciplinary ordering and structuring of citizens generally. I say this too as I encounter the re-entrenchment of colonial vocabularies that attribute behavioral and attitudinal characteristics as racially determined under the crude and simplistic nomenclature of "white," "black," or "of color." Indeed, the terms "Indigenous" and "Aboriginal" also have a totalizing effect on the plural ontologies and epistemologies of peoples of mixed lineages through intermarriages and the like, presenting a false picture of the complexities and specificities of peoples and place. Such is the success of the British imperial project in its policing and erasure of difference. Such is its success in its modeling of itself as Canadian. Being good, therefore, is to participate in and defend the normalization of a British queen "owning" all Crown land, not as personal property obviously but as an act that valorizes, reifies, and sanctions the existence of the Canadian state as a perpetually colonial enterprise that is mandated to control, occupy, and use Indigenous people's lands. Being good is to directly participate in this British Canadian colonial project by cocreating the material reality for, and giving meaning to, the possibility for performing one's sense of belonging, membership, and identity as a Canadian.

Clouded Title, therefore, sidestepped local networks of political actors and gatekeepers within the community, especially those who organize, endorse, facilitate, channel, and entrench the archetype of the British Canadian citizen through local government agencies (in the management of community activities), grassroots (historical and other) societies, and so forth. I needed to bypass local political actors who broker who can speak and how. To evidence the reality of this, on one occasion I was offered some unsolicited "advice," subtly but nonetheless pointedly, not to act independently but to follow what was already being managed by the model citizens of Pender Island. It was therefore necessary to act outside any local endorsements so as to ensure that *Clouded Title* and *Kinship* would stand apart from these social networks and not only do the work of disturbing what is seen as of political importance but also chart another path and alter who is visible as a political actor.

Fourth, I wanted to tap into the local gossip and chat that always percolates within small communities. I anticipated that perhaps one hundred residents from the 820 homes might initially read and take seriously the contents of the paper, or parts of it, and then talk about it to their friends and neighbors. In small communities, word travels fast and has deep effects on how people orient themselves within a place. I anticipated that the informal social networks would do the work of expanding and sustaining attention to the newspaper's contents.

Fifth, I was interested in not only exploring how the intervention could stage new ways of doing politics through practice but testing the possibilities of what was possible for forging a new mode of citizenship that started not from the assumption of ownership and the conferral of a state-sanctioned status but from an act. As we saw in chapter 4, the work of Tania Bruguera and Jonas Staal framed the performance of nonstatist citizenship in new and novel ways. By comparison, I was interested to explore what new relationships might manifest in the performance of this act of citizenship. What might these relationships suggest as a new way to live with the W̱SÁNEĆ People and within their territory? Can new, nonstatist practices of membership be enacted in the reworking of perceptions of place and among new assemblages of interlocutors?

For the first intervention, *Clouded Title*, not only did I post newspapers to people's homes, but I also sent some copies to a few individuals in government, including the local Green Party representatives for the Gulf Islands/Pender Island (the federal minister of Parliament and the local minister of the British Columbia Legislative Assembly) and to some individuals at the provincial courthouse to extend the "experiment" to those who constitute the apparatus of the state. Copies were also delivered to individuals at arts institutions such as the Emily Carr University of Art + Design (to faculty and the library collection), the Interference Archive in Brooklyn, New York, and the Street Road Artists' Space in Pennsylvania to ensure that some copies could be accessed within a few public archives. As described in chapter 5, one week after the initial posting, I and Emily Artinian (of Street Road) hosted a pop-up art exhibition and workshop (also called *Clouded Title*) on Pender Island that marked the formal launch of the newspaper. Approximately 150 copies of the newspaper were distributed during the event, with some visitors taking additional copies to pass on to others. Two of the event's guest speakers from Tsawout First Nation offered to distribute copies to Tsawout First Nation's band office, including to the chief and the band council and others on the reserve (approximately fifty copies). This launch concluded the first wave of the dissemination of the newspaper.

From these initial acts, the ground quickly shifted, so to speak, and the first intervention then took on a life of its own. Within a few days of its posting, out of the 820 newspapers that were delivered to private residences, twenty-three copies were immediately returned, by hand, to the post office. Members of Tsawout who distributed copies to individuals on the reserve told me that some elders were emotionally moved by the reference to the Douglas Treaty as a peace treaty, not a sale of land—reference to it as the latter has long frustrated W̱SÁNEĆ relations with the state and settlers. There was much appreciation too of the portrayal of their own history and perspectives of the land. I assumed that this response was based on the fact that the direct quotes of W̱SÁNEĆ and other First Nations authors were seen as having been re-spected and not distorted. The intervention had also taken on another dimen-sion of performativity: passages from the newspaper were read out to others by members of Tsawout Nation at local schools and during a Kairos Blanket Exercise Workshop (a public workshop that introduces non-Indigenous par-ticipants to the affective experience of having your land appropriated; Kairos 2018). I received emails and telephone calls from a local journalist and an elected member of the local branch of government (responsible for the infra-structure of the built environment such as roads). These people sought me out and quizzed me about my personal life and social connections (questions that I refused to answer). I assumed (perhaps wrongly) that they were per-turbed by the sudden presence of a new political voice in the community, and I wondered if they were scouting out ways to close down discussion of the topic because its message takes to task underlying rationales for their public authority. When I delivered copies to the local library, one of its volunteers greeted the gift with derision and did not want to include them in the col-lection. Again, I saw this as part of the intervention's success in disrupting local sensibilities and an example of the kind of gatekeeping that is enacted within local archives. (I nevertheless did leave copies on the main desk.) Alternatively, I received an email of thanks from one of the church leaders on the island who co-organized the reading circle, as mentioned previously, and a personal letter from Elizabeth May, the then leader of the Green Party and a member of Parliament, who wrote encouragingly (and with surprising specificity) of the necessity for such citizen art interventions. It was clear from her letter that she had carefully read the newspaper. She also referenced a passage from it in one of her newsletters sent to residents on the island. I was told by one island resident that they took their copy to their workplace (a government job in Vancouver) and then shared and discussed it with col-leagues. One of the interlocutors expressed surprise at First Nations People having any entitlement to the lands he was living on. Another person bluntly concurred with the literal reading of treaty as lands being "sold," asserting that this was conclusive. Some island residents had reported that they had de-tailed discussions with friends and neighbors who were shocked and ashamed by the language of the treaty and saw its phrasing as demonstrative of an inex-cusable arrogance and ignorance on the part of the British agents. Others had turned up with copies of the newspaper at a community meeting (the reading circle) hoping to have an evening set aside for the discussion of its content (which subsequently happened in June 2019). City hall, in Victoria, British Columbia, had requested copies for the mayor and all the elected members of council, having heard of the newspaper's existence through the band council offices of Tsawout First Nation. The mayor's office also asked to be sent any future editions of *Citizen Artist News*. Numerous people have thanked me in person for drawing their attention to the existence (and problems) of the treaty. They also appreciated that it was explained through detailed and thorough research, prompting deeper reflection on the dilemmas that it posed. Many commented that they found the newspaper to be an important exposé on the appropriation of, specifically, Pender Island. I also met with some hostility and alarm and have been patronized by some individuals who positioned themselves as managing reconciliation activities on the island.

It was noticeable too that, in the wake of the intervention, a local grassroots historical society had eliminated from its website references to the purported sale of land to early settlers (Pender Islands Museum 2005). Interestingly, a new website and timeline have since been constructed (replete within inaccuracies about the history of the W̱SÁNEĆ Peoples' reserve lands on the island) to narrate the island's history (http://penderislandsmuseum.ca), but again, and unsurprisingly, a British colonial history is being valorized. Random events of the nascent colonial state are set in chronological order, having the effect of aggrandizing individual British settler arrivals and their "purchases," "preemptions," or "inheritances" of land (Pender Islands Museum 2021). There is no transparency about how exactly these Scottish and English farmers actually acquired ownership of appropriated W̱SÁNEĆ lands or even why they were so motivated to make the long journey from the United Kingdom in the first place. Nor is there any mention of the actions that the nascent state undertook to privilege these British farmers, such as barring the W̱SÁNEĆ (and other First Nations) from coming to the islands by incarcerating them on the reserve and in residential schools and banning their reef-net fishing. Nor is there any mention of the policing of the W̱SÁNEĆ (and other First Nations) by Indian agents (some of whom resided on the island) employed to ensure the execution of the Indian Act and its repressive legislation, and so forth. Equally, this British colonial narrative with its tacit attempt to script a benign migration also apes ethnographic museological techniques used to historicize Indigenous peoples as but a specter of a Chalcolithic past, with more "recent" (i.e., nineteenth-century) events, such as the Douglas Treaties, inaccurately described as applying to the W̱SÁNEĆ People's unceded territory of Pender Island. Was this the result of an intentional misreading of *Clouded Title*? Or is it simply an example of the deflection that persists among British Canadian settlers in the moment when W̱SÁNEĆ voices and counternarratives become visible and begin to circulate? I noticed too that following the intervention, descriptions of the history of Pender Island on Wikipedia had been modified to include mention of Coast Salish Peoples (Wikipedia, n.d.d) but, again, no mention of any of the past or current violence of colonial appropriation.

Some island residents and also some readers wider afield (such as members of faculty at Emily Carr University of Art + Design) reported that they had to spend time reading the newspaper, to think through the complexity of the internal arguments presented in each footnote and, having done so, found it to be emotionally demanding and a challenge to their own understandings and assumptions. One island resident reported that they carefully read it twice so as to fully digest its various points. Others have said that they struggled with it, finding its contents too demanding. I was told by one island resident, who is a descendant of one of the early British farming families, that her father was annoyed and that she spent time talking him through it. No further information was offered about what was discussed. I can only speculate that it was a difficult conversation for them. Some confided that they hadn't read it all. This again was evidence of the contractual dimension of the intervention and its efficacy in doing politics. That is, these readers had obviously read enough of the newspaper to feel the burden of the obligation of its request to engage in the experiment. I see the confession of nonengagement as a direct withdrawal from the intervention's tacit mini social contract.

In the months that followed, some friends and neighbors introduced me to people as the artist who created the newspaper. It obviously was being widely talked about, and on one occasion a woman told me that she was struck by the "oddness" of it when she received it in the post. She hadn't read it but had put it away to read on another occasion. This tallied with my impression that perhaps more people than I expected had, at least, kept hold of their copy. I kept loose tabs on the number of papers being discarded at the recycling center on the island (the main hub for processing waste packaging and printed matter), asking staff to put aside any copies that they saw. Approximately fifteen copies were collected and returned to me over a period of three months. Wider afield, a friend who was a law student at the University of Victoria (and who is also First Nations) presented it to colleagues and faculty for discussion in class. She then asked for a digital copy so that she could distribute it to others. Street Road Artists Space (Pennsylvania) included it in numerous public events and exhibition openings throughout 2018 and 2019 (see Street Road 2018), including scheduling a day of discussion in August 2019 to draw out and trouble Street Road's own presence on the lands of the Lenape People. It has also been the subject of Skype/Zoom discussions among me, Emily Artinian, and Street Road's visitors in the continuance of the *Clouded Title* project (Street Road 2018). And requests for copies continue through email or face to face.

In short, it is no exaggeration to claim that this first newspaper and its invitation to participate in a thought experiment had entered into the bloodstream of the local community and even reached others beyond the island. It also deepened my personal relationships of trust with friends from Tsawout First Nation—relationships that I highly value because of what they hold as possibilities for new modes of belonging and membership within their territory, potentially centered on W̱SÁNEĆ laws and governance but also, importantly, from a position of "recognition" of what lies between us in the inescapable reality of colonial violence. From this first intervention, there was also a flourishing of new relationships with other members of the W̱SÁNEĆ community living on the reserve. I was asked to join an organizing committee hosted by the band office for a rally in support of Tsawout Nation's land claim ("Paddle for ȽEL,ŦOS" 2018). Again, I was introduced to people as the artist responsible for the newspaper and asked to share copies with those involved in the meetings. This smoothed the way for me and two colleagues[2] to produce a short film in support of the rally (Ibid.) that involved interviewing elders on the reserve. I also felt a sense of confidence, too, to reach out again to Robert Clifford, who spoke (via phone) at the launch of *Clouded Title* workshop on Pender, to interview him and explore further the notion of kinship relations to nonhuman actors as expressed in W̱SÁNEĆ culture and law.

With *Clouded Title* in circulation, I was able to press ahead with preparations for the second intervention, *Kinship*, which had been set in motion eight months earlier, having secured funding for a collaboration with the artist Doug LaFortune (supported by a Research to Creation Grant funded by the Canada Council for the Arts), who lives on the reserve at Tsawout. Initially, we did not plan a newspaper per se, and in the early phases of the project, we were both excited to develop artwork with the aim of disseminating printed matter to residents' homes on Pender Island, on the reserve, and wider afield. We were also excited to do the work of exploring the issue of kinship to more-than-human beings by focusing on the divergent aesthetic and affective relations to "trees, fish and deer" as signifiers within both colonial and W̱SÁNEĆ culture. Over the course of two years (2017–2019), Doug, his wife Kathy, and I met frequently, and they were extraordinarily generous (and brave, given my skin color and all that that represented) in inviting me into their home to discuss, plan, and organize the intervention, including two 1-day land-based workshops (i.e., holding our meetings at sites of significance within W̱SÁNEĆ territory). This involved us in working with other elders from Tsawout and some of the island's settler-residents. These occasions and our numerous meetings at the LaFortune home not only afforded opportunities to ground Doug's and my work but also enriched our new friendship and created space for us to talk about the various registers of colonial violence that lay between us. Our relationship further vivified (for me) what I had learned through previous research and discussions and also gave depth and new meaning to the value of the intervention itself. These encounters also afforded an opportunity to experience the protocols and aesthetic tenor of the community and made palpable the real effects of the state's partitioning of people. At times it felt as if I were passing through a vibrating, dense wall on the border of the reserve—Tsawout's ancient winter village—and the colonial state, with each side pulsating at different speeds, encompassing different logics and realities of place.

As the project progressed, it became apparent that the newspaper was an appropriate format for handling the complexity of the topic and for anchoring W̱SÁNEĆ voices as audible and visible within "this" place and "now." And it did prove to be an important material support for expanding and instantiating W̱SÁNEĆ presence and perspectives on the island and within the community's wider territory. I will discuss this point further. With regard to the design of the newspaper, my interview with Clifford proved to be a cornerstone of the publication and helped to structure the visual arrangement of the newspaper's contents, where the placement of images and text could activate cross readings, leaving readers to digest and discover its layered meanings. The final assemblage of content featured Doug's illustrations, which further illuminated the interview with Clifford and a selection of cosmological stories about transformations of human ancestors into trees, salmon, and deer told by Elder Earl Claxton Jr. and other W̱SÁNEĆ speakers (the latter reprinted from a collection of published W̱SÁNEĆ stories [Richling 2016]). The back page and center spread of the newspaper featured Doug's imagery, but doubled up as large, interactive posters (see figures 7.1 and 7.2), so as to break the framing of the newspaper's format and prompt people to read across, through, and (literally) around its pages. The aim was to increase people's handling of the newspaper and make it as multifunctional as possible, so as to encourage using the posters in other contexts, if they so wished. The result was a magnificent, visually compelling, and intellectually provocative artwork that we were all proud to put into circulation and share with others living in W̱SÁNEĆ territory.

I launched the newspaper at the end of September 2019 and followed the same distribution strategies as with the first intervention. Copies were posted to resident's homes on Pender, placed in the newsstand at the local supermarket and Tsawout Nation's band office, and sent to members of the provincial legislature, the mayor's office, and leaders of the Green Party. However, new venues had become available, and hundreds of copies were delivered to the

Figure 7.1. Center spread of *Citizen Artist News: Kinship* showing double-page pull-out poster (originally horizontal within the newspaper). Illustrations by Doug LaFortune, designed in collaboration with Fawn Daphne Plessner and Denise Holland, featuring the W̱SÁNEĆ story "How the People Got Salmon." *Photo courtesy of F. D. Plessner*

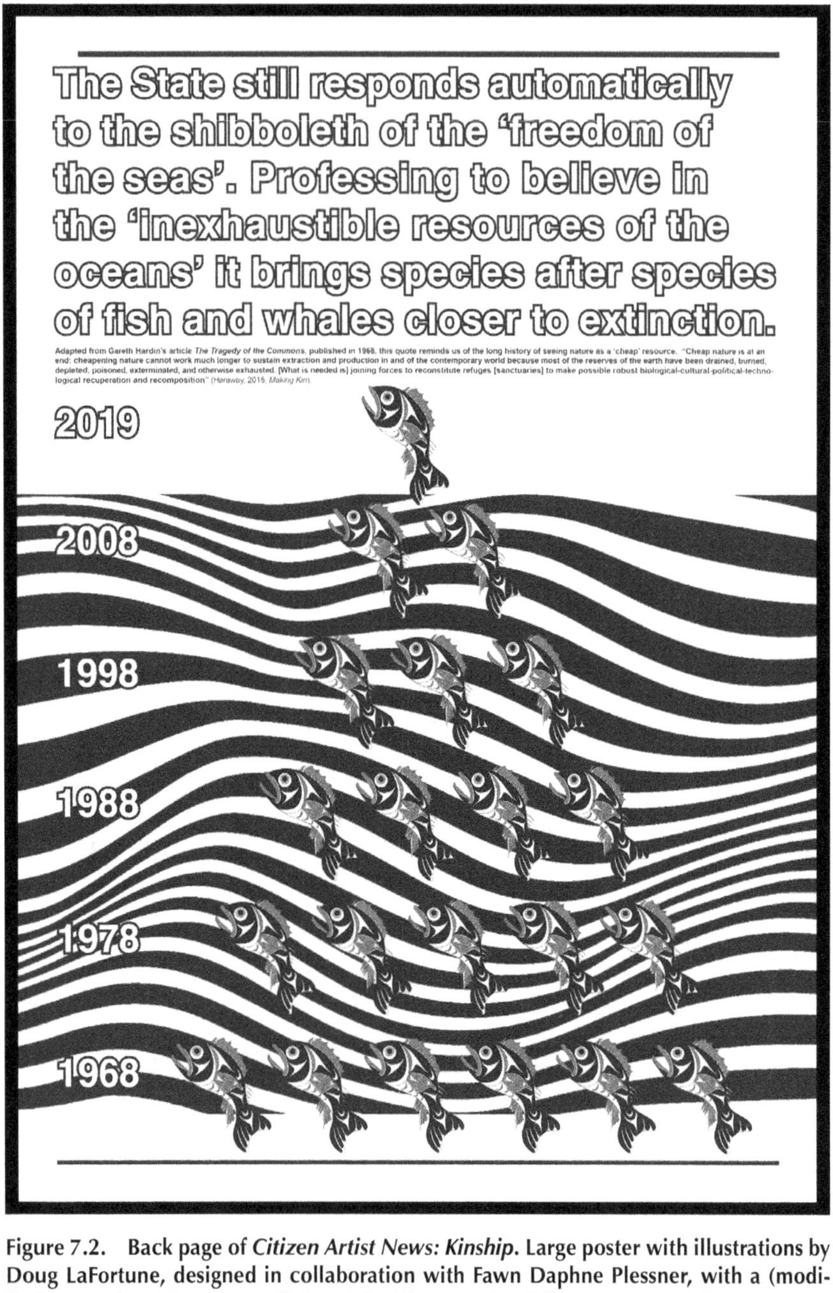

Figure 7.2. Back page of *Citizen Artist News: Kinship*. Large poster with illustrations by Doug LaFortune, designed in collaboration with Fawn Daphne Plessner, with a (modified) quote from Gareth Hardin's article "The Tragedy of the Commons." *Photo courtesy of F. D. Plessner*

W̱SÁNEĆ School Board offices and the First Peoples House at the University of Victoria. The intervention again focused the attention of residents and others to engage with the politics of place. No one returned their copies to the post office this time, and copies quickly disappeared from the local supermarket's newsstand. Doug's imagery was key to attracting people's attention. I was approached in person or received emails from some local residents expressing their enjoyment of its visual display. People based in Victoria, who came across the newspaper at the First Peoples House, emailed to express their appreciation of its focus on kinship, excited by its relevance to the politics of the day. A neighbor who works for an environmentalist group based on Vancouver Island, but also within W̱SÁNEĆ territory, reported that one of her colleagues (who was not an island resident) brought a copy to share in their workplace, excited by its creative and provocative content. The LaFortunes distributed hundreds of copies among their personal and professional network, giving copies to friends, fellow artists, and local and provincial museum curators. In late January 2020, a group of community organizers asked for copies of the newspaper for a series of educational workshops they were cohosting on the island, to commence in February, on the topic of climate crisis. I furnished them with fifty copies for the event and directed them also to the local supermarket where people could acquire additional copies if they so wished. These workshops were headed up by an alliance of the W̱SÁNEĆ School Board and a branch of local government (Southern Gulf Island's Community Resource Center). It was noticeable too that one of their panel discussions imitated the speaker's list from Artinian's and my *Clouded Title* workshop (launched in April 2018)—a coincidence perhaps? Or simply a sign of the effects of the citizen art interventions as they played out in their public reenactment? Whatever the case, these workshops, unlike the *Clouded Title* session, required participants to pay a considerable fee and thus restricted islander's access. By narrowing and limiting community participation, the workshops had the effect of excluding residents from discussions about community (climate action) problems and muting the contribution of its W̱SÁNEĆ speakers. However, it was subsequently reported to me by people who attended the workshops that *Kinship* had a considerable impact on the discussions that circulated within those spaces. The newspaper intervention took participants by surprise: It prompted extensive discussions about the politics of place, especially in the newspaper's foregrounding of W̱SÁNEĆ perspectives, beliefs, and values. It also had the effect of disrupting the local political status quo: Who set in motion this W̱SÁNEĆ discussion about kinship and reciprocal responsibilities—and long before this workshop? Who took action without the knowledge or endorsement of local hierarchies and networks of political actors?!

A few months later, in early July 2020, a small group of local activists approached me about using the design of one of the newspaper's posters (its back page) for a campaign to raise awareness about the southern resident killer whales as endangered species. They wanted to emulate the poster's impactful design and the directness of its message (see figure 7.2) for a series of posters they were envisaging for their campaign. During a face-to-face meeting with some of its members, I was astonished by one person who animatedly related the details of the contents of *Clouded Title* back to me, performing a kind of expertise about the fine-grained problems that the newspaper presented. This person had not understood that I was responsible for its production, and it was fascinating to witness how much of its details and problematics had been digested and internalized. It was impressive that they had so carefully engaged in the newspaper's thought experiment, and I was struck by how the text was transformed from the page to an oral retelling. It was odd to experience my first intervention circling back to my own ears in an unselfconscious performance of its contents (two years after it was launched!). It also left me contemplating the different registers of speech and action of the interventions, who listened, who heard the voices of W̱SÁNEĆ speakers in the act of reading, how many times the intervention was reenacted or rebounded, and who instead closed it off as noise. I saw in this moment, too, that in the intimacy of listening, there exists a great capacity for citizen art interventions to affectively forge new beginnings, new orientations, new ways to be present "here" in real and substantive ways.

In closing, the interventions delivered into the proverbial "belly of the (colonial) beast" two thought experiments that carved out a new civil space for doing politics on the island by directly soliciting residents to engage in a public exercise of "reconsidering place" (Plessner 2018, 1). In anchoring W̱SÁNEĆ voices within this place and now, thus dispelling any pretense of W̱SÁNEĆ invisibility or erasing the W̱SÁNEĆ in (historical) time, disrupting the smooth, omnipresent assumption of colonial entitlement to garner, possess, and use their unceded land (i.e., manipulate, exploit, extract, and commodify it), the interventions troubled who is present "here" and what is said "here" about here and now. The interventions also made it clear that those whose land one occupies see the land/here profoundly differently from the local settlers that reside here. And they continue to subtly puncture local fictions of benign occupation, calling into question British Canadian narratives by altering what is seen as a political topic and who is seen as a political actor. Targeting unwitting residents and reaching into the private spaces of individual households, they created a public disturbance to the social and political construction of lives lived as settled (i.e., entitled and satisfied) occupants and, in turn, troubled normative notions of status citizenship.

The newspapers also made visible that inscribed in the peace treaty are vivid markers and histories of the W̱SÁNEĆ people's aesthetic relations to the land, a cosmological history, and the legacy of their ancestral relations to the (is)lands as more-than-human beings—relations that are wholly without cognizance within colonial imaginaries of land and animals but nevertheless are introduced to island residents as a real possibility for new beginnings. The interventions take seriously these insights about nonhuman kinship and reciprocal responsibilities as a foundation for new relations, new modes of (nonstatist) membership, within their wider territory. They therefore demonstrate that to be here encompasses more-than-human beings (e.g., islands, forests, animals) as entangled in the conception and practice of political membership and governance.

The relationships that have been formed because of the interventions have brought into view the fact that new and nascent modes of citizenship are possible by not misrecognizing the W̱SÁNEĆ and their experiences and perspectives or leaving unacknowledged the real violence that persists through the actions of settlers and the state. The interventions decenter the colonial state and forge new orientations for seeing this terrain as centered on the W̱SÁNEĆ People's accounts of place, their laws and their ways of being, allowing for new aesthetic (perceptual and affective) pathways and imaginaries to take shape within the locale. They puncture what has been partitioned and rupture what is sensible within the local colonial imaginary. By inviting residents to perform an act of seeing anew, they have provided a material support for enacting new and nascent modes of membership.

Citizen art interventions, including the examples of other artists' projects discussed in previous chapters, demonstrate that, through their performance, the practice of citizenship is a mode of becoming that produces new possibilities and organizational realities of belonging and membership. The significance of citizen art is in its capacity to perform politics and shape alternative, non-statist modes of citizenship that circumvent the inherent pitfalls of status citizenship regimes and cosmopolitan imaginaries. Of course, further exploration of the differing manifestations of nonstatist citizenship in citizen art (e.g., its making visible the problematics of status and cosmopolitan citizenship, further interrogation of how citizen art structures and supports solidarities and assemblies, or its affective challenges to entrenched political beliefs and behaviors) would build on this book in practicable ways. More critical work on the various forms of citizen art interventions would be a worthwhile endeavor and would further evolve an understanding of the manifestation of these new practices of citizenship.

NOTES

1. Bourdieu 2008 argues that it is important for intellectuals to counter the doxa of neoliberal ideology within the (French) state: "This all makes particularly necessary the intervention of researchers who are well enough informed and equipped to combat on an equal basis those fine speakers [journalists] who are often poorly trained, and appeal to the authority of a science that they have not mastered to impose a completely political vision of the world of economics" (277).

2. Karen Kunzo and Adiba Muzzafar.

Appendix A

THE DOUGLAS TREATY: NORTH SAANICH

Know all men, that we the chiefs and people of the Saanich Tribe, who have signed our names and made our marks to this deed on the eleventh day of February, one thousand eight hundred and fifty-two, do consent to surrender, entirely and for ever, to James Douglas, the agent of the Hudson's Bay Company in Vancouver Island, that is to say, for the Governor, Deputy Governor, and Committee of the same, the whole of the lands situated and lying as follows, viz:—commencing at Cowichan Head and following the coast of the Canal de Haro North-west nearly to Saanich Point, or Qua-na-sung; from thence following the course of the Saanich Arm to the point where it terminates; and from thence by a straight line across country to said Cowichan Head, the point of commencement, so as to include all the country and lands, with the exceptions hereafter named, within those boundaries.

The conditions of our understanding of this sale is this, that our village sites and enclosed fields are to be kept for our own use, for the use of our children, and for those who may follow after us and the land shall be properly surveyed hereafter. It is understood, however, that the land itself, with these small exceptions, becomes the entire property of the white people for ever; it is also understood that we are at liberty to hunt over the unoccupied lands, and to carry on our fisheries as formerly.

We have received, as payment (amount not stated)

(Signed)

Hotutstun his X mark and 117 others.
Witness to signatures, (signed)

Joseph William McKay, Clerk H.B.Co's service
Richd. Golledge, Clerk

Source: "Saanich Tribe—North Saanich," "Treaty Texts—Douglas Treaties," Government of Canada, https://www.rcaanc-cirnac.gc.ca/eng/110010002905 2/1581515763202#saanichNorth.

Appendix B

THE W̱SÁNEĆ PEOPLE'S COVENANT WITH XÁLS

A long time ago when the Creator, XÁLS, walked the Earth, there were no islands in the W̱SÁNEĆ territory. The islands that are there today were human beings (our ancestors). At this time XÁLS walked among the W̱SÁNEĆ People, showing them the proper way to live. In doing this he took a bunch of the W̱SÁNEĆ People and threw them back into the ocean. Each of the persons thrown into the ocean became the islands there today. Each of those islands were given a particular name that reflects the manner in which they landed, their characteristics or appearance, or the significance they have to the W̱SÁNEĆ People. "James Island" was named ȽEL,ŦOS, meaning "Splashed in the Face." ȽEL,ŦOS reflects the way the island landed in the ocean. The southeast face of ȽEL,ŦOS is worn by the wind and the tide.

After throwing the W̱SÁNEĆ People into the ocean, XÁLS turned to speak to the islands and said, "Look after your relatives, the W̱SÁNEĆ People". XÁLS then turned to the W̱SÁNEĆ People and said, "You will also look after your 'Relatives of the Deep.'" This is what XÁLS asked us in return for the care of our "Relatives of the Deep" provide for us."

Source: Clifford 2016b.

189

Bibliography

Addley, Ester. 2010. "Student Fees Protests: Who Started the Violence?" *Guardian*. December 10. www.theguardian.com/education/2010/dec/10/student-protests -tuition-fees-violence (accessed May 23, 2013).

Agamben, Giorgio. 2005. *State of Exception*. Chicago: University of Chicago Press.

Al Jazeera. 2018. "The UK's Windrush Generation: What's the Scandal About?" *Al Jazeera*. April 18. www.aljazeera.com/news/2018/04/uk-windrush-generation -scandal-180418074648878.html (accessed August 25, 2018).

Alfred, Taiaiake. 2005. *Wasáse: Indigenous Pathways of Action and Freedom*. Toronto: University of Toronto Press.

Anderson, Benedict. 2006. *Imagined Communities*. London: Verso.

Annan, Kofi. 1999. "Two Concepts of Sovereignty." *The Economist*. September 16. www.economist.com/node/324795 (accessed December 12, 2015).

Appadurai, Arjun. 1990. "Disjuncture and Difference in the Global Cultural Economy." *Theory, Culture & Society* 7 (2–3): 295–310. www.arjunappadurai.org/articles /Appadurai_Disjuncture_and_Difference_in_the_Global_Cultural_Economy.pdf (accessed August 12, 2018).

Appiah, Kwame Anthony. 1997. "Cosmopolitan Patriots." *Critical Inquiry* 23, no. 3: 617–39.

Arendt, Hannah. 1972. *Crises of the Republic: Lying in Politics; Civil Disobedience; On Violence; Thoughts on Politics and Revolution*. Orlando: Harcourt Brace & Co.

———. 1976. *Totalitarianism: Part Three of the Origins of Totalitarianism*. San Diego: Harvest Books.

———. 1990. *On Revolution*. London: Penguin Group.

———. 1998. *The Human Condition*. Chicago: University of Chicago Press.

———. 2009. *The Origins of Totalitarianism*. Oxford: Benediction Classics.

———. 2018. *Thinking without a Bannister: Essays in Understanding, 1953–1975*. Edited by Jermone Kohn. New York: Shocken Books.

Aristotle. 1992. *The Politics*. Translated by T. A. Sinclair and Trevor J. Saunders. New York: Penguin Books.

Austin, John L. 1975. *How to Do Things with Words*. Oxford: Oxford University Press.

Azoulay, Ariella. 2008. *The Civil Contract of Photography*. New York: Zone Books.

———. 2011. "A Civil State of Emergency." *Verso* (blog). February 20. www.verso books.com/blogs/918-a-civil-state-of-emergency-a-photoessay-by-ariella-azoulay (accessed September 10, 2011).

———. 2012. "Regime-Made Disaster: On the Possibility of Nongovernmental Viewing." In *Sensible Politics: The Visual Culture of Nongovernmental Activism*, edited by Meg McLagan and Yates McKee, 29–41. New York: Zone Books.

———. 2019. *Potential History: Unlearning Imperialism*. London: Verso.

"Background of the Douglas Treaties." n.d. Governor's Letters. www.govlet.ca/en /pdf/cc2-blm-1.pdf (accessed December 1, 2016).

Bajoria, Jayshree, and Robert McMahon. 2013. "The Dilemma of Humanitarian Intervention." Council on Foreign Relations. June 12. www.cfr.org/backgrounder /dilemma-humanitarian-intervention (accessed March 21, 2015).

Bakhtin, Mikhail. 1984. *Rabelais and His World*. Translated by Helene Iswolsky. Bloomington: Indiana University Press.

Balibar, Etienne. 2002. *Politics and the Other Scene*. London: Verso.

———. 2004. *We, the People of Europe: Reflections on Transnational Citizenship*. Princeton, NJ: Princeton University Press.

BBC News. 2021. "Kamala Harris Tells Guatemala Migrants: 'Do Not Come to US.'" *BBC News*. June 8. www.bbc.com/news/world-us-canada-57387350.

Beck, Ulrich. 2003. "Toward a New Critical Theory with a Cosmopolitan Intent." *Constellations* 10, no. 4: 453–68.

———. 2008. *Cosmopolitan Vision*. Malden, MA: Polity Press.

———. 2012. "The Cosmopolitan Society and Its Enemies." *Theory, Culture & Society* 19, nos. 1–2: 17–44.

Becker, Howard S. 1982. *Art Worlds*. Berkeley: University of California Press.

Bellamy, Alex. J. 2012. "Kosovo and the Advent of Sovereignty Responsibility." In *Kosovo, Intervention and Statebuilding: The International Community and the Transition to Independence*, edited by Aiden Hehir, 38–59. London: Routledge.

Benhabib, Seyla, and Judith Resnick. 2009. *Migrations and Mobilities: Citizenship, Borders, and Gender*. New York: New York University Press.

Bennett, Jane. 2010. *Vibrant Matter: A Political Ecology of Things*. Durham, NC: Duke University Press.

Berardi, Franco "Bifo." 2009. *The Soul at Work: From Alienation to Autonomy*. Cambridge, MA: Semiotext(e).

———. 2010. "Cognitarian Subjectivation." *e-flux Journal* 20 (February): 1–8. www.e-flux.com/journal/cognitarian-subjectivation (accessed February 6, 2011).

Berthoin Antal, Ariane. 2014. "The Studio in the Firm: A Study of Four Artistic Intervention Residencies." *Academia*. www.academia.edu/9769137/The_Studio _in_the_Firm_A_Study_of_Four_Artistic_Intervention_Residencies (accessed May 21, 2016).

Berthoin Antal, Ariane, and Ilana Nussbaum Bitran. 2015. *Artistic Interventions in Organizations: Data Reports from Multi-stakeholder Surveys in Spain 2011–2014.* SPIII 2015-603. August. Berlin: Wissenschaftszentrum für Sozialforschung.

Berthoin Antal, Ariane, and Anke Strauss. 2013. "Artistic Interventions in Organisations: Finding Evidence of Values-Added." Creative Clash Report. *Academia.* www.academia.edu/4055751/Artistic_interventions_in_organizations_Finding_evidence_of_values-added (accessed July 21, 2017).

Bishop, Claire. 2004. "Antagonism and Relational Aesthetics." *October* 110 (autumn): 51–79. https://academicworks.cuny.edu/gc_pubs/96 (accessed October 2, 2018).

———. 2006a. "The Social Turn: Collaboration and Its Discontents." *Artforum* 44, no. 6 (February): 179–85.

———, ed. 2006b. *Participation: Documents of Contemporary Art.* Cambridge, MA: MIT Press.

———. 2012. *Artificial Hells: Participatory Art and the Politics of Spectatorship.* London: Verso.

Blaagaard, Bolette B. 2018. *Citizen Journalism as Conceptual Practice: Postcolonial Archives and Embodied Political Acts of New Media.* London: Rowman & Littlefield International.

Bluntschli, Johann Kaspar. 2000. *The Theory of the State.* Authorized English translation from sixth German edition. Kitchener, Ontario: Batoche Books.

Bosniak, Linda. 2000. "Citizenship Denationalized." *Indiana Journal of Global Legal Studies* 7, no. 2: 447–510.

———. 2006. *The Citizen and the Alien: Dilemmas of Contemporary Membership.* Princeton, NJ: Princeton University Press.

Bourdieu, Pierre. 2008. *Political Interventions.* Edited by Franck Poupeau and Thierry Discepolo. Translated by David Fernbach. London: Verso.

Bourriaud, Nicolas. 2002. *Relational Aesthetics.* Translated by Simon Pleasance, Fronza Woods, and Mathieu Copeland. Dijon, France: La Presse du Réel.

Bowman, Wayne D. 2016. "Artistry, Ethics, and Citizenship." In *Artistic Citizenship*, edited by David J. Elliott, Marissa Silverman, and Wayne Bowman, 59–80. Oxford: Oxford University Press.

Braidotti, Rosi, Patrick Hanafin, and Bolette Blaagaard. 2013. *After Cosmopolitanism.* New York: Routledge.

Bruguera, Tania. 2010–2015. *Migrant People Party* (Partido del pueblo migrante). www.taniabruguera.com/cms/586-0-Migrant+People+Party+MPP.htm (accessed October 4, 2012).

———. 2011. "Make a Movement Sundays." Immigrant Movement International. https://immigrant-movement.us/wordpress/make-a-movement (accessed October 4, 2012).

Bühnemann, Marc, Timmi Tillmann, and Anan Ganjanapan. 2013. "Report on the Workshop and Panel on Indigenous Knowledge (IK) and Natural Commons in Myanmar." Beyond Borders: Building a Regional Commons in Southeast Asia. Third International Conference on International Relations and ICIRD Development, Chulalongkorn University, Bangkok, Thailand, August 21–23. www.th.boell

.org/sites/default/files/uploads/2013/11/icird_report_ik.pdf (accessed March 10, 2014).

Bulman, May. 2018. "Windrush Generation to Be Refused Citizenship." *Independent*. September 21. www.independent.co.uk/news/uk/home-news/windrush-citizens-latest-citizenship-refused-home-office-sajid-javid-a8549101.html (accessed October 10, 2018).

Butler, Judith. 2011. "Bodies in Alliance and the Politics of the Street." *Transversal Texts*. https://transversal.at/transversal/1011/butler/en (accessed July 26, 2018).

Byock, Jesse. 2002. "The Icelandic Althing: Dawn of Parliamentary Democracy." In *Heritage and Identity: Shaping the Nations of the North*, edited by Jan Magnus Fladmark, 1–18. Heyerdahl Institute and Robert Gordon University. Shaftesbury, UK: Donhead.

Byrne, Eleanor, and Berthold Schoene. 2013. "Cosmopolitanism as Critical and Creative Practice: An Introduction." *Open Arts Journal* 1 (summer): 2–7. https://openartsjournal.org/issue-1/2013s01ebbs (accessed May 9, 2016).

Cairns, Alan C. 2000. *Citizens Plus: Aboriginal Peoples and the Canadian State*. Vancouver: University of British Columbia Press.

Calhoun, Craig. 2007. *Nations Matter: Culture, History and the Cosmopolitan Dream*. New York: Routledge.

Canadian Centre for Architecture. 2009. "Tools for Actions." *Canadian Centre for Architecture*. www.cca. qc.ca/actions (accessed March 16, 2016).

Canadian Encyclopedia. n.d. "The White Paper, 1969." *Canadian Encyclopedia*. www.thecanadianencyclopedia.ca/en/article/the-white-paper-1969 (accessed October 21, 2017).

Cannizzaro, Enzo. 2015. "Responsibility to Protect and the Competence of the UN Organs." In *Responsibility to Protect (R2P): A New Paradigm of International Law?* Edited by Peter Hilpold, 207–18. Leiden: Brill Nijhoff.

Carlile, Alex, Michael Clarke, Tobias Feakin, Margaret Gilmore, and Benedict Wilkinson. 2012. "UK Terrorism Analysis. Re-balancing Security and Justice: The Reform of UK Counter-terrorism Legislation." Royal United Services Institute (RUSI): *Open Briefing* 3 (May). www.openbriefing.org/issuedesks/uksecurity/reformukctlegislation (accessed June 20, 2013).

Carroll La, Khadija. 2016. "Object to Project: Artists' Interventions in Museum Collections." In *Sculpture and the Museum*, edited by Christopher R. Marshall, 217–39. London: Routledge.

Cartiere, Cameron, and Martin Zebracki. 2016. *The Everyday Practice of Public Art*. New York: Routledge.

Castillo, Moisés. 2012. "We Are All Migrants." *Animal Político: Mexico D.F.* May 26. www.taniabruguera.com/cms/593-0-We+are+all+Migrants.htm (accessed October 9, 2016).

Chambers, Georgia. 2018. "The Windrush Scandal Made Me Realise I'm Still Seen as a Foreigner in My Own Country, So I've Applied for Jamaican Citizenship." *Independent*. April 24. www.independent.co.uk/voices/windrush-scandal-uk-jamaican-citizenship-racism-prejudice-a8319516.html (accessed August 29, 2018).

Chandler, Ann Marie, and Norie Neumark. 2006. *At a Distance: Precursors to Art and Activism on the Internet*. Cambridge, MA: MIT Press.

Chatterjee, Partha. 1993. *The Nation and Its Fragments: Colonial and Postcolonial Histories*. Princeton, NJ: Princeton University Press.

Chen, Michelle, and Tania Bruguera. 2012. "You Define the Space." *CultureStr/ke*. October11.www.taniabruguera.com/cms/files/2012_-_you_define_the_space_-_eng .pdf (accessed June 9, 2015).

Chernilo, Daniel. 2006."Social Theory's Methodological Nationalism: Myth and Reality." *European Journal of Social Theory* 9, no. 1: 5–22.

Chishti, Muzaffar, and Claire Bergeron. 2011. "Post-9/11 Policies Dramatically Alter the US Immigration Landscape." *Migration Policy Institute*. September 8. www .migrationpolicy.org/article/post-911-policies-dramatically-alter-us-immigration -landscape (accessed March 28, 2014).

Claxton, Earl, Jr. 2017. Interview and conversations with Fawn Daphne Plessner, August–December 2017.

Claxton, Nick. 2003. "The Douglas Treaty and WSÁNEĆ Traditional Fisheries: A Model for Saanich Peoples Governance." PhD diss, University of Victoria. http:// citeseerx.ist.psu.edu/viewdoc/download?doi=10.1.1.531.3534&rep=rep1&type =pdf (accessed March 18, 2016).

Clifford, Robert Justin. 2011. *WSÁNEĆ Law and the Fuel Spill at Goldstream*. LL.M. thesis, University of Victoria. https://dspace.library.uvic.ca/bitstream /handle/1828/5648/Clifford_Robert_LL.M_2014.pdf (accessed May 9, 2017).

Clifford, Robert YELḰÁT̵E. 2016a. "Listening to Law." *Windsor Yearbook of Access to Justice*. https://ojs.uwindsor.ca/ojs/leddy/index.php/WYAJ/article/view File/4809/4033 (accessed January 6, 2018).

———. 2016b. "WSÁNEĆ Theory and the Fuel Spill at SELEKT̵EŁ (Goldstream River)." *McGill Law Journal* 61, no. 4: 755–93.

———. 2019. "Saanich Law and the Trans-Mountain Pipeline." *Centre for International Governance Innovation*. July 4. www.cigionline.org/articles/saanich-law -and-trans-mountain-pipeline-expansion.

Cole, David. 2007. "Against Citizenship as a Predicate for Basic Rights." *Fordham Law Review* 75: 2541–48.

———. 2010. "Are Foreign Nationals Entitled to the Same Constitutional Rights as Citizens?" *Thomas Jefferson Law Review* 25: 367–88.

Cole, Harris. 2012. "The Native Land Policies of Governor James Douglas." *BC Studies: The British Columbian Quarterly* (summer): 101–22.

Connor, Maureen. 2013. "The Artists Placement Group: Context Is Not Everything." In *Artists Reclaim the Commons: New Works, New Territories, New Publics*, edited by Glen Harper and Twylene Moyer, 144–50. Hamilton, NJ: ISC Press.

Coughlan, Sean. 2010. "How the Student Fees Protest Turned Violent." *BBC News*. November 10. www.bbc.co.uk/news/education-11729912 (accessed May 23, 2013).

Coulthard, Glen. 2014. *Red Skin, White Masks: Rejecting the Colonial Politics of Recognition*. Minneapolis: University of Minnesota Press.

Coward, Roger. 1975. *Arting Is Knowing—Knowing Is Creating: Report of Feasibility Study and Proposal for the Main Placement with the Department of Environment.* Llandrindod Wells, Powys, Wales: Self-published.

———. 1976. *All Fine & Context & Other Papers.* Llandrindod Wells, Powys, Wales: Self-published.

Cramerotti, Alfredo. 2009. *Aesthetic Journalism: How to Inform without Informing.* Bristol, UK: Intellect Books.

Cunliffe, Phillip. 2014. "The Responsibility to Protect and the New Liberal Dystopianism." *Into the Eleventh Hour: R2P, Syria and Humanitarianism in Crisis*, edited by Robert W. Murray and Alasdair McKay. Bristol, UK: e-International Relations. www.e-ir.info/publication/into-the-eleventh-hour-r2p-syria-and-humanitarianism -in-crisis (accessed April 12, 2016).

Danto, Arthur. 1964. "The Artworld." *Journal of Philosophy* 61, no. 19: 571–84.

De Certeau, Michel. 1984. *The Practice of Everyday Life.* Translated by Steven Rendell. Berkeley: University of California Press.

De Genova, Nicholas. 2009. "Conflicts of Mobility, and the Mobility of Conflict: Rightlessness, Presence, Subjectivity, Freedom." *Subjectivity* 29: 445–66.

———. 2010. "The Queer Politics of Migration: Reflections on 'Illegality' and Incorrigibility." *Studies in Social Justice* 4, no. 2: 101–26.

Debord, Guy, and Gil J. Wolman. 1956. *A Users Guide to Détournement.* Translated by Ken Knabb. *Collaboratory for Digital Discourse and Culture @ Virginia Tech.* www.cddc.vt.edu/sionline/presitu/usersguide.html.

Dederer, Hans-Georg. 2015. "'Responsibility to Protect' and 'Functional Sovereignty.'" In *The Responsibility to Protect (R2P): A New Paradigm in International Law*, edited by Peter Hilpold, 156–83. Leiden: Brill Nijhoff.

Delanty, Gerard. 2000. *Citizenship in a Global Age: Society, Culture, Politics.* Maidenhead, UK: Open University Press.

Della Porta, Donatella. 2005. "Making the Polis: Social Forums and Democracy in the Global Justice Movement." *Mobilization: An International Quarterly*10, no. 1: 1–41.

———. 2006. *Social Movements: An Introduction.* Oxford, UK: Blackwell Publishing.

———. 2007. *The Global Justice Movement: Cross-National and Transnational Perspectives.* London: Paradigm Publishers.

Della Porta, Donatella, and Sidney Tarrow. 2005. *Transnational Protest and Global Activism.* Lanham, MD: Rowman & Littlefield.

Democracy Now. 2018. "Trump Declares 'I'm a Nationalist' in Texas Rally." *Democracy Now.* October 24. www.democracynow.org/2018/10/24/headlines/trump _declares_im_a_nationalist_in_texas_rally (accessed October 10, 2018).

Democratic Self-Administration of Rojava (DSAR) and New World Summit: Studio Jonas Staal. 2016. *New Worlds.* www.jonasstaal.nl/site/assets/files/1521/new _worlds.pdf (accessed August 7, 2018).

Demos, T. J. 2013. *The Migrant Image: The Art and Politics of Documentary during Global Crisis.* Durham, NC: Duke University Press.

Derrida, Jacques. 2002. "The Future of the Profession or the University without Condition." *Without Alibi*. Edited and translated by Peggy Kamuf. Stanford, CA: Stanford University Press.

Dewey, Caitlin. 2013. "What It Means That Egypt Is Entering a 'State of Emergency.'" *Washington Post*. August 14. www.washingtonpost.com/blogs/worldviews /wp/2013/08/14/what-it-means-that-egypt-is-entering-a-state-of-emergency (accessed February 18, 2014).

Dietachmair, Philipp, and Pascal Gielen. 2017. *The Art of Civil Action and Cultural Dissent*. Amsterdam: Valiz.

Diverlus, Rodney. 2016. "Re/imaging Artivism." In *Artistic Citizenship*, edited by David J. Elliott, Marissa Silverman, and Wayne Bowman, 189-209. Oxford: Oxford University Press.

Dolphijn, Rick, and Iris van der Tuin. 2012. *New Materialism: Interviews and Cartographies*. University of Michigan Library. Ann Arbor: Open Humanities Press.

Dzenko, Corey, and Theresa Avilla. 2018. *Contemporary Citizenship, Art and Visual Culture: Making and Being Made*. London: Routledge.

Eastside Projects. 2015. *Roger Coward: You and Me, Here We Are*. Eastside Projects Gallery, London. May 16–July 11. https://eastsideprojects.org/projects/roger -coward-you-and-me-here-we-are (accessed June 9, 2017).

Economist. 2010. "Foreign University Students: Will They Still Come?" *Economist*. August 5. www.economist.com/britain/2010/08/05/will-they-still-come (accessed March 9, 2012).

Elliott, Dave, Sr. 1990. *Saltwater People as Told by Dave Elliott Sr.: A Resource Book for the Saanich Native Studies Program*. Edited by Janet Poth. Contributions by Earl Claxton Sr., John Elliott, Linda Underwood, and Charles Elliott. Saanich, BC: Native Education, School District 63.

Elliott, David J., Marissa Silverman, and Wayne Bowman. 2016a. *Artistic Citizenship: Artistry, Responsibility and Ethical Praxis*. Oxford: Oxford University Press.

———. 2016b. "Hamilton and Artistic Citizenship." *Artistic Citizenship* (blog). www.artistic-citizenship.com/2016/11/23/hamilton-and-artistic-citizenship (accessed May 5, 2018).

———. 2016c. "Artistic Citizenship: Introduction, Aims, Overview." In *Artistic Citizenship*, edited by David J. Elliott, Marissa Silverman, and Wayne Bowman, 1–21. Oxford: Oxford University Press.

Evans, Gareth. 2006. "From Humanitarian Intervention to the Responsibility to Protect." Humanitarian Intervention Symposium, University of Wisconsin, Madison, March 31. www.fh-muenster.de/humanitaere-hilfe/downloads/Evans_-_Responsi bility_To_Protect.pdf (accessed August 12, 2015).

Facing History and Ourselves. n.d. "Until There is Not a Single Indian in Canada." *Facing History and Ourselves*. www.facinghistory.org/stolen-lives-indigenous -peoples-canada-and-indian-residential-schools/historical-background/until-there -not-single-indian-canada (accessed March 16, 2016).

Faulks, Keith. 2000. *Citizenship: Key Ideas*. London: Routledge.

Feiss, Ellen. n.d. "What Is Useful? The Paradox in Tania Bruguera's 'Useful Art.'" *Art & Education Papers*. www.artandeducation.net/paper/what-is-useful-the-para dox-of-rights-in-tania-brugueras-useful-art (accessed May 10, 2015).

Fenton, Natalie. 2010. "Drowning or Waving? New Media, Journalism and Democracy." In *New Media, Old News: Journalism and Democracy in the Digital Age*, edited by Natalie Fenton, 3–16. London: Sage.

Fine, Robert. 2007. *Cosmopolitanism: Key Ideas*. London: Routledge.

First Nations Study Program. 2009. *Indian Status*. https://indigenousfoundations.arts .ubc.ca/indian_status (accessed October 20, 2021).

For Freedoms. n.d. "50 State Initiative." *For Freedoms*. https://forfreedoms-web-prod .s3.amazonaws.com/documents/50state-toolkit.pdf (accessed August 12, 2018).

"For Freedoms, the First Artist-Run Super PAC." n.d. *Crowdpac*. www.crowdpac .com/campaigns/19969/for-freedoms-the-first-artist-run-super-pac (accessed August 4, 2018).

Fort Nelson First Nation. 2004. "Fort Nelson First Nation Membership Code." *Fort Nelson First Nation*. www.fortnelsonfirstnation.org/uploads/1/4/6/8/14681966 /fnfn_membershipcode_2004march31_.pdf (accessed July 10, 2017).

Foucault, Michel. 2013. "Right of Death and Power over Life." In *Biopolitics: A Reader*, edited by Timothy Campbell and Adam Sitze, 41–81. Durham, NC: Duke University Press.

Freee Art Collective. 2017. *Citizen Ship. City Club*. June 26 to October 21. http:// cityclubmk.org/projects/citizen-ship (Accessed October 18, 2021).

Frieling, Rudolf, ed. 2008. *The Art of Participation: 1950 to Now*. San Francisco: San Francisco Museum of Modern Art.

Frogner, Raymond. 2010. "Innocent Legal Fictions: Archival Convention and the North Saanich Treaty of 1852." *Archivaria: The Journal of the Association of Canadian Archivists*. 70 (fall): 45–94.

Frye Burnham, Lynda, and Stephen Durland. 1998. *The Citizen Artist: 20 Years of Art in the Public Arena: An Anthology from High Performance Magazine, 1978–1998*. New York: Critical Press.

Garfinkel, Harold. 1964. "Studies of the Routine Grounds of Everyday Activities." *Social Problems* 11, no. 3 (winter): 225–25.

———. 2014. *Studies in Ethnomethodology*. Malden, MA: Polity Press.

Geiger-Gerlach, Martina. 2018. *Raumwunder: Für Das Leere Haus* (For the empty house). Karlshofstrasse 42, Stuttgart, Germany.

Geuss, Raymond. 2001. *History and Illusion in Politics*. Cambridge: Cambridge University Press.

———. 2008. *Philosophy and Real Politics*. Princeton, NJ: Princeton University Press.

———. 2010. *Politics and the Imagination*. Princeton, NJ: Princeton University Press.

Gibson, J. J. 1986. *The Ecological Approach to Visual Perception*. Hillsdale, NJ: Lawrence Erlbaum Associates.

Giegerich, Wolfgang. n.d. "Definitional Statement." *International Society for Psychology as the Discipline of Interiority*. www.ispdi.org (accessed April 12, 2013).

Gilmore, Margaret. 2012. "Is the Government's Communications Bill a Charter for Snoopers?" *Royal United Services Institute.* June 13. www.rusi.org/analysis/com mentary/ref:C4FD90660F2BE1/#.UX08UXDFVlA (accessed April 28, 2013).

Gilmore, Margaret, Alex Carlile, Michael Clarke, Tobias Feakin, and Benedict Wilkensen. 2012. "UK Terrorism Analysis. Re-balancing Security and Justice: The Reform of UK Counter-terrorism Legislation." *Royal United Services Institute.* May 21. www.rusi.org/analysis/commentary/ref:C4FBA0672E54E6/#.UX0-cHD FWrd (accessed January 20, 2013).

Giokas, John. 1995. *The Indian Act Evolution, Overview and Options for Amendment and Transition: Final Report.* March 22. Government of Canada. http://publica tions.gc.ca/collections/collection_2016/bcp-pco/Z1-1991-1-41-130-eng.pdf (accessed November 28, 2015).

Glick Schiller, Nina. 2009. *A Global Perspective on Transnational Migration: Theorizing Migration without Methodological Nationalism.* Working Paper No. 67. Centre on Migration, Policy and Society (COMPAS). University of Oxford.

Goodin, Robert E., and Philip Pettit. 1998. *A Companion to Contemporary Political Philosophy.* Oxford, UK: Blackwell Publishers.

Government of Canada Indigenous and Northern Affairs. n.d. "Robinson Treaties and Douglas Treaties, 1850." www.aadnc-aandc.gc.ca/eng/1360945974712 /1360946016409 (accessed December 1, 2016).

Graeber, David. 2007. *Possibilities: Essays on Hierarchy, Rebellion, and Desire.* Edinburgh: AK Press.

———. 2009. *Direct Action: An Ethnography.* Edinburgh: AK Press.

Graham, Gordon. 2002. *The Case against the Democratic State: An Essay in Cultural Criticism.* Thorverton, UK: Imprint Academic.

Graham, Janna, and Nicolas Vass. 2014. "Intervention/Art." *P/Art/icipate: Kultur Aktiv Gestalten.* 5, no. 10. www.p-art-icipate.net/cms/intervention-art (accessed July 16, 2017).

Gray, John. 1993. *Action Art: A Bibliography of Artists' Performance from Futurism to Fluxus and Beyond.* Westport, CT: Greenwood Press.

Green, Jeffrey Edward. 2010. *The Eyes of the People: Democracy in an Age of Spectatorship.* Oxford: Oxford University Press.

Gullestad, Anders M. 2010. "Demand Everything! Interview with Simon Critchley." *Art & Research* 3, no. 2. www.artandresearch.org.uk/v3n2/gullestad.php (accessed February 2, 2014).

HafenCity Universität, Hochschule für Angewandte Wissenschaft, Fundus Theater and K3: Centre for Choreography/Tanzplan Hamburg. 2018. "Graduate School Performing Citizenship." *Performing Citizenship.* http://performingcitizenship.de /data/en/info (accessed May 25, 2018).

Haraway, Donna J. 2015. "Anthropocene, Capitalocene, Plantationocene, Chthulucene: Making Kin." *Environmental Humanities* 6: 159–65. www.environmentand society. org/sites/default/files/key_docs/environmental_humanities-2015-haraway-159-65 .pdf (accessed August 10, 2018).

———. 2016. *Staying with the Trouble: Making Kin in the Chthulucene.* Durham, NC: Duke University Press.

Hardin, Garrett. 1968. "The Tragedy of the Commons." *Science, New Series* 162, no. 3859: 1243–48. http://science.sciencemag.org/content/sci/162/3859/1243.full.pdf (accessed July 22, 2018).

Hardt, Michael, and Antonio Negri. 2000. *Empire*. Cambridge, MA: Harvard University Press.

Harman, Graham. 2007. *Heidegger Explained: From Phenomenon to Thing*. Chicago: Open Court.

Harper, Glen. 1998. *Interventions and Provocations: Conversations on Art, Culture, and Resistance*. Albany: State University of New York Press.

Harper, Glen, and Twylene Moyer. 2013. *Artists Reclaim the Commons: New Works/New Territories/New Publics*. Hamilton, NJ: ISC Press.

Harrison, Angela. 2010. "Violence at Tory HQ Overshadows Student Fees Protest." *BBC News*. November 10. www.bbc.co.uk/news/education-11726822 (accessed May 23, 2013).

Hartley, Alex. 2012. *Nowhere Island*. Coastal Journey from Svalbard to Bristol. www.nowhereisland.org (accessed November 10, 2012).

Hartman, Ben. 2010. "Peace Now Holds 'Masquerade Carnival' to Protest Gov't." *Jerusalem Post*. February 21. www.jpost.com/Israel/Peace-Now-holds-masquerade-carnival-to-protest-govt.

Heater, Derek. 1999. *What Is Citizenship?* Cambridge, UK: Polity Press.

Hehir, Aidan. 2010. *Kosovo, Intervention and Statebuilding: The International Community and the Transition to Independence*. Abingdon, UK: Routledge.

Held, David, and Anthony McGrew. 2002. *The Global Transformations Reader: An Introduction to the Globalization Debate*. Cambridge, UK: Polity Press and Blackwell Publishing.

Helfrich, Silke. 2014. "Recent Landmarks in the Growing Commons Movement." *Commonsblog*. January 17. http://commonsblog.wordpress.com/2014/01/17/recent-landmarks-in-the-growing-commons-movement (accessed August 8, 2014).

Helfrich, Silke, Rainer Kuhlen, Wolfgang Sachs, and Christian Siefkes. 2009. *The Commons: Prosperity by Sharing*. Berlin: Heinrich Böll Foundation.

Helguera, Pablo. 2011. *Education for Socially Engaged Art: A Materials and Techniques Handbook*. New York: Jorge Pinto Books.

Hendricks, Jon, and Jean Toche. 1978. *GAAG: The Guerilla Art Action Group: 1969–1976: A Selection*. New York: Printed Matter.

Hewitt, Andy. 2011. "Privatizing the Public: Three Rhetorics of Art's Public Good in Third Way Cultural Policy." *Art & the Public Sphere* 1, no. 1: 19–36. www.ingentaconnect.com/content/intellect/aps/2011/00000001/00000001/art00003 (accessed September 3, 2013).

———. 2012. *Art and Counter-publics in Third Way Cultural Policy*. PhD diss., University of the Arts London. http://ualresearchonline.arts.ac.uk/5679/1/HEWITT.A.TPh.D2012%2D1.pdf (accessed February 6, 2016).

Hewitt, Andy, and Mel Jordan. 2004. *Futurology: Issues, Contexts and Conditions for Contemporary Art Practice Today*. Walsall, UK: New Art Gallery Walsall.

Hildebrandt, Paula, Kerstin Evert, Sibylle Peters, Mirjam Schaub, Kathrin Wildner, and Gesu Ziemer. 2019. *Performing Citizenship: Bodies, Agencies, Limitations.* Cham, Switzerland: Palgrave Macmillan.

Hobbes, Thomas. 1999. *Leviathan: Cambridge Texts in the History of Political Thought.* Edited by Richard Tuck. Cambridge: Cambridge University Press.

Hopper, Tristan. 2013a. "B.C. First Nation Leads Historic and Controversial Move toward Aboriginal Private Home Ownership." *National Post.* November 8. http://nationalpost.com/news/canada/b-c-first-nation-leads-historic-and-controversial-move-toward-aboriginal-private-home-ownership (accessed April 28, 2016).

———. 2013b. "How Canada Forgot about More Than 1,308 Graves at Former Residential Schools." *National Post.* July 13. https://nationalpost.com/news/canada/how-canada-forgot-about-more-than-1308-graves-at-former-residential-schools

Hosein, Gabrielle Jamela. 2012. "Transnational Spirituality, Invented Ethnicity and Performances of Citizenship in Trinidad." *Citizenship Studies* 16, nos. 5/6 (August): 737–49.

Hudek, Antony, and Alex Sainsbury. 2012. *The Individual and the Organization: Artists Placement Group, 1966–79.* London: Raven Row.

Human Rights Watch. 2013. "Detention without Judicial Review; Trials Lacking Appeal Rights." *Human Rights Watch.* January 30. www.hrw.org/news/2013/01/30/egypt-emergency-powers-excessive (accessed February 18, 2014).

Hutnyk, John. 2013. "The Malignant Teaching Factory." *Citizen Artist News.* Special Edition 2012–2013. www.citizenartist.org.uk/ca-articles/CitizenArtistNews3.pdf, 1.

Independent. 2013. "Nationwide Emergency Powers Extended in Egypt." *Independent.* September 12. www.independent.co.uk/news/world/africa/nationwide-emergency-powers-extended-in-egypt-8812981.html (accessed February 18, 2014).

Indigenous and Northern Affairs. 2010. "Chapter 18: An Act to Amend and Consolidate the Laws Respecting Indians." *Indigenous and Northern Affairs.* www.aadncaandc.gc.ca/eng/1100100010252/1100100010254 (accessed March 10, 2017).

International Commission on Intervention and State Sovereignty (ICISS). 2001. *The Responsibility to Protect: Report of the International Commission on Intervention and State Sovereignty.* Ottawa: International Development Research Centre. http://responsibilitytoprotect.org/ICISS%20Report.pdf (accessed April 2, 2016).

Internationale Sommerakademie für Bildende Kunst. 2013. *Arte Útil: A Colloquium with Tania Bruguera.* Salzburg: Internationale Sommerakademie für Bildende Kunst, 233–50. www.taniabruguera.com/cms/files/atl-54-bruguera.pdf (accessed August 1, 2015).

Isin, Engin. 2002. *Being Political: Genealogies of Citizenship.* Minneapolis: University of Minnesota Press.

———. 2012. *Citizens without Frontiers.* London: Bloomsbury.

———. 2019. "Doing Rights with Things: The Art of Becoming Citizens." In *Performing Citizenship: Bodies, Agencies, Limitations,* edited by Paula Hildebrandt, Kerstin Evert, Sibylle Peters, Mirjam Schaub, Kathrin Wildner, and Gesu Ziemer, 45–56. Cham, Switzerland: Palgrave Macmillan.

Isin, Engin, and Greg N. Nielsen. 2008. *Acts of Citizenship.* London: Zed Books.

Isin, Engin, and Peter Nyers. 2014. *Routledge Handbook of Global Citizenship Studies*. London: Routledge.

Isin, Engin, and Bryan Turner. 2002. *Handbook of Citizenship*. London: Sage Publications.

Jackson, Shannon. 2011. *Social Works: Performing Art, Supporting Publics*. London: Routledge.

Jewkes, Yvonne, and Majid Yar, eds. 2009. *Handbook on Internet Crime*. Devon, UK: William Publishing.

Joseph, Bob and Cindy. 2002. *Guide to Terminology: Working Effectively with Aboriginal Peoples*. Port Coquitlam, BC: Indigenous Corporate Training Inc. www.ictinc.ca/indigenous-peoples-a-guide-to-terminology (accessed March 16, 2016).

Kairos. 2018. "Blanket Exercise Workshop." *Kairos*. www.kairoscanada.org/what-we-do/indigenous-rights/blanket-exercise (accessed July 12, 2018).

Kant, Immanuel. 1987. *Critique of Pure Reason*. Translated and edited by Paul Geyer and Allen W. Wood. Cambridge: Cambridge University Press.

Kapler, Maija. 2017. "Reconciliation More Than Land Acknowledgements, Indigenous Groups Say." *CBC News*. January 14. www.cbc.ca/news/canada/manitoba/reconciliation-more-than-land-acknowledgments-indigenous-groups-say-1.3936171 (accessed February 24, 2016).

Kaprow, Allan. 2003. *Essays on the Blurring of Art and Life*. Edited by Jeff Kelley. London: University of California Press.

Kardas, Saban. 2001. "Humanitarian Intervention." *Perception: Journal of International Affairs* 6, no. 2 (June–July). http://sam.gov.tr/tr/wp-content/uploads/2014/02/SabanKardas.pdf (accessed May 21, 2017).

Kelly, Susan. 2005. "The Transversal and the Invisible: How Do You Really Make a Work of Art That Is Not a Work of Art?" *EIPCP: European Institute for Progressive Cultural Policies*. www.republicart.net/disc/mundial/kelly01_en.htm (accessed March 10, 2017).

Kerber, Linda K. 2009. "The Stateless and the Citizen's Other: A View from the United States." In *Migrations and Mobilities: Citizenship, Borders and Gender*, edited by Seyla Benhabib and Judith Resnick, 76–123. New York: New York University Press.

Kershaw, Alex. 2015. "Immigrant Movement International: An Interview with Tania Bruguera." *Field* 1 (spring): 12–26 (accessed October 12, 2015).

Kester, Grant, ed. 1998. *Art, Activism, and Oppositionality: Essays from Afterimage*. London: Duke University Press.

———. 2004. *Conversation Pieces: Community and Communication in Modern Art*. Oakland: University of California Press.

———. 2011. *The One and the Many: Contemporary Collaborative Art in a Global Context*. Durham, NC: Duke University Press.

"Khaled Jarrar: State of Palestine (Interview)." 2012. Video posted to YouTube by GPRBLN. September 27, 2012. www.youtube.com/watch?v=qpHRbncBmJQ (accessed August 12, 2018).

Kleinfeld, Rachel, and John Dickas. 2020. "Resisting the Call of Nativism: What U.S. Political Parties Can Learn from Other Democracies." *Carnegie Endowment*.

March 5. https://carnegieendowment.org/2020/03/05/resisting-call-of-nativism-what-u.s.-political-parties-can-learn-from-other-democracies-pub-81204

Kleingeld, Pauline. 2012. *Kant and Cosmopolitanism: The Philosophical Ideal of World Citizenship*. Cambridge: Cambridge University Press.

Klicperova-Baker, Martina. 2010. "'Citizenship' and 'European Citizenship' as Qualitative and Legal Concepts—Typology of Citizenship and the EU." 60th Annual Conference of Political Studies Association, Edinburgh, United Kingdom, March 29.

Korsgaard, Christine M. 2018. *Fellow Creatures: Our Obligations to the Other Animals*. Oxford: Oxford University Press.

Krauss, Rosalind. 1979. "Sculpture in the Expanded Field." *October* 8 (spring): 31–44. https://doi.org/10.2307/778224.

Kwon, Miwon. 2002. *One Place after Another: Site-Specific Art and Locational Identity*. Cambridge, MA: MIT Press.

Kymlicka, Will. 1990. *Contemporary Political Philosophy: An Introduction*. Oxford, UK: Clarendon Press.

Lebourdais, Chief Michael. 2013. "Dear Canada: First Nations Do Not Want to Be Wards of the State." *Globe and Mail*. January 8. www.theglobeandmail.com/opinion/dear-canada-first-nations-dont-want-to-be-wards-of-the-state/article7028879 (accessed November 12, 2016).

Leduc, Sarah. 2015. "The Kurds: The World's Largest Stateless Nation." *France 24: International News 24/7*. July 30. www.france24.com/en/20150730-who-are-kurds-turkey-syria-iraq-pkk-divided (accessed August 10, 2018).

Levy, Jacob T. 2015. "Against Fraternity: Democracy without Solidarity." *Berkeley Law*. www.law.berkeley.edu/wp-content/uploads/2015/04/Against-Fraternity-Democracy-Without-Solidarity-2015.pdf (accessed August 10, 2018).

Linden, Christina. 2011. "Interview with Shannon Jackson." *Art Practical Performance: The Body Politic*. 2, no. 15. www.artpractical.com/feature/interview_with_shannon_jackson (accessed May 12, 2013).

Lippard, Lucy. 1973. *Six Years: The Dematerialization of the Art Object, 1966–1972*. Oakland, CA: University of California Press.

Lippard, Lucy, and John Chandler. 1999. "The Dematerialization of Art." In *Conceptual Art: A Critical Anthology*, edited by Alexander Alberro and Blake Stimson, 46–51. Cambridge, MA: MIT Press.

Locke, John. 1690. *Second Treatise on Civil Government*. In *The Founders Constitution*, edited by Philip B. Kurland and Ralph Lerner. Chicago: University of Chicago Press.

———. 1823. *Two Treatises of Government*. Edited by Rod Hay. Toronto: York University. www.yorku.ca/comninel/courses/3025pdf/Locke.pdf (accessed May 26, 2013).

London School of Economics. 2008. "Foreign National ID Cards Will Do Little to Improve Security in the Near Future Says LSE Academic." *London School of Economics and Political Science*. September 25. www.lse.ac.uk/newsAndMedia/newsarchives/2008/IDCards.aspx (accessed August 13, 2013).

Love, Nancy S., and Mark Mattern. 2013. *Doing Democracy: Activist Art and Cultural Politics*. Albany: State University of New York.

Lyon, Alynna J., and Mary Fran T. Malone. 2012. "Responding to Kosovo's Call for Humanitarian Intervention: Public Opinion, Partisanship and Policy Objectives." In *Kosovo, Intervention and Statebuilding: The International Community and the Transition to Independence*, edited by Aiden Hehir, 17–37. London: Routledge.

Mackey, Eva. 2016. *Unsettled Expectations: Uncertainty, Land and Settler Decolonization*. Winnipeg: Fernwood Publishing.

MacSweeny, Eoghan. n.d. "The Doctrine of Humanitarian Intervention: A Double Standard?" *Cork Online Law Review*. http://corkonlinelawreview.com/editions/2003/2003viii.pdf (accessed September 15, 2015).

Marquand, David. 2004. *Decline of the Public: The Hollowing Out of Citizenship*. Cambridge: Polity Press.

Martin, James. 2013. *Chantal Mouffe: Hegemony, Radical Democracy and the Political*. London: Routledge.

May, Todd. 2008. *The Political Thought of Jacques Rancière: Creating Equality*. Edinburgh: Edinburgh University Press.

Maynor, John. 2018. "Civic-Republicanism." *Encyclopaedia Britannica*. www.britannica.com/topic/civic-republicanism (accessed March 15, 2018).

McGettigan, Andrew. 2013. *The Great University Gamble: Money, Markets and the Future of Higher Education*. London: Pluto Press.

Meier, Prita Sandy, Jessica Horton, and Freya Hartzell, et al. 2014. "Objects, Objectives, Objections: The Goals and Limits of New Materialisms in Art History." Conference Panel Discussion. College Art Association Conference, Chicago, Illinois.

Meschini, Emanuele Rinaldo. 2013. "Arte Útil Part 1: A Practical Theorization." *Luxflux: Art in Theory* 49 (September). http://luxflux.net/arte-util-parte-1-una-teorizzazione-pratica (accessed October 10, 2016).

Meskimmon, Marsha. 2011. *Contemporary Art and the Cosmopolitan Imagination*. London: Routledge.

———. 2013. "The Precarious Ecologies of Cosmopolitanism." *Open Arts Journal* 1 (summer): 15–26. https://openartsjournal.files.wordpress.com/2013/07/oaj_issue1_meskimmon.pdf (accessed May 9, 2016).

Mezzadra, Sandro, and Brett Neilson. 2008. "Border as Method, or, the Multiplication of Labor." *European Institute for Progressive Cultural Policies (EIPCP)*. March. http://eipcp.net/transversal/0608/mezzadraneilson/en (accessed March 4, 2013).

———. 2012. "Between Inclusion and Exclusion: On the Topology of Global Space and Borders." *Theory Culture Society* 29: 58–75.

Miessen, Markus. 2011. *The Nightmare of Participation*. Berlin: Sternberg Press.

Miller, Abigail. 2017. "'No Trump, No KKK, No Racist UVA': Black Lives Matter Group Targets Monument of University's Founder Thomas Jefferson in Charlottesville." *Daily Mail*. September 13. www.dailymail.co.uk/news/article-4880272/Black-Lives-Matter-targets-UVA-Thomas-Jefferson-monument.html (accessed October 10, 2018).

Miller, J. R. 2007. "Compact, Contract, Covenant." Miller-Keenan Lecture. St. Thomas More College. February 13. www.collectionscanada.gc.ca/obj/g4/11/780973 431612_13244st.pdf (accessed April 12, 2017).

Montgomery, David T. 2016. "Applied Theatre and Citizenship in the Puerto Rican Community: Artistic Citizenship in Practice." In *Artistic Citizenship*, edited by David J. Elliott, Marissa Silverman, and Wayne Bowman, 447–468. Oxford: Oxford University Press.

Monument Lab. 2017. "Monument Lab: Philadelphia (Citywide Exhibition, 2017)." *Monument Lab.* September–November. https://monumentlab.com/projects/monu ment-lab-philadelphia-citywide-exhibition-2017.

Mouffe, Chantal. 2007. "Art Activism and Agonistic Spaces." *Art & Research: A Journal of Ideas, Contexts and Methods* 1, no. 2 (summer): 1–5.

Museum of Contemporary Art, Los Angeles. 2012. *Engagement Party: Practice at MOCA 2008–2012*. Los Angeles: Museum of Contemporary Art.

Nair, Parvati. 2012. "The Body Politic of Dissent: The Paperless and the Indignant." *Citizenship Studies* 16, no. 5–6: 783–92.

National Centre for First Nations Governance. n.d. "Reclaiming Our Identity: Band Membership, Citizenship and the Inherent Right." *Centre for First Nations Governance.* https://fngovernance.org/wp-content/uploads/2020/06/Reclaiming_Our _Identity.pdf (accessed November 29, 2017).

National Inquiry into Missing and Murdered Indigenous Women and Girls. 2019. *Reclaiming Power and Place: The Final Report of the National Inquiry into Missing and Murdered Indigenous Women and Girls*. Vol. 1a. National Inquiry into Missing and Murdered Indigenous Women and Girls. www.mmiwg-ffada.ca/final-report.

Neue Slowenische Kunst (NSK). 1984–1992. *NSK State: Neue Slowenische Kunst 1984–1992.* Exhibition. Chelsea Space. https://nskstate.com/article/neue -slowenische-kunst-1984-1992 (accessed October 18 2021).

———. 2010. *First NSK Citizens Congress.* http://congress.nskstate.com (accessed March 15, 2011).

"Nicolas Bourriaud. *Excerpts from Relational Aesthetics*." 1998. mariabuszek.com. http://mariabuszek.com/mariabuszek/kcai/PoMoSeminar/Readings/BourriaudRA .pdf (accessed September 16, 2015).

Novick, Ilana. 2016. "For Freedoms—a Super PAC Where Art Meets Politics." *Alternet.* www.alternet.org/culture/super-pac-run-artists (accessed August 12, 2018).

Nozick, Robert. 1974. *Anarchy, State and Utopia.* New York: Basic Books.

Nussbaum, Martha. 1994. "Patriotism and Cosmopolitanism." *Boston Review: A Political and Literary Forum* 19, no. 5. www.oneworlduv.com/wp-content/uploads /2011/06/patriotism_cosmopolitanism.pdf (accessed April 1, 2015).

———. 1996. *For Love of Country?* Edited by Joshua Cohen. Boston: Beacon Press.

Nyers, Peter. 2008. "No One Is Illegal between City and Nation." In *Acts of Citizenship*, edited by Engin Isin and Greg M. Nielsen, 160–81. London: Zed Books.

Occupy Wall Street. 2011. "#OccupyTogether." https://web.archive.org/web /20130514230107/http://www.occupytogether.org.

Oliveri, Federico. 2012. "Migrants as Activist Citizens in Italy: Understanding the New Cycle of Struggles." *Citizenship Studies* 16, nos. 5–6: 793–806.

Osborne, Samuel. 2017. "France Declares End to State of Emergency Two Years after Paris Terror Attacks." *Independent.* October 31. www.independent.co.uk/news/world/europe/france-state-of-emergency-end-terror-attacks-paris-isis-terrorism-alerts-warning-risk-reduced-a8029311.html (accessed March 28, 2018).

Ostrom, Elinor. 1990. *Governing the Commons: The Evolution of Institutions for Collective Action.* Cambridge: Cambridge University Press.

Oxford Reference. n.d. "Jus Soli." *Oxford Reference.* www.oxfordreference.com/view/10.1093/acref/9780199551248.001.0001/acref-9780199551248-e-2148.

"Paddle for LEL,ŦOS (James Island) and the Salish Sea." 2018. Video posted to YouTube by Plessner Plessner. August 14, 2018. www.youtube.com/watch?v=TeVIuOdnzrY.

Panagia, Davide. 2018. *Rancière's Sentiments.* Durham, NC: Duke University Press.

Papastergiadis, Nikos. 2012. *Cosmopolitanism and Culture.* Cambridge, UK: Polity Press.

Paul, Philip Kevin, Philip Christopher Paul, Eddy Carmack, and Eddy MacDonald. 1995. "The Care Takers." *Institute of Ocean Sciences Department of Fisheries and Oceans.* www.dfo-mpo.gc.ca/Library/181814.pdf (accessed May 13, 2017).

Payton, Bre. 2017. "Here's a List of All the Monuments Liberals Want to Tear Down So Far." *Federalist.* August 17. http://thefederalist.com/2017/08/17/heres-list-monuments-liberals-want-tear-far (accessed October 10, 2018).

Paz, Danielle. 2013. "Interview between Dan Paz and Tania Bruguera." *Shifter Magazine* 20 (May): 124–30. www.taniabruguera.com/cms/6640Interview+between+Dan+Paz+and+Tania+Bruguera.htm (accessed May 6, 2015).

Pelosi, Nick. 2012. "Ecuadorian President Responds to Criticism." *First Peoples Worldwide.* December 13. http://firstpeoples.org/wp/tag/conaie (accessed March 4, 2014).

Pender Islands Museum. 2005. "The Pender Islands Timeline." *Pender Islands Museum.* www.penderislandmuseum.org/content/pender-islands-time-line (accessed May 6, 2017).

———. 2021. "Time Line." *Pender Islands Museum.* http://penderislandsmuseum.ca/timeline?field_time_period_target_id=All&title=&body_value=&page=3 (accessed August 3, 2021).

Performigrations. 2014. "Mobile Interventions." http://performigrations.eu/project/art-installation/mobile-interventions (accessed September 9, 2016).

Peters, Sibylle. 2016. "Performing Citizenship: Performance Art and Public Happiness." In *Artistic Citizenship*, edited by David J. Elliott, Marissa Silverman, and Wayne Bowman, 469–79. Oxford: Oxford University Press.

Plessner, Daphne. 2010. Citizen Artist. www.citizen artist.org.uk (accessed November 18, 2018).

———. 2011. "The Mobile Armband Exhibition." March 26. www.citizenartist.org.uk/ca-articles/citizenartistMobileArmbandInfo.pdf.

———. 2012. "Political Activism and Art: A Consideration of the Implications of New Developments in Practice." *Art & Education.* July 21: 1–5. www.citizenartist.org.uk/ca-articles/Political%20Activism%20and%20Art:%20A%20Consider

ation%20of%20the%20Implications%20of%20New%20Developments%20in%20
Practice.%20%7C%20Art%20&%20Education.pdf (accessed December 06, 2012).
———. 2013a. "Citizen Artist News: The University as a Border Regime." May 12.
http://citizenartist.org.uk/ca-articles/CitizenArtistNews3.pdf
———. 2013b. "National Student Surveys." *Central St. Martins College of Art and
Design, London.* March 23. www.citizenartist.org.uk.
———. 2014. "What Is a University?" *Journal of Artistic Research* 6 (accessed
October 10, 2014).
———. 2018. "Citizen Artist News: Clouded Title." April 12. Pender Island, B.C.
Canada. www.citizenartist.org.uk/ca-articles/Plessner-CitizenArtistNews-clouded
%20title.pdf.
———. 2019. "Citizen Artist News: Kinship." October. www.citizenartist.org.uk
/ca-articles/Citizen_Artist_News_Kinship-small.pdf.
Polisi, Joseph W. 2005. *The Artist as Citizen.* Cambridge, MA: Amadeus Press.
Pollis, Adamantia, and Peter Schwab, eds. 1980. *Human Rights: Cultural and Ideological Perspectives.* New York: Praeger Publishers.
Public Domain Review. n.d. "Yellow Journalism: The 'Fake News' of the 19th Century."
Public Domain Review. https://publicdomainreview.org/collections/yellow-jour
nalism-the-fake-news-of-the-19th-century (accessed August 12, 2018).
Ramsden, Ché. 2016. "Artivism: Art as Activism, Activism as Art." *Open Democracy: 50.50.* September 10. www.opendemocracy.net/ch-ramsden/artivism-art-as
-activism-activism-as-art (accessed May 10, 2018).
Rancière, Jacques. (2004) 2009. *The Politics of Aesthetics.* London: Continuum.
———. 2010. *Dissensus: On Politics and Aesthetics.* London: Continuum.
———. 2011a. *The Emancipated Spectator.* London: Verso.
———. 2011b. "The Thinking of Dissensus: Politics and Aesthetics." In *Reading
Rancière,* edited by Paul Bowman and Richard Stamp, 1–17. London: Continuum.
Raunig, Gerald. 2013. *Factories of Knowledge: Industries of Creativity.* Intervention
Series 15. Los Angeles: Semiotext(e).
Rawls, John. 1971. *A Theory of Justice.* Cambridge, MA: Belknap Press of Harvard
University Press.
Readings, Bill. 1996. *The University in Ruins.* Cambridge, MA: Harvard University
Press.
Regina v. Bartleman. 1984. "British Columbia Court of Appeal: R v. Bartlemen." Brit-
ish Columbia Court of Appeal. CanLII 547. June 27. www.canlii.org/en/bc/bcca
/doc/1984/1984canlii547/1984canlii547.pdf (accessed September 6, 2017).
Regina v. Morris. 2006. "Supreme Court Judgments." Judgments of the Supreme
Court of Canada. 2 SCC 915; 2006 SCC 59. Case No. 30328. December 21. https://
scc-csc.lexum.com/scc-csc/scc-csc/en/item/2334/index.do (accessed September 6,
2017).
Richling, Barnett. 2016. *The W̱SÁNEĆ and Their Neighbours: Diamond Jenness on
the Coast Salish of Vancouver Island, 1935.* Oakville, Ontario: Rock Mills Press.
Robinson, Dylan. 2020. *Hungry Listening: Resonant Theory for Indigenous Sound
Studies.* Minneapolis: University of Minnesota Press.

Rose, Joel. 2018. "A Toddler's Death Adds to Concerns about Migrant Detention." *NPR*. August 28. www.npr.org/2018/08/28/642738732/a-toddlers-death-adds-to -concerns-about-migrant-detention (accessed October 10, 2018).

Rygiel, Kim. 2010. *Globalizing Citizenship*. Vancouver: University of British Columbia Press.

Ryniker, Ann. 2001. "The ICRC's Position on 'Humanitarian Intervention.'" *International Review of the Red Cross (ICRC)* 83, no. 842: 527–32. https:// studylib.net/doc/8231919/the-icrc-s-position-on-%E2%80%9Chumanitarian-inter vention%E2%80%9D (accessed February 10, 2017).

Salter, Mark B., ed. 2008. *Politics at the Airport*. Minneapolis: University of Minnesota Press.

Sassen, Saskia. 1999. "Who's City Is It? Globalization and the Formation of New Claims." In *Cities and Citizenship*, edited by James Holsten, 177–94. Durham, NC: Duke University Press.

———. 2000. "The Need to Distinguish between Denationalized and Postnational." *Indiana Journal of Global Legal Studies* 7, no. 2: 575–58.

———. 2002a. "The Repositioning of Citizenship: Emergent Subjects and Spaces for Politics." *Berkeley Journal of Sociology* 46: 4–25. http://transnationalism .uchicago.edu/RepositioningCitizenship.pdf (accessed June 12, 2012).

———. 2002b. "Towards Post-national and Denationalized Citizenship." In *Handbook of Citizenship Studies*, edited by Engin Isin and Brian Turner, 277–91, London: Sage Publications.

———. 2007. "A Sociology of Globalization." In *Contemporary Societies*, edited by J. C. Alexander, 129–63. New York: W. W. Norton.

Schininá, Guglielmo. 2017. "Objectification and Abjectification of Migrants: Reflections to Help Guide Psychological Workers." *Intervention* 15, no. 2: 100–5. www .interventionjournal.com/sites/default/files/Objectification_and_abjectification _of_migrants__.2.pdf (accessed July 9, 2018).

Schlingensief, Christoph. 2000. "Please Love Austria: First Austrian Coalition Week." June 9–16. www.schlingensief.com/projekt_eng.php?id=t033 (accessed November 13, 2014).

Schmidt Campbell, Mary, and Randy Martin. 2006. *Artistic Citizenship: A Public Voice for the Arts*. New York: Routledge.

Schneider, Florian. 1997. *Kein Mensch Ist Illegal*. Germany, United Kingdom, Canada, Online. June 28–present. www.kein-mensch-ist-illegal.org/ and http:// museumarteutil.net/projects/kein-mensch-ist-illegal (accessed February 2, 2014).

Schnugg, Claudia. 2014. "The Organisation as Artist's Palette: Arts-Based Interventions." *Journal of Business Strategy* 35, no. 5: 31–37. www.emeraldinsight.com /doi/abs/10.1108/JBS-02-2013-0015?journalCode=jbs (accessed June 7, 2016).

Scholl, Christian. 2010. "Bakunin's Poor Cousins: Engaging Art for Tactical Interventions." In *Cultural Activism: Practices, Dilemmas, and Possibilities*. Thramyris /Intersecting: Place, Sex and Race 21: 157–78.

Schwartz, Stephanie. 2012. "Tania Bruguera: Between Histories." *Oxford Art Journal* 35, no. 2: 215–32.

Schwarzenbach, Sibyl A. 2015. "Fraternity, Solidarity and Civic friendship." *Amity: The Journal of Friendship Studies* 3, no. 1: 3–18. https://amityjournal.leeds .ac.uk/issues/volume-3/fraternity-solidarity-and-civic-friendship (accessed August 9, 2018).

Shahzad, Ramna. 2017. "What Is the Significance of Acknowledging the Indigenous Land We Stand On?" *CBC News*. July 15. www.cbc.ca/news/canada/toronto /territorial-acknowledgements-indigenous-1.4175136 (accessed July 21, 2017).

Sheikh, Simon. 2009. "Objects of Study or Commodification of Knowledge? Remarks on Artistic Research." *Art & Research: A Journal of Ideas, Contexts and Methods* 2, no. 2 (spring). www.artandresearch.org.uk/v2n2/pdfs/sheikh.pdf (accessed May 16, 2012).

Sholette, Gregory. 2011. *Dark Matter: Art and Politics in the Age of Enterprise Culture*. London: Pluto Press.

Sigona, Nando. 2013. "UK Migration Policy: We Need to Talk about Citizenship." *Open Democracy*. February 4. www.opendemocracy.net/en/5050/uk-migration -policy-we-need-to-talk-about-citizens (accessed February 6, 2013).

Simpson, Audra. 2014. *Mohawk Interruptus: Political Life across the Borders of Settler States*. Durham, NC: Duke University Press.

Slater, Howard. 2000. "The Art of Governance: On the Artist Placement Group, 1966–1989." *Variant* 2, no. 11 (summer). www.variant.org.uk/pdfs/issue11/Howard _Slater.pdf (accessed June 9, 2017).

Smith, Barry. 1990. "Towards a History of Speech Act Theory." In *Speech Acts, Meanings and Intentions: Critical Approaches to the Philosophy of John R. Searle*, edited by A. Burkhardt, 29–61. Berlin: de Gruyter.

Soila-Wadman, Marsha, and Oriana Haselwanter. 2014. "Design Thinking and Artistic Interventions: Tools for Understanding and Developing Organizational Creativity?" *Swedish Design Research Journal* 2: 32–42. www.svid.se/upload/Forskning /Design_Research_Journal/Design_Research_Journal_nr_2_2014/Design_think ing_and_artistic_interventions.pdf (accessed May 12, 2016).

Sources on the Douglas Treaties. n.d. *Douglas Treaty Documents #1–#16*. CC2-Treaties Docs. www.govlet.ca/en/pdf/cc2-blm-6.pdf (accessed September 1, 2016).

Sputnik. 2018. "Windrush: Britons Asked to 'Prove They Are Worthy of Citizenship.'" *Sputnik*. April 25. https://sputniknews.com/analysis/201804251063878508 -windrush-citizens-prove-worthy-expert (accessed August 25, 2018).

Staal, Jonas. 2012. *New World Summit*. Academia. www.academia.edu/27983112 /New_World_Summit (accessed April 10, 2015).

———. 2013. *New World Academy Reader #1. Toward a People's Culture with the Democratic Movement of the Philippines*. Utrecht: Basis voor Actuele Kunst.

———. 2015–2018. "New World Summit—Rojava." Jonas Staal. www.jonasstaal.nl /projects/new-world-summit-rojava (accessed September 24, 2021).

———. 2015a. *New World Academy Reader #5. Stateless Democracy*. Utrecht: Basis voor Actuele Kunst.

———. 2015b. "To Make a World, Part III: Stateless Democracy." *e-flux Journal* 63 (March): 1–12. http://worker01.e-flux.com/pdf/article_8996631.pdf (July accessed, 2015).

Staal, Jonas, Florian Malzacher, and Joanna Warsza. 2015. Artist Organizations International and HAU (Haupt Stadt Kultur Fonds). www.artistorganisations inter national.org (accessed June 10, 2017).

Stanford Encyclopedia of Philosophy. n.d. "Liberalism." https://plato.stanford.edu /entries/liberalism/#PolLib (accessed August 12, 2018).

Stark, Alex, Thomas Weiss, Ramesh Thakar, Mary Ellen O'Connell, Aidan Hehir, Alex J. Bellamy, David Chandler, et al. 2011. "The Responsibility to Protect: Challenges and Opportunities in Light of the Libyan Intervention." *e-International Relations*. November. www.e-ir.info/wp-content/uploads/R2P.pdf (accessed July 17, 2015).

Stevini, Barbara. 2001. "Organisation + Imagination: Pioneering Art in the Social Context." PDF. https://s3.amazonaws.com/arena-attachments/566821/026fab1fccc 53d1c09f75c76250e3ebc.pdf?1457950653 (accessed July 28, 2017).

Stewart, Kathleen. 2007. *Ordinary Affects*. Durham, NC: Duke University Press.

Street Road. 2018. "Clouded Title." Street Road. February 12–18 and April 14. www .streetroad.org/clouded-title.html.

Styhre, Alexander, and Jonas Fröberg. 2016. "Artist in Residence Work as Détournement and Constructed Situations: Theorizing Art Interventions in Organizations." Department of Business Administration, School of Business, Economics and Law, University of Gothenburg, Sweden. https://slidex.tips/download/artist-in-res idence-work-as-detournement-and-constructed-situations-theorizing-a (accessed August 10, 2017).

Sullivan, Jeffrey. 2017. "Black Lives Matter Activists Rally for Removal of Confederate Monument." *Rivard Report*. July 4. https://therivardreport.com/black-lives -matter-activists-rally-for-removal-of-confederate-monument (accessed October 10, 2018).

Supreme Court of British Columbia v. Tsawout First Nation. 2018. Notice of Civil Claim. Court Fine no. VIC-S-S-180472. First Peoples Law. www.firstpeopleslaw .com/database/files/library/18_01_24_Tsawout_Notice_of_Civil_Claim_(Filed) .pdf (accessed February 10, 2018).

Tancons, Claire. 2011. "Occupy Wall Street: Carnival against Capital? Carnivalesque as Protest Sensibility." *e-flux Journal* 30 (December). www.e-flux.com/journal /30/68148/occupy-wall-street-carnival-against-capital-carnivalesque-as-protest -sensibility (accessed May 24, 2013).

———. 2012. "Carnival to Commons: Pussy Riot Punk Protest and the Exercise of Democratic Culture." *e-flux Journal* 37 (September). www.e-flux.com/journal /carnival-to-commons-pussy-riot-punk-protest-and-the-exercise-of-democratic -culture (accessed May 23, 2013).

Tate. n.d. "Art Intervention." Tate. www.tate.org.uk/art/art-terms/a/art-intervention (accessed July 19, 2017).

Teitel, Ruti. 1997. "Human Rights Genealogy." *Fordham Law Review* 66, no. 2: 301–17. http://ir.lawnet.fordham.edu/flr/vol66/iss2/3 (accessed June 19, 2013).

Thanawala, Sudhin, and Andrew Dalton. 2018. "Judge Blocks Trump Decision to End Young Immigrant Program." *Associated Press*. January 9. https://finance.yahoo.com

/news/judge-blocks-trump-decision-end-041658365.html (accessed October 10, 2018).

Thom, Brian. 2009. "The Paradox of Boundaries in Coast Salish Territories." *Cultural Geographies* 16, no. 2: 179–205. https://dspace.library.uvic.ca/bitstream /handle/1828/6281/Thom_Brian_CultGeog_2009.pdf (accessed March 3, 2016).

Thompson, Nato. 2012. *Living as Form: Socially Engaged Art from 1991–2011*. Cambridge, MA: MIT Press.

———. 2015. *Seeing Power: Art and Activism in the 21st Century*. London: Blackstone and Melville House Publishing.

———. 2017. *Culture as Weapon: The Art of Influence in Everyday Life*. London: Melville House.

Thompson, Nato, Gregory Sholette, Joseph Thompson, Nicholas Mirzoeff, and Ondine C. Chavoya, eds. 2004. *The Interventionists: Users Manual for the Creative Disruption of Everyday Life*. North Adams, MA: MASS MoCA Publications.

Times of Israel. 2017. "The Kurds: One Stateless People across Four Countries." *Times of Israel*. September 25. www.timesofisrael.com/the-kurds-one-stateless -people-across-four-countries (accessed August 10, 2018).

Timm, Jane C. 2017. "Donald Trump's Border Wall: A 'Progress' Report." *NBC News*. May 30. www.nbcnews.com/politics/donald-trump/donald-trump-s-border -wall-progress-report-n764726 (accessed October 10, 2018).

Torolab Collective. 2005. "Region of Transborder Trousers (LRPT)." GPS Tracking of Border Crossings: Tijuana–San Diego. Arco Contemporary Art Fair, Madrid. http://torolab.org/blog/lrpt (accessed September 30, 2012).

Torpey, John. 2000. *The Invention of the Passport: Surveillance, Citizenship and the State*. Cambridge: Cambridge University Press.

Truth and Reconciliation Commission of Canada. 2015. *Honouring the Truth, Reconciling for the Future: Final Report of the Truth and Reconciliation Commission of Canada*. Vol. 1: *Summary*. Toronto: James Lorimer & Company.

Tsawout First Nation. n.d. "About SȾÁ,UTW̱ First Nation." Tsawout First Nation. https://tsawout.ca/about-tsawout. (accessed October 13, 2017).

———. 2015. *Tsawout Marine Use Study: Prepared for Tsawout First Nation's Review of the Proposed Kinder Morgan Trans Mountain Expansion, Marine Shipping Component*. Edited by Peter Evans, Beth Keats, and Dave King. Victoria, BC: Trailmark Systems and Consulting.

Tsawout First Nation v. Attorney General of Canada, Her Majesty the Queen in Right of British Columbia and J. I. Properties Incorporated. 2018. Notice of Civil Claim. Court file no: VIC-S-S-180472. First Peoples Law. www.firstpeopleslaw.com /database/files/library/18_01_24_Tsawout_Notice_of_Civil_Claim_(Filed).pdf (accessed May 9, 2016).

Tuck, Eve, and Wayne K. Yang. 2012. "Decolonization Is Not a Metaphor." *Decolonization: Indigeneity, Education & Society* 1, no. 1: 1–40. www.academia.edu /2721597/Decolonization_is_not_a_metaphor (accessed December 12, 2015).

Underwood, Mavis Kathleen. 2018. *The Education of an Indigenous Woman: The Pursuit of Truth, Social Justice, and Healthy Relationships in a Coast Salish Community Context*. MA thesis, University of Victoria.

Union of BC Indian Chiefs (UBCIC). 1981. "UBCIC 13th Annual General Assembly: Minutes." UBCIC. October 28–30, 1981. http://constitution.ubcic.bc.ca/node/138 (accessed January 6, 2016).

United Kingdom Office of the Prime Minister. 2014. "Summary of the Government Legal Position on Military Action in Iraq against ISIL: Policy Paper." GOV.UK. September 25. www.gov.uk/government/publications/military-action-in-iraq-against-isil-government-legal-position/summary-of-the-government-legal-position-on-military-action-in-iraq-against-isil (accessed July 19, 2015).

United Nations. 2007. "United Nations Declaration on the Rights of Indigenous Peoples." United Nations. www.un.org/esa/socdev/unpfii/documents/DRIPS_en.pdf (accessed July 29, 2013).

United Nations General Assembly. 2005. "2005 World Summit Outcome." A/60/L.1. World Health Organization. September 15. www.who.int/hiv/universalaccess2010/worldsummit.pdf (accessed August 12, 2015).

———. 2009. "Implementing the Responsibility to Protect: Report of the Secretary General." A/63/677. United Nations. https://documents-dds-ny.un.org/doc/UNDOC/GEN/N09/206/10/PDF/N0920610.pdf?OpenElement (accessed November 13, 2015).

United Nations High Commission for Refugees (UNHCR). 2010a. "Preventing and Reducing Statelessness: The 1961 Convention on the Reduction of Statelessness." UNHCR. September. www.unhcr.it/wpcontent/uploads/2016/01/preventing_and_reducing_statelessness.pdf (accessed November 2, 2014).

———. 2010b. "Protecting the Rights of Stateless Persons: The 1954 Convention Relating to the Status of Stateless People." UNHCR. September. www.unhcr.org/4ca5941c9.pdf (accessed November 2, 2014).

———. 2011. "Mapping Statelessness in the United Kingdom." UNHCR. November. www.unhcr.org/4ecbc3c09.html (accessed November 2, 2014).

———. 2014. "Convention on the Reduction of Statelessness." UNHCR. November. www.unhcr.org/protection/statelessness/3bbb286d8/convention-reduction-statelessness.html (accessed November 2, 2014).

University and College Union (UCU). n.d. "University and College Union Report on Points Based Immigration." UCU. www.ucu.org.uk/media/pdf/k/g/pbs_seminar report_apr09.pdf (accessed August 22, 2013).

University of the Arts London. 2012. "University of the Arts London Joining Information 2012–13." University of the Arts London. www.arts.ac.uk/study-at-ual/international/application-advice (accessed August 8, 2013).

US Department of Arts and Culture (USDAC). n.d. "Statement of Values." USDAC. https://usdac.us/statement-of-values.

Van Abbemuseum. 2018. "The Museum as Parliament." *Van Abbemuseum*. https://vanabbemuseum. nl/en/programme/programme/museum-as-parliament (accessed August 15, 2018).

Van der Ploeg, Piet, and Laurence Guérin. 2016. "Questioning Participation and Solidarity as Goals of Civic Education." *Critical Review: A Journal of Politics and Society* (June 29): 1–17. http://verenigingvantaalspecialisten.nl/wp-content

/uploads/2014/12/vdPloeg_Guerin_Questioning-Participation-and-Solidarity-as
-Goals-of-Citizenship-Education.pdf (accessed August 8, 2018).

Vasiljević, Jelena. 2016. "The Possibilities and Constraints of Engaging Solidarity
in Citizenship." *Filozofija i društvo* 27, no. 2: 373–86. http://instifdt.bg.ac.rs/wp
-content/uploads/2016/04/06-Jelena-Vasiljevic.pdf (accessed August 9, 2018).

Verellen, Thomas. 2012. "A Few Words on the Responsibility to Protect." *Katholieke
Universiteit Leuven, Faculteit Rechtsgeleerdheid Jura Falconis* 48, no. 2: 151–87.
https://limo.libis.be/primoexplore/fulldisplay?docid=LIRIAS1854751&context
=L&vid=Lirias&search_scope=Lirias&tab=default_tab&lang=en_US
&fromSitemap=1 (accessed October 25, 2015).

Vine, John. 2012. "An Inspection of Tier 4 of the Points Based System (Students)."
GOV.UK. November 29. https://assets.publishing.service.gov.uk/government
/uploads/system/uploads/attachment_data/file/546577/An-inspection-of-Tier-4-of
-the-Points-Based-System-29.11.2012.pdf (accessed January 1, 2013).

Vujanović, Ana. 2016. "Art as a Bad Public Good." In *Artistic Citizenship*, edited by
David J. Elliott, Marissa Silverman, and Wayne Bowman, 104–22. Oxford: Oxford
University Press.

Waldron, Daniel, and Sanwar Ali. 2018. "UK Tier 4 Visa Restrictions Eased for International Students." *workpermit.com.* September 16. http://workpermit.com/news
/uk-tier-4-visa-restrictions-eased-international-students-20180916 (accessed
November 14, 2018).

Webster, Stephen C. 2011. "Under 'Emergency' for Decades, Egypt's Special Powers
Mirrored in Post-9/11 US." *Raw Story.* January 28. www.rawstory.com/rs
/2011/01/28/perpetual-emergency-1981-egypt-gave-government-uslike-spe
cial-powers (accessed February 18, 2014).

Weibel, Peter. 2015. *Global Activism: Art and Conflict in the 21st Century.* Karlsruhe:
ZKM: Centre for Art and Media.

Werthein, Judi. 2005. *Brinco. inSite.* https://insiteart.org/people/judi-werthein (accessed October 20, 2021).

Wesemann, Anne. 2020. "EU Court Case Sees British Citizen Seek Post-Brexit
Rights in France." *Global Citizenship Observatory.* https://globalcit.eu/eu-court
-case-sees-british-citizen-seek-post-brexit-rights-in-france.

Wikipedia. n.d.a. "Carnival Against Capital." *Wikipedia.* https://en.wikipedia.org
/wiki/Carnival_Against_Capital_(accessed November 4, 2016)

———. n.d.b. "Cloud on Title." *Wikipedia.* https://en.wikipedia.org/wiki/Cloud_on
title(accessed June 7, 2018).

———. n.d.c. "For Freedoms." *Wikipedia.* https://en.wikipedia.org/wiki/For_Freedoms
(accessed September 22, 2021).

———. n.d.d. "Pender Island." *Wikipedia.* https://en.wikipedia.org/wiki/Pender_Island
(accessed August 8, 2017).

———. n.d.e. "Post-truth Politics." *Wikipedia.* https://en.wikipedia.org/wiki/Post-truth
_politics (accessed October 10, 2018).

———. n.d.f. "UK Border Agency." *Wikipedia.* https://en.wikipedia.org/wiki/UK
_Border_Agency.

————. n.d.g. "Windrush Scandal." *Wikipedia.* https://en.wikipedia.org/wiki/Windrush
   _scandal (accessed October 1, 2120).

Wiles, David. 2016. "Art and Citizenship: The History of a Divorce." In *Artistic
   Citizenship*, edited by David J. Elliott, Marissa Silverman, and Wayne Bowman,
   22–40. Oxford: Oxford University Press.

Wilk, Elvia. 2016. "The Artist-in-Consultance: Welcome to the New Management."
   e-flux Journal 74 (June): 1–9.

Wilson, Kevin. n.d. *Public Art Community Toolkit.* Nottingham: Arts Service, Not-
   tinghamshire County Council.

Wilson, Mick. 2007. "Autonomy, Agonism, and Activist Art: An Interview with Grant
   Kester." *Art Journal* 66, no. 3 (fall): 107–18.

————. 2010. "Higher Arts Public Education, Research and Citizenship." In *Art
   Futures: Current Issues in Higher Arts Education*, K. Corcoran, C. Delfos, and
   F. Solleleveld, 20–29. Amsterdam: European League of Institutes of the Arts
   (ELIA).

Wochenklausur. 2009. "From the Object to the Concrete Intervention." In *Institutional Critique: An Anthology of Artists' Writings*, edited by Alexander Alberro and
   Blake Stimson, 462–77. Cambridge, MA: MIT Press.

Zannos, Iannis. 2014. "The Secret School." *Performigrations.* www.performigrations
   .eu/the-secret-school (accessed November 12, 2015).

Zapotosky, Matt, David Nakamura, and Abigail Hauslohner. 2017. "Revised Executive
   Order Bans Travelers from Six Muslim-Majority Countries from Getting New Visas." *Washington Post.* March 6. www.washingtonpost.com/world/national-security
   /new-executive-order-bans-travelers-from-six-muslim-majority-countries-apply
   ing-for-visas/2017/03/06/3012a42a-0277-11e7-ad5b-d22680e18d10_story.html
   (accessed October 10, 2018).

Zeiger, Mimi. 2011. "The Interventionists' Toolkit." *Places Journal.* https://places
   journal.org/series/interventionists-toolkit (accessed May 14, 2016).

Zurcher, Anthony. 2016. "The Birth of the Obama 'Birther' Conspiracy." *BBC News.*
   September 16. www.bbc.com/news/election-us-2016-37391652.

WEBSITES

Art Not Oil Coalition: www.artnotoil.org.uk

Arte Útil: www.arte-util.org

Bambitchell: www.bambitchell.com

Basis voor Actuele Kunste (BAK): www.bakonline.org

Centre for Political Beauty: www.politicalbeauty.com

Chto Delat?: http://chtodelat.org

Citizen Artist Incubator (2015–2017): www.citizenartist.eu

Citizen Artist: http://citizenartist.com

Cornerstone Theatre: https://cornerstonetheater.org

Critical Art Ensemble: www.critical-art.net

David Bollier: News and Perspectives on the Commons: www.bollier.org
Democracia: www.democracia.com.es
For Freedoms: https://forfreedoms.org
Free Class FaM: http://freeclassfrankfurt.wordpress.com
Governor's Letters: http://govlet.ca/en/index.php
Immigrant Movement International: https://immigrant-movement.us
Indigenous Foundations: https://indigenousfoundations.arts.ubc.ca
Janez Janša: www.janezjansa.si
Jonas Staal: www.jonasstaal.nl
Kochi Biennale Foundation: https://kochimuzirisbiennale.org
Laboratory of Insurrectional Imagination: https://labofii.wordpress.com
Liberate Tate: www.liberatetate.org.uk/liberating-tate
Museum de Lakenhal de Veenfabriek, Leiden: www.lakenhal.nl/en
Pender Islands Museum: http://penderislandsmuseum.ca
Public Art Online. 2008. Public Art Online. www.public artonline.org.uk
RAVEN Trust: https://raventrust.com
7th Berlin Biennale 2012: www.berlinbiennale.de/en/biennalen/22/forget-fear
Silent University, The: http://thesilentuniversity.org
Stop Ecocide International: www.stopecocide.earth
Street Road: www.streetroad.org
Suzanne Lacy: www.suzannelacy.com
Tania Bruguera: www.taniabruguera.com
Tree Museum: tree-museum.com
Tsawout First Nation: https://tsawout.ca
US Department of Arts and Culture: http://usdac.us
Wochenklausur: www.wochenklausur.at
Yes Men: http://theyesmen.org

Index

Aboriginal peoples: in UN, 15n5. *See also* Indigenous people; W̱SÁNEĆ First Nation People

Academic Technology Approval Scheme, 105

action art, 64

activism, 7; at local level, 43–44; in public domain, 44–45; solidarity in, 57n9; in transnationalism, 44

activist art, 1n14, 7, 18; ethics of, 24–25

Acts of Citizenship (Isin and Nielsen), 20, 47

aesthetic journalism, 7

aesthetics: of APG, 72; of citizen art, 3; of *Citizen Artist News: Clouded Title*, 131–32; of citizenship, 11; *New World Summits* and, 99; in politics, 50–56; relational, 76; of settlers, 161; of status citizenship, 162; of W̱SÁNEĆ First Nation People, 124, 163–64

Alfred, Taiaiake, 134

All Fine & Context & Other Papers (Coward), 84n19

Anderson, Benedict, 57n10

Annan, Kofi, 80, 86n30

Anonymous Hacktivists, *66*

"Anthropocene, Capitalocene, Plantationocene, Chthulucene" (Haraway), 152–53

antiterrorist legislation, in UK, 21

APG. *See* Artist Placement Group

Appadurai, Arjun, 56n3

Appiah, Kwame Anthony, 40–41, 57n10

Arendt, Hannah, 57n5, 96, 100–101, 115n6, 117n16

Aristotle, 37, 53

"Art and Citizenship" (Wiles), 28

Arte Útil, 89–90

Artificial Hells (Bishop), 43–44

Artinian, Emily, 144n8, 175, 178–79

art interventions, 7, 22; as artists-in-residence, 83n6; Bourriaud and, 74–77; citizenship in, 78–79; descriptions of, 83n4; distribution of the sensible and, 67–68, 70; as generative frictions, 79, 85n26; performance art and, 64; politics and, 61–82; projects in, 63, 70–77; RtoP and, 77–82; status citizenship and, 11–12, 81–82; usefulness of, 78. *See also specific examples*

Artistic Citizenship (Elliot, Silverman, and Bowman), 25–26

Artist Placement Group (APG), 3, 11, 64, 71–75, 84n18

artists-in-residence. *See* art interventions

Art Not Oil Coalition, 64

art object, 22, 31n14; projects and, 82n3

About the Author

Fawn Daphne Plessner is a professional artist and Associate Professor at Emily Carr University of Art + Design, Canada. She holds a BA (Hons) Philosophy, from Birkbeck College, University of London and a PhD in Art & Politics from Goldsmiths College, University of London, United Kingdom. She studied Fine Art at the Akademie der Bildenden Kunste, Munich, Germany, under the artist Robin Page, an early member of the Fluxus movement. She has won numerous research grants and her artwork has been exhibited in countries such as the United Kingdom, Ireland, Germany, the United States, and Canada. Since 2008, her work has focused on public art interventions under the banner of citizen artist.

www.ingramcontent.com/pod-product-compliance
Lightning Source LLC
Chambersburg PA
CBHW050427280326
41932CB00013BA/2019